Help! for Teachers

Strategies for Reaching All Students

Second Edition

Help! for Teachers

Strategies for Reaching All Students

Second Edition

Grant Martin

purposeful design.
publications
A Division of ACSI

Colorado Springs, CO

A Division of ACSI

Books, Textbooks, and Educational Resources
for Christian Educators and Schools Worldwide

Purposeful Design Publications is the publishing division of ACSI and is committed to the ministry of Christian school education, to enable Christian educators and schools worldwide to effectively prepare students for life. As the publisher of books, textbooks, and other educational resources within ACSI, Purposeful Design Publications strives to produce biblically sound materials that reflect Christian scholarship and stewardship, and that address the identified needs of Christian schools around the world.

Help! for Teachers: Strategies for Reaching All Students
Second Edition

ISBN 1-58331-060-6   Catalog #6514

Purposeful Design Publications
A Division of ACSI
PO Box 35097 • Colorado Springs, CO 80935-3509
www.acsi.org

To my wife, Jane,
for her constant encouragement,
her willingness to sacrifice our social calendar
when a deadline is near,
her constant provision of nourishment
while I'm typing away at the computer,
and her proofreading of the finished manuscript.
Above all, I thank her for the years of love
and friendship she has given me.
She truly is a loving helpmate.

TABLE OF CONTENTS

PREFACE

Imagine you are a high school student who has significant problems with reading. You might feel like the young man who authored the following poem. This seventeen-year-old learning-disabled student was significantly limited in his ability to read fluently and take tests, yet he was quite intelligent. Can you get a glimpse of his suffering? The poem is entitled "Different."

> I am a prisoner
> Charged with no crime,
> But imprisoned just the same.
>
> Is there no justice?
> Can't I plead my case?
> I was sentenced before my birth,
> Sentenced to a life of ridicule and laughter.
>
> How much more time must I serve?
> When will this torment end?
> Please, please,
> Tell me how much more must I stand?

There are many students like this in our schools, crying out for help. They may not be as articulate, but they still feel the pain and anguish caused by failure in the classroom. The numbers are significant:
- Between 5 and 10 percent of school children have some type of learning disability (LD) (Bradley, Danielson, and Hallahan 2002; U.S. Department of Education 2001).
- Around 3 to 5 percent have attention-deficit/hyperactivity disorder (ADHD) (American Academy of Pediatrics 2001).

- Another 5 to 15 percent experience emotional or behavioral problems that require mental health services. This category includes students who have experienced the trauma of parental divorce and those who exhibit noncompliance, aggression, depression, and social problems (Kazdin 1989).

There is no reason to believe these incidence rates are much different in Christian schools. In spite of high admission standards or emphasis on a college preparatory curriculum, special-needs students sit in many of our classrooms. I believe we must make every effort to try to reach these students. The mandate to serve them certainly falls within the stated purpose of most Christian schools.

Your school has most likely established a mission or some goals very similar to the following:
- Students, teachers, and families will work together to glorify God while offering an opportunity for all students to reach their full potential in a Christian atmosphere.
- Our purpose is to equip and train students to discover and develop their unique, God-given design ... to the end that they may glorify God by fulfilling His purpose for their lives.
- We strive to provide a program and environment in which all individuals may develop to their optimum potential spiritually, mentally, and physically, as well as socially, culturally, and vocationally.
- Our goal is to educate students according to their developmental needs.
- We endeavor to help all students develop their personalities on the basis of a proper understanding and acceptance of themselves as unique individuals created in the image of God, and on the basis of the fullest possible development of their own capabilities.

God gives every child certain potentialities at birth. Exceptional students are just as much a part of God's creation (Psalm 139:13–14), of the body of Christ (Ephesians 4:25), and of God's eternal purpose (Ephesians 3:11) as any other students in your school.

In reality, however, many special-needs students do not survive in the standard school environment. For example, students with ADHD often face failure. About 50 percent repeat a grade by high school. About 35 percent will drop out of school and only 5 percent will complete college. One study found that 46 percent of students with ADHD are suspended, and 11 percent are expelled. In addition, 50 percent or more of students with ADHD also have learning disabilities (Biederman, Faraone, and Lapey 1992; Pastor and Rueben 2002). These statistics clearly reveal that a huge number of students are not achieving at the level of their God-given potential.

If student achievement were permanent and immutable, we wouldn't need schools or teachers. However, environment and experience play major roles in student development and learning. Therefore, schools exist to facilitate each child's God-given endowment. The point I am making—and the reason for this book—is that we have fallen far short of the goal of meeting the needs of all students.

Assuming that we really care about reaching all students academically, the probable reason for the shortfall is lack of knowledge or resources for reaching those special-needs students. The reality is that many schools would love to be doing more for kids who learn differently, but they simply don't know what can be done or don't have the budget, materials, or staff to set up any kind of special program. This book is intended to help close the gap between educational goals and instructional reality for students with ADHD, learning disabilities, or emotional barriers to learning.

As Christian educators with a calling to help students learn in the best way possible, what can we do? Let me give an analogy. Everybody needs a balanced diet. For many of us, a normal menu or array of meals provides the nutrition we need to stay reasonably healthy and to carry out our daily functions. However, some folks need adjustments in their diet, such as extra iron or vitamin B. They need more of certain nutrients to meet the unique needs of their body. The same principle applies to the special-needs student. Many of the teaching methods that work for regular students will also work with most special-needs students. It's just that these students require more of the basic elements of quality teaching, and in more consistent doses. Yes, sometimes these students need a specialized diet containing intensive and customized instruction. However, quality instruction provided in a consistent manner will go a long way in helping all students achieve to their maximum potential.

Historically, Christian parents have had to rely on public school resources or private secular schools or tutors to get services for their special-needs child. Many of these resources are beneficial. However, parents who seek a Christian education for their special-needs child have had limited alternatives. I would like to see Christian schools provide more of these resources.

With greater awareness of special needs, improved diagnostic procedures, and perhaps even increased numbers of special-needs children, the challenge and the opportunity are wide open for Christian schools. I would argue that the need is urgent and that a concerted effort to meet it is long overdue.

Christian educators must realize such biologically based conditions as learning disabilities and ADHD are not just the results of a spiritual problem, poor parenting, or irresponsible temperament. While these can contribute to the dilemma, they are not the core cause. Deficiencies in specific brain functions are at the heart of the matter. For example, the inability of ADHD students to inhibit behavior and control responses prevents them from meeting the classroom demands for self-control, goal-setting, and problem-solving. They don't stay in their seats, raise their hands before talking, follow directions accurately, or complete their assignments. But these students don't just wake up one morning and decide to be impulsive or inattentive any more than learning-disabled students decide to reverse words or letters as they read. Through some combination of genetics, injury, illness, and environmental influences, up to 20 percent of our students have barriers to learning that they did not choose. Our job is to help them learn more effectively and handle their situation in a responsible manner.

A diagnosis of ADHD or an LD should be used as an explanation that will lead to improved management and instruction. Such a diagnosis should not be used as an excuse. At the same time, students are not helped by being labeled as immature or irresponsible. The mission of educators is to understand how they can alter in-school variables to better accommodate the requirements of these students. The goal of this book is to assist Christian school administrators and teachers in identifying special-needs students more accurately, and then establishing plans and procedures that are effective in facilitating classroom success.

A Comment About Learning Differences and Learning Disabilities

More recently, *learning differences* has been used as a less negative term for learning features found in students who are struggling in school. The term denotes a broad range and a wide variety of learning challenges, including diagnosed learning disabilities and ADHD.

Learning disability is a term defined in federal law. The Individuals with Disabilities Education Act (IDEA) has set out guidelines to determine a child's eligibility for special education services through the public school system.

The two terms are neither synonymous nor interchangeable. *Learning differences* is not an alternative to the legal definition of *learning disabilities*. When speaking or writing of the rights, services, and eligibility classifications mandated in IDEA legislation, the term *learning disabilities* is more appropriate.

Learning disability is an umbrella term covering conditions that vary considerably in their nature and the degree of their impact. LDs may affect a single aspect of learning, or they may impact multiple learning modalities. They may occur alone or in combination with other conditions, such as ADHD or emotional problems. They appear in individuals who have their own unique strengths and weaknesses, their own identity and personality. We must always focus on what children can do, not just on what they cannot do.

Learning differences is an expansive and inclusive term which recognizes that many children with learning problems are not identified as learning disabled and/or do not receive special education services because they do not meet federal and state eligibility requirements. While around 5 percent of school-age children in public school receive special education services because they have an identified learning disability, it's estimated that as many as 20 percent experience significant learning challenges. Thus the number of children dealing with learning differences is much larger than the official figures would indicate. It is on *all* the students possibly included under the *learning differences* label that this book will focus.

An advantage of the term *learning differences* is that it reflects the fact that there are inherent differences in children's growth, development, and learning characteristics. It emphasizes that children who struggle with academics because of learning and attention problems are capable of learning; they just learn in different ways.

Given that this umbrella term must cover so much, I have chosen to use the term *learning disability* in order to suggest that for many individuals there remains a degree of deficit in the area affected. Also, the term has a history both in common usage and in pertinent laws. It is certainly not a precise term. *Learning disability* does not tell us what kind of problem the student is having. However, it is a useful term to start us thinking about why a particular student is struggling.

More details about the exact definition of *learning disabilities* will be included in chapter 2. While the term *learning differences* has value in being more inclusive, I will use the term *learning disabilities* more often in this book because I will usually be talking about an area of deficit that is defined in federal and state law, or that has been identified by a comprehensive assessment.

Organization of the Book

This book is organized into two major sections. Part I provides the Christian educator with descriptions and diagnostic details for identifying learning problems. ADHD and LDs are the areas of major focus in this book. Space restrictions won't permit a comprehensive discussion of all types of learning problems. However, part I will include summaries of emotional barriers to learning and of underachievement in talented and gifted students.

Part II presents detailed material on teaching students with learning problems, including accessing community resources, management and teaching strategies, and examples of accommodation and remediation methods and materials for ADHD and learning disabilities. Also included is some material on dealing with emotional barriers to learning. Extensive lists of resources are provided in the final portion of the book.

I have spent thirty-six years working with preschool through college students. I have taught in the classroom at the primary and secondary levels, and I have worked as a district school psychologist. Following my doctoral work in educational and clinical psychology, I served as a special education clinical professor in a field-based teacher-training project. And for the past twenty-eight years I have been in private practice in the Seattle area, specializing in emotional and learning problems of children and adolescents. In my career, I have probably worked with almost 9,000 students. This practical experience, combined with the research necessary to write a dozen books and numerous articles, is what I bring to the task of preparing this book. My prayer is that you will find it beneficial.

There are no instant cures or quick fixes. There is no easy way to teach special-needs students. However, with the educational components described in the following chapters, you should be able to make significant contributions to helping students reach more of their God-given potential.

May God bless you in your ministry to *all* your students.

Grant L. Martin, Ph.D.
Seattle, Washington

References

American Academy of Pediatrics. 2001. Prevalence and assessment of attention-deficit/hyperactivity disorder in primary care settings. *Pediatrics* 107, no. 3:e43.

Biederman, J., S. V. Faraone, and K. Lapey. 1992. Comorbidity of diagnosis in attention deficit disorder. In *Attention-deficit hyperactivity disorder.* G. Weiss, ed. Philadelphia, PA: WB Saunders.

Bradley, R., L. Danielson, and D. P. Hallahan, eds. 2002. *Identification of learning disabilities.* Mahwah, NJ: Lawrence Erlbaum Associates, Inc.

Kazdin, A. E. 1989. Developmental psychopathology: Current research, issues and directions. *American Psychologist* 44:180–87.

Pastor, P. N., and C. A. Rueben. 2002. Attention deficit disorder and learning disability: United States, 1997–98. National Center for Health Statistics. *Vital and Health Statistics* 10, no. 206. http://www.cdc.gov/nchs/data/series/sr_10/sr10_206.pdf.

U.S. Department of Education. 2001. OSERS twenty-third annual report to Congress on the implementation of the IDEA. http://www.ed.gov/about/reports/annual/osep/2001/index.html.

PART I

Identification of Learning Problems

CHAPTER 1

Learning Problems in the Classroom

There are many reasons why students have trouble with the learning process. This chapter will present illustrations and descriptions of learning disabilities (LDs), attention-deficit/hyperactivity disorder (ADHD), some emotional barriers to learning, and student underachievement. These are not the only reasons students may struggle with reading, writing, math, study skills, or compliance with classroom rules and procedures. However, these descriptions and their accompanying methods of intervention can go a long way in helping you teach your special-needs students more effectively.

Learning Disabilities

Roger's teacher was concerned that he wasn't making adequate progress in reading. Mrs. Johnson knew that Roger was bright. He did quite well in math. However, his reading skills had not improved much over the first half of the school year. Something wasn't right, and she was worried.

Mrs. Johnson asked permission to have Roger tested because she thought he might have some type of learning disability. If the test results proved positive, the school could provide some extra help. The news was disheartening for Roger's parents, Marj and Gary. For Gary, it was particularly difficult because it reminded him of his own struggles as a child. He had never been a good reader. Teachers were always telling him he had the potential to do better. However, reading and writing had always caused him to feel frustrated. Now his son was facing the same kinds of humiliation and discouragement.

A psychologist tested Roger for learning disabilities. The report indicated that Roger had above-average intelligence. His math ability was a bit above grade level, but his silent reading comprehension and writing skills were significantly low. The psychologist pointed out that if Roger heard a passage read to him, his comprehension was excellent. When he had to read to himself, however, he had significant trouble. The tests also highlighted deficiencies in word-attack, or phonics, skills. Roger consistently miscalled words when he read to himself, often substituting incorrect words for the ones in the text. As a result, his understanding of what he read was faulty.

The description instantly made sense to his parents. "Yes," they said, "we can read part of a book or an article from the newspaper, and Roger never misses a beat. It's only when he has to read to himself that he gets mixed up." Roger's teacher added, "That makes sense to me. It's as if Roger missed out on some of his early word-attack skills. However, the odd thing is that he's inconsistent. Some sound combinations he knows, and others seem to give him fits."

A learning disability like Roger's is only one reason students may not be learning as effectively as possible. Let's look at another type of learning problem.

Attention-Deficit/Hyperactivity Disorder

Some children can't sit still. Others are highly distractible, forgetful, or inattentive. Some appear distracted by every little thing and don't seem to learn from their mistakes. Many of these children disregard rules, even when they are punished repeatedly. There are also those who tend to act without thinking, resulting in many accidents and reprimands. This collection of problems is called attention-deficit/hyperactivity disorder (ADHD).

ADHD can make classroom learning and family life disruptive and stressful. No matter how hard parents and teachers try to do the right thing, these children persist in acting out, daydreaming, missing homework assignments, and neglecting chores. Here are a few examples of experiences common with attention-deficit children:

Fred is constantly out of his seat. He seldom raises his hand for permission before doing something. When ideas come into his head, he acts impulsively, without thinking. Fred never stops. He's always going about ninety miles an hour. At recess he is constantly getting into trouble for his impulsive behavior. Yet the amazing thing is that he can repeat everything his teacher says, even when he doesn't seem to be listening.

Terry's mother hates to pick her son up at school. Every day, it seems, his teacher tells her about Terry's talking out in class, making animal noises, or getting out of his seat. He can't seem to concentrate. Every little thing that happens in the classroom is a major distraction for him. He's only six years old, but he's already beginning to dislike school.

There appear to be several types of ADHD. Some children are primarily impulsive and hyperactive, while others are inattentive and distractible. A third group of children seem to be both impulsive and inattentive.

Children with hyperactivity exhibit aggression and bizarre behavior, and they appear impulsive. They are more noisy, disruptive, messy, irresponsible, and immature than typical children, earning labels like "whirling dervish" and "Dennis the Menace." These children have a higher risk for serious aggressive or oppositional behavior and antisocial or acting-out behavior.

In contrast, the ADHD children who are predominantly inattentive tend to be anxious, shy, socially withdrawn, moderately unpopular, and poor in sports. They often stare into space and daydream, and they perform poorly in school. They are often forgetful, low in energy, sluggish, and drowsy. They have difficulty becoming sufficiently aroused and vigilant to give attention to academic tasks. These students are often lost in thought, apathetic, and lethargic, and they may be described as "space cadets" or "couch potatoes." They are less aggressive, impulsive, and overactive at home and school than those with hyperactive characteristics, and they have fewer problems in peer relationships. These children probably make up the largest category of ADHD children, yet they may be the most underdiagnosed.

Some children have a combination of both inattention and hyperactive-impulsive features. They exhibit most of the behavioral manifestations of inattention—making careless mistakes, failing to give attention to details, and being easily distracted by extraneous stimuli. In addition, they display hyperactive-impulsive characteristics—fidgeting with hands or feet, being unable to remain seated, appearing often on the go, interrupting others, and having difficulty waiting their turn.

Although hyper focusing is not one of the official criteria, some attention-deficit children appear to have a tendency to hyper focus. They become so absorbed in and preoccupied with an activity that they tune out everything around them. It is as if a bomb could go off in the same room and they wouldn't deviate from the television program they are watching, the book they are reading, or the model they are building. A few people seem to be the extreme opposite of hyperactive. They are said to be hypoactive. They move like cold molasses on a winter morning. Lethargy, apathy, apparent indifference, and slow motion are their way of life. They do not complete projects or school assignments because doing tasks takes so long.

All children sometimes exhibit inattentiveness, impulsiveness, or high energy levels. However, for attention-deficit children these symptoms are part of the daily routine rather than the exception. Also, they manifest these behaviors everywhere they go—home, school, church, grandma's house, the grocery store. The rule is that these children are consistently inconsistent.

Emotional Barriers to Learning

Some years ago, I met Carla, a sixteen-year-old girl who was showing signs of depression. She was struggling in school, and her grades had dropped drastically. School officials asked me to talk to her and determine whether I could help.

Carla was articulate, artistic, and sensitive. She came from an upper-middle-class home. Her father was a professional, and her mother was a homemaker. She was the middle child of three, having a brother and a sister. In spite of her talent, good looks, and material comfort, Carla was often miserable and distressed. She would have episodes, or "breakdowns" as she called them, when she would pull out some of her hair, pound her head against the wall until it bled, and wail in emotional agony for long periods.

Carla took the time to write about her inner turmoil. Let's look at brief sections of her journal for more of her story:

> I am me ... at least I try to be. I guess, though, that I am a whole lot of
> different types all scrunched up into one person. I don't think I am a very
> real person. Not even my handwriting is real. I write in so many different

7

hands … just whatever strikes my fancy. Sometimes I like to imitate other people's handwriting. For some reason it makes me feel good inside and calms me down if I'm mad or nervous. I guess the real, true me comes out whenever I have those … I call them small breakdowns. Just who or what the real me is, I don't know. I try to figure it out sometimes, but I always get confused and frustrated and give up.

I'm always wondering what it would be like to be hugged and kissed and stuff, and I wish ever so much that I would be. Often I try hugging and kissing myself, but that doesn't help much.

I guess Daddy loves me, but I don't think my mother does. I like Daddy best, and I don't like my mother at all. I think that most of the time I don't even love her. Daddy respects us kids and what we have to say. He understands us, and if we're mad and are a little disrespectful, he doesn't mind because he knows how we feel. Mom just slaps us and is always telling us how terrible we are and how we can never do anything right and how hard she works for us.

Another part of me has a nice family and stuff but is crazy. That part of me has to go to a psychologist. She has breakdowns like the one my poem's about, and she goes to sleep and wakes up in another world—her own world. Sometimes it is good. She can fly and go anywhere with the wave of her hand. The world is beautiful … sunny and green and birds singing. There is no war, no suffering … just beautiful people and peacefulness and happiness.

The other world is dark … gray … like a spinning pit. There is a hole at the top, and she can see this world and anybody in it through this hole. But she can't get out. She is tormented and sad and speaks a different language. Gradually she rises up toward the hole. As soon as she is half out, she looks down. She can see the spinning gray pit. She grabs on to something and pulls herself out onto the earth. Then she is with her happy family again.

Here is a poem I wrote last year. It's not very good, but I think I captured my feelings that I get when I have those little breakdowns.

Breakdown

Oh God, for not another full minute

Can I stand this crazy wreck of my life.

How I crave to be from this puzzling din cut—

Forever dead … forever free from strife.

Feel my tension building up from my toes;

Hear my weeping, tired and despondent dread;

Taste the salty tears of my depressing woes;

See the clumps of hair I pull from my head.

Whether lying here in a wretched heap,

Or smashing everything with a rod,

I am all alone … all alone … oh God,

Someone help me … lull me to eternal sleep.

So ends Carla's description of herself. It's painfully clear she is living in a home with little affection and a great deal of conditional acceptance. Her fantasies are a tool to help her avoid feeling her internal pain. At times, her emotional pain becomes so intense that she substitutes physical pain to try to numb the emotions. Depression plagues her, and she creates alternate personalities and scenarios to escape her strife.

Depression is only one of the emotional barriers to learning that can result from various personal and family stressors. Family conflict, including parental divorce, can also affect schoolwork. Obviously, traumatic events such as being abused and witnessing family violence can severely limit students' learning. In later sections of this book, we'll examine these kinds of emotional obstacles.

Underachievement

Ruth had been different from the beginning. As an infant, she had an alertness and curiosity about her that her two siblings didn't have. Sharon and Stan, Ruth's parents, had been good students, and both had college degrees. Yet they had never thought of themselves as gifted or especially bright. Ruth, on the other hand, had been precocious in many ways. She talked fluently at the age of ten months and was reading at age two.

Her questions were incessant. She wanted to know about everything that happened around her. Although her thirst for knowledge was usually a source of delight for her parents, it also resulted in some frustration. There was seldom a quiet or calm moment when Ruth was around.

One day Sharon was busily trying to get dinner on the table while monitoring the homework of Ruth's older brother. The family had to finish eating in order for Sharon and Stan to get to a PTA meeting at seven o'clock. In the middle of all that activity, Ruth, who was eighteen months old at the time, was standing on a chair, trying to follow along in her mother's cookbook. After about the twentieth question, Ruth's mother, responding in exasperation, said, "Ruth, won't you ever stop asking questions? Now get out of my road. I don't want to hear another word from you until dinner is on the table."

With that, Ruth got down from the chair, walked over to the bulletin board next to the phone, picked up a piece of chalk, and wrote, "No, I won't."

While most children at that age are struggling to string several words together in a spoken sentence, Ruth was writing complete thoughts. Events like that helped her parents realize that Ruth was no ordinary learner. She was going to need a stimulating combination of experiences to keep her satisfied and challenged.

Things went along well until Ruth's fourth grade in school. Over the first three or four months of the school year, Ruth seemed to settle into some kind of academic funk. She began missing assignments, faltering on some of her tests, doing little homework, and spending all her time on the phone.

At the time, Ruth was in a regular fourth-grade class, but she was pulled out a half day a week for enrichment activities for talented students. The pullout program had started in the second grade, and for the past two years Ruth had seemed to enjoy it very much. Now she was complaining that it bored her and made her miss some activities in her regular class.

The enrichment teacher noticed the decline in Ruth's motivation, so she asked Ruth's parents to come in for a conference. During the discussion, Ruth's regular class teacher commented that Ruth seemed to be doing fine socially. She was well liked and had many friends. In fact, everyone wondered if friends had taken on more importance for Ruth than her schoolwork. There was also some evidence to suggest that Ruth was intentionally downplaying her ability and making errors in her assignments. The impression of the teachers and parents was that Ruth was displaying some of the classic signs of underachievement often seen in capable students. The question was what to do about it.

Ruth's situation illustrates the status of many talented students. We know they have high potential in one or more areas such as music, mathematics, language, or problem solving. Yet they're not achieving at a level commensurate with their demonstrated ability. So again the question arises, *Why aren't these students learning?*

Of course, students don't have to be gifted to be underachievers. "Average" students may experience times when they aren't working up to their capabilities. Their underachievement isn't due to learning disabilities. They don't have an attention deficit, they're not particularly stressed or depressed, and they are not dealing with a traumatic home situation. They just aren't motivated to work as hard as they should.

A Look Ahead

We've looked at examples of each of the major types of problems that will be discussed in the following chapters. Learning disabilities, attention deficits, underachievement, and emotional barriers such as stress, depression, and family problems will be discussed in detail in this book. I know you are concerned about some of the students in your class or school. You want them to be as successful as possible. You're keenly interested in both knowing why some students are not progressing as they should and learning what you and others can do to help.

Answering those concerns is the purpose of this book. I hope you've already identified with some of the learning problems included in this chapter. Now keep reading for the information you need. The next chapters will give you an overview of the four types of learning problems so that you can start to understand what may be troubling some of your students.

CHAPTER 2

The Nature of Learning Problems

This chapter will present an overview of the barriers to learning that were introduced and illustrated in chapter 1. Each type of learning problem will be defined and described, and its prevalence and possible causes will be discussed. My hope is that you have connected emotionally to one of the stories in chapter 1 and that you'll now begin to gain a solid understanding of these problems.

Learning Disabilities

Few topics have generated more controversy than the attempt to define learning disabilities (LDs). From 1960 to 1975, learning disability emerged as a formal category. Dr. Samuel Kirk is credited with having originated the term *learning disabilities* when he used it in a speech in 1963. Since that time, professionals, parents, and government agencies have tried to develop a definition that's valid, fair, and reliable. The use of a single term for this category of learning problems may help separate them from other types of special needs. However, there are many conflicting theories about the nature and causes of learning disabilities. The label is all-embracing. It identifies a syndrome, not a specific student with specific problems.

A clear definition allows professionals to identify learning difficulties accurately, treat them effectively, and motivate students who have them sufficiently so that their quality of life improves. At least that's the ideal. The problem is that children with learning disabilities usually exhibit a combination of characteristics. No two learners are the same, but some common themes are present in those with learning disabilities.

Definitions of Learning Disability

A widespread premise underlying many definitions is that people who have a learning disability have more difficulty acquiring, applying, and retaining information than would be predicted from other facts about them. Most definitions emphasize a discrepancy between presumed intellectual capacity and actual school achievement. Students with learning disabilities are not dumb or lazy. In fact, they usually have average or above-average intelligence. However, their brains process information in a different way than do the brains of other students.

Learning disabilities arise from a deficiency in basic thinking processes, a deficiency that contributes to academic failure. A learning disability can be seen as the presence in a student of one or more specific cognitive deficits that create unique educational needs.

One definition was developed by the U.S. Office of Education (USOE) in 1977 and incorporated into subsequent federal legislation. It's the most widely accepted definition because it's the one used by most federal and state agencies to administer programs for students. It is now included in the most recent special education law, the Individuals with Disabilities Education Act (IDEA). This act defines a specific *learning disability* as "a disorder in one or more of the basic psychological processes involved in understanding or in using language, spoken or written, that may manifest itself in an imperfect ability to listen, think, speak, read, write, spell, or do mathematical calculations, including conditions such as perceptual disabilities, brain injury, minimal brain dysfunction, dyslexia, and developmental aphasia" (U.S. Department of Education 2001). However, learning disabilities do not include "learning problems that are primarily the result of visual, hearing, or motor disabilities, of mental retardation, of emotional disturbance, or of environmental, cultural, or economic disadvantage" (U.S. Congress 1997).

The second major definition was adopted first in 1981 and modified several times by the National Joint Committee on Learning Disabilities (NJCLD), a consortium of ten national organizations with interests in learning disabilities. The NJCLD tried to improve on the USOE's definition by reinforcing the idea that learning disabilities can exist at all ages, by distinguishing between learning disabilities and learning problems, and by making clear that learning disabilities can coexist with other handicapping conditions. The NJCLD concluded, "*Learning disabilities* is a general term that refers to a heterogeneous group of disorders manifested by significant difficulties in the acquisition and use of listening, speaking, reading, writing, reasoning, or mathematical skills" (NJCLD 1994).

These disorders are intrinsic to the individual, are presumed to be due to central nervous system dysfunctions, and may occur across the life span. Problems in self-regulatory behaviors, social perception, and social interaction may exist with learning disabilities but do not, by themselves, constitute a learning disability. Learning disabilities may occur along with other disabilities such as sensory impairment, mental retardation, and serious emotional disturbance or with extrinsic influences such as cultural differences and insufficient or inappropriate instruction. However, learning disabilities are not the result of those conditions or influences (NJCLD 1998).

The NJCLD definition is commonly acknowledged because of its broad support by professional organizations. The USOE/IDEA definition is widely used because of its official legislative status.

IDEA must be reauthorized every few years, and arguments and ideas are being presented to Congress as this book is being written. There may very well be some changes made to the definition of learning disabilities as well as to the delivery of services to special-needs students attending private schools. Some suggestions being considered for changing the definition of LDs include (1) specifying precise characteristics in reading, mathematics, written expression, and oral language; (2) using a direct comparison of a student's age and grade with academic functioning (instead of using the IQ-achievement discrepancy); (3) not excluding children because of inadequate instruction, cultural and social factors, and emotional disturbance; and (4) considering a student's response to well-designed and well-implemented early intervention (Lyon et al. 2001).

Each of these major components of the definition for *learning disabilities* can be expanded and critiqued, though most such discussions are outside the scope of this book. The one area that we need to mention is the criterion used by most states: There must be a severe discrepancy between potential and achievement. Usually some type of formula is used to identify such a discrepancy. A typical criterion would be that a fourth-grade student must be at least two years behind in an area of academic achievement in order to qualify for services outside the normal classroom offerings.

The problem with using the criterion of an IQ-achievement discrepancy is that it is predicated on failure. This "wait-and-fail" model requires a student to fall significantly behind some predicted level of performance to be eligible for services. Therefore, students often do not receive services until the third grade or later because they can't be shown to meet the required discrepancy until they have several years of school failure under their belt. The result is that students cannot use public school special education resources until they have experienced two or three years of school failure, low self-esteem, and loss of motivation.

Obviously, there are problems with this approach, and considerable discussion is taking place to make changes that will allow struggling students to receive help earlier. One major change would be to identify discrepancies in the student's basic psychological or cognitive functioning. For example, if a psychologist finds that a student has at least average abilities in all areas except that of processing information through the auditory modality, a significant learning disability can be established. We'll explore this further in the next chapter as we look at different types of learning disabilities and learning modalities.

The fourth edition of the *Diagnostic and Statistical Manual of Mental Disorders* (DSM-IV), used by most medical and mental health professionals, doesn't list *learning disability*. Instead, the manual describes disorders in reading, math, and written expression. Such a diagnosis is determined by measuring a child's academic achievement with standardized tests and determining whether the scores are below expectations for the child's chronological age, intelligence, and age-appropriate education (American Psychiatric Association 2001). Most of the other categories described in this book will have a DSM-IV definition.

Summary Definition
The various definitions of learning disabilities have some common elements. For example, students with an LD have difficulty with academic and learning tasks, and they exhibit a discrepancy between potential and achievement. These students are characterized by uneven growth patterns and psychological processing deficits. Their learning disability results from some type of central nervous system dysfunction. Other causes are not major contributors.

The best we can say at this point is that a learning disability likely has a neurological origin and that it affects specific areas of learning and behavior in an otherwise competent person. An LD is not a result of emotional disturbance, mental retardation, or hearing, visual, or other sensory impairments as in cerebral palsy. It also does not have environmental causes, such as inadequate parenting, poor teaching, economic disadvantages, neglect, or abuse. An LD can, however, coexist with other handicapping conditions. Unfortunately, it may not be curable and may therefore be a lifelong condition. And finally we have to acknowledge that learning disabilities are not completely understood.

The affected areas of learning may include the input, output, storage, retention, retrieval, or processing of information. That means a student can have difficulty in acquiring, remembering, organizing, recalling, or expressing information. The skills most often affected are reading, writing, listening, speaking, reasoning, and doing math.

Learning disabilities vary from person to person. In one person the disability may show up in reading comprehension. With another person, the problems may be in written expression. Sometimes there will be a combination of problems in more than one component of the learning process.

Influence of Postmodernist Thought on Definitions of LD

I don't want to get too philosophical, but I want to point out a kind of contemporary thinking that influences a great deal of secular education. A stream of thought that has created a high level of discord within the field is called postmodernism. While hard to define, postmodernism might be described as the idea that "beauty is found only in the eye of the beholder."

Before I proceed, let me try to give a quick summary of some attempts to explain the place of humanity in the world. Descriptions of the history of various worldviews will usually begin with the premodern era, from the time of the early Greeks until the dawn of the Enlightenment in the eighteenth century. While there were many outlooks on the nature of truth, the prevailing worldview included a strong belief in the supernatural and in absolute truth. As Christian thought developed, it asserted that God is the foundation of truth and that the purpose of humans is to discern their relationship to God. These assumptions were nonnegotiable. Most contemporary Christians would still subscribe to them.

A shift in the worldview of the majority came in the nineteenth century with the advances in science and human understanding about the natural world. People believed that they no longer needed the supernatural to guide them. Reason and science alone could give them the answers they needed to find their place in the world. Thus there came about a shift in the thinking of most people, from a premodern to a modern worldview.

During this period in intellectual history (approximately 1790–1990), beginning with what is often called the Enlightenment, many viewed God as neither concerned nor involved in His creation. Reason and science were the hope for humans, and any answers they needed were obtainable by rational study and the application of scientific principles. A major tenet was that knowledge of ourselves and the world was certain and possible. Truth was available through application of the scientific method. People saw the world as a closed, static system of natural laws waiting to be discovered, and they rejected the supernatural. Rational people did not need to trust anything beyond what logic and their own senses told them. The basic tenets of Christianity—belief in miracles, the Incarnation, and other supernatural doctrines—were totally rejected. People decided they did not need the Bible since they had developed their powers of observation and scientific inquiry. They thought they should consult textbooks and not the Bible with its myths and simplistic stories.

However, the Enlightenment did not bring about unity and peace. The institution of slavery, two world wars, and nuclear proliferation, for example, made people begin to question whether reason and science alone could make the world a better place. Scientists, scholars, and others in an intellectual environment were ready to find a new way of explaining the nature and purpose of humankind. Their attempts to discover truth led to postmodernism, the next worldview, which is held by many today.

The ideology of postmodernism is one of anti-foundationalism. It denies the existence of any universal truth or standards, labeling "oppressive" any belief system that claims to be foundational or absolute. The job for the postmodernist is to critique or "deconstruct" such worldviews and level them out so that no single idea or belief is thought to be any more "true" than any other. For thinkers of this type, there is no absolute truth or foundation. A postmodernist, of course, must reject Christianity because it claims to be true. Christian beliefs are simply examples of personal or cultural bias. It is all right to have Christian beliefs as long as you don't claim they are any more true than those of another religious persuasion. Every person's moral code is to be respected no matter what it is. Of course, our language must be revised—in other words, made "politically correct"—so we don't appear to favor a particular outlook.

Where does the postmodernist view of the world leave us? Futile and hopeless, I would say. Without a sense of direction and purpose, we are left on our own to explore our world without a road map or a destination. If nothing else, postmodernism highlights the finiteness of our existence. It shows us the futility of our supposed individual autonomy. For the truth is that God is our Creator and we are His creation. Apart from His truth, we know nothing. It is Christ who gives meaning and purpose to our lives. And it is in God's Word that we find standards for living. The Christian worldview is true, and it gives hope to all people. It provides us both an absolute basis for dealing with the realities of life and a sense of purpose and direction.

What does all the above have to do with education, and with learning disabilities in particular? Many tenets of postmodernist thought about special education are in direct conflict with those of modernism. Yet we know that modernism is not complete either. Certainly Christians don't hold science and logic as the ultimate sources of knowledge. The scientific method is useful, but it does not replace God's revelation.

Knowing there are limits, even in the modernist worldview, we can explore how the competing ideologies work out in the classroom. Modernists hold that the current state of knowledge in special education, developed through scientific inquiry, is promising and that it provides a solid foundation for building more knowledge and implementing "best practices." It would say that there are educational standards for establishing literacy or reading levels, for example. Therefore, if a child is having problems in learning, we want to find out why and then bring the child up to a functional level.

Modernism holds that a learning disability is a phenomenon to address in a way that is consistent with the medical model of illness and wellness. That is, like an illness, it can be treated, accommodated, or endured. Modernists believe that special education should use instruction to enhance the functioning, knowledge, skills, and socialization of those with disabilities (Bradley, Danielson, and Hallahan 2002).

Postmodernism rejects the modern view of scientifically determined standards of proficiency. Instead, postmodernists support a socially constructed view of knowledge in which logical inquiry is a social enterprise. They see "disability," then, as a social construction based on incorrect and immoral assumptions about differences. According to that view, there can be no diagnosis of "learning disability." The primary focus of a postmodernist would be on deconstructing or changing social opinions that limit people with disabilities. A postmodernist idea of remediation would not be to improve a child's ability to read, but rather to change our cultural expectations that all children *should* be able to read. The goal of education would not be to help students conform to some external level of knowledge. Instead, it would be to "empower" them by accepting their own standards of literacy. Furthermore, it would assert that students don't acquire knowledge from the teacher; rather, they create their own knowledge, and they can do so most effectively in a collaborative, social environment.

These philosophical issues may not be a problem for Christian school educators in your own setting. Yet if you ever try to use pubic school resources, you need to be alert to these perspectives and their implications for your students. You can find in-depth discussions on these issues in *A Primer on Postmodernism* (Grenz 1996) and *The Death of Truth: What's Wrong with Multiculturalism, the Rejection of Reason and the New Postmodern Diversity* (McCallum 1996).

Incidence of Learning Disabilities

Because specialists can't agree on a precise definition, and people use different ways to diagnose them, it's difficult to know exactly how many students have learning disabilities. Most estimates suggest that from 5 to 10 percent of the school population have some type of learning disorder. Whatever the exact numbers may be, the general impression is that learning disabilities are a problem of great magnitude and importance.

As many as one out of every five people in the United States has a learning disability. Fifty-one percent of students receiving special education services through the public schools are identified as having learning disabilities. Therefore, almost three million students who are ages six through twenty-one have some form of a learning disability and receive special education in the public schools (U.S. Department of Education 2001).

A national survey by the Centers for Disease Control and Prevention (CDC) found that over 2.6 million children ages six through eleven were reported to have had a diagnosis of either ADHD or LD. In all, 3 percent had been diagnosed with only ADHD, 4 percent with only LD, and 4 percent with both conditions (Pastor and Rueben 2002).

In most reports comparing the incidence of learning disabilities, boys outnumber girls by about six to one. Estimates and studies of the gender difference have ranged from five boys for one girl to nine boys for one girl. The CDC survey mentioned above found that the percentage of boys with only ADHD was almost three times greater than the percentage of girls. The percentage of boys with both ADHD and LD was over two times greater than the percentage of girls with both diagnoses. However, in this study, the percentage of boys and girls with only LD was similar, although this finding contrasts with many other reports (Pastor and Rueben 2002).

Some experts believe this gender imbalance results from biased referrals. Boys are more likely to act out and cause problems when they're frustrated in the classroom. Girls with learning problems may withdraw and not bring attention to themselves, and therefore they are not identified as readily. Other researchers believe that the higher male incidence has something to do with both heredity and some of the basic causes of learning disabilities. No one knows whether there would really be a difference in incidence if all biases were removed. All we can say is that boys have been identified much more often than girls.

Causes of Learning Disabilities

Learning disabilities have no single or primary cause. Rather, they stem from a combination of biological and environmental influences. Learning depends on the proper operation of defined brain circuits that transfer information and ultimately store it in a form accessible for retrieval. Most researchers are looking at interferences in the operations of those mechanisms in order to identify the causes of learning disabilities.

There is also evidence that genetics plays an important role. Researchers have known for a long time that some learning problems seem to be hereditary. In fact, studies suggest that between 25 and 40 percent of disabled children have inherited their problem. Some studies, for example, have concluded that one out of three cases of dyslexia can be linked to a defective chromosome. Scientists suspect that under certain conditions the defective gene can cause a specific brain malfunction. Consistent findings by several research groups have indicated that loci at chromosomes six and fifteen may well be linked to reading and spelling difficulties (Raskind 2001). Since the causes of reading disabilities, for example, are so complex, it is likely that genetic information will become a tool for assigning relative risk for reading or spelling disability more than a true diagnostic test. However, it appears that a major contribution to the cause of learning disabilities is genetic.

We know that genetics determines most of our brain function. Therefore, a great deal of the current research attempts to link abnormal brain functioning with specific features of learning disabilities. We have learned much about these connections. Brain imaging studies have suggested there are measurable neuroanatomical differences between children with poor phonological awareness and those with difficulties in listening comprehension (Leonard 2001). Functional neuroimaging studies of the brain in children with reading disabilities have demonstrated a biological basis for the disorder (Richards 2001).

Much more research is needed. Some disabilities may be related to a biological or brain-functioning predisposition, but whether one actually develops an LD may depend on such environmental influences as medical condition, family structure, or instructional opportunities. The genetic or brain-functioning conditions may simply make a disability much more likely.

In short, learning disabilities probably come from a variety of sources. Inherited tendencies, biological factors, and immature development may all play a part. Environmental factors such as inappropriate schooling and harmful surroundings may complicate a disability that's already present.

Someday, we may be able to use what we know about brain functioning to match specific types of instruction to an identified category of disability. It's not possible now, but that kind of neurologically based intervention will likely be available in the future. Meanwhile, we must do the best we can with the understanding we have.

Learning Styles and Learning Disabilities

The basic idea of learning styles, though not the whole story, is that students have unique approaches to learning. Everyone has certain ways of learning that work best for that person. Each person's modality strengths, to use the technical term, translate into preferences for communicating and learning in certain ways. Some students learn best with a visual approach, while others are auditory learners. Some are kinesthetic and learn best by doing rather than by seeing or listening. Learning-style preferences also include such considerations as whether one learns better in a quiet or busy setting, with high or low levels of light, and with or without group interaction.

While learning styles determine how individuals receive and process information, learning disabilities are deficits in their ability to learn to their full potential. Their learning styles can be seen as their general pattern of strengths, and their learning disabilities as specific areas of weakness. To help students, it's important to understand their strengths as well as their liabilities. Thus, in planning educational strategies, it is useful to identify both learning styles and learning disabilities.

Before we leave this topic, a word of caution is in order. All the popular learning-style descriptions seem to have consensus value and are quite intriguing. The assumption of the proponents of learning styles is that each of us is unique in how we receive and process information. These teachers make every effort first to identify how their students learn best and then to teach to those specific styles. They practice a variety of teaching strategies in order to accommodate the variety of learning styles they find in their classroom. Many of their teaching strategies make sense and benefit certain students.

My concern is that the research to support the effectiveness of using learning-style methods to improve student performance is limited (Curry 1990; Ellis and Fouts 1993). Teachers should be open-minded but cautious about programming recommendations. It's important for teachers to know and work with their students' learning styles, as I'll stress in chapters to come. However, when receiving accommodation or remediation suggestions for a certain student, a teacher should be sure to ask what evidence there is that the proposed interventions have worked with similar students.

Attention-Deficit/Hyperactivity Disorder

Some children have problems with attention, impulse control, and overarousal, and these problems are another cause of difficulties with learning. This collection of problems has been called hyperactivity disorder or attention deficit disorder. Currently, its official name is attention-deficit/hyperactivity disorder (ADHD).

ADHD may be one of the most prevalent problems of childhood. Every classroom in the country has, on average, one child who has an attention disorder. ADHD is the most common neurobehavioral disorder of childhood and is among the most prevalent chronic health conditions affecting school-age children. It is a major clinical and public health problem because of its associated morbidity and disability in children, adolescents, and adults.

ADHD is not a benign disorder. Its core symptoms include inattention, hyperactivity, and impulsivity (Barkley 1998). It can cause devastating problems. Follow-up studies of clinical samples suggest that people with ADHD are far more likely than others to drop out of school (32 to 40 percent), to rarely complete college (5 to 10 percent), to have few or no friends (50 to 70 percent), to underperform at work (70 to 80 percent), to engage in antisocial activities (40 to 50 percent), and to use tobacco or illicit drugs. Moreover, children growing up with ADHD are more likely to experience teen pregnancy (40 percent) and sexually transmitted diseases (16 percent), to speed excessively and have multiple car accidents, to experience depression (20 to 30 percent) and personality disorders (18 to 25 percent) as adults, and in hundreds of other ways to mismanage and endanger their lives (Barkley 2002a, 2002b; Gorski 2002).

As I have traveled around the country giving seminars on this topic, I'm often asked whether ADHD is real or just a current psychological fad. I can definitively say that ADHD is real. I am not saying every case called ADHD has been diagnosed accurately. However, there are strong data to support the existence of ADHD. For example, the American Medical Association (AMA) commissioned a study to review the relevant evidence. The study concluded that ADHD is one of the best-researched disorders in medicine, and that the overall data on its validity are far more compelling than for most mental disorders and even for many medical conditions (Goldman et al. 1998).

Early recognition, assessment, and management of ADHD can redirect the education and psychosocial development of most children who have it. Yet despite its serious consequences, studies indicate that fewer than half of those with the disorder are receiving treatment (Baumgaertel, Copeland, and Wolraich 1996).

Definition and Types of ADHD

ADHD has long been viewed as an issue of attention or behavior. The disorder was termed minimal brain dysfunction in 1960, hyperkinetic reaction of childhood in 1968, attention deficit either with or without hyperactivity in 1980, and attention-deficit/hyperactivity disorder in

1987 (Barkley 1998). In 1994, the three subtypes were defined, and those with ADHD were said to be primarily inattentive, primarily hyperactive, or a combination of both. There will likely be some significant changes in the next *Diagnostic and Statistical Manual of Mental Disorders* (DSM-V), scheduled for publication in 2004 or 2005.

Thus there appear to be several types of ADHD. The current terminology as found in DSM-IV identifies three categories similar to those described above under the general heading of ADHD (American Psychiatric Association 1994). Some children are primarily impulsive and hyperactive, while others are inattentive and distractible. A third group seem to have both impulsive and inattentive characteristics. Most rating scales and questionnaires used for assessment draw on the symptoms listed in the DSM-IV. Professional debate continues on the exact features of attention disorders. However, most authorities agree that they include inattention, impulsivity, and overactivity.

Clinical experience and research strongly suggest there are two main categories of attention disorders—those with hyperactivity and those without. One consists of motor hyperactivity and impulsive behavior; the other of inattention, disorganization, and difficulty completing tasks.

It's also important to remember that while hyperactivity used to be the primary feature in descriptions of attention disorder, it actually appears in fewer than 30 percent of children who have such a disorder. Most attention-deficit children are not hyperactive, though those who are get much of the attention because of their highly visible behaviors. The terminology has been confusing. Sometimes *hyperactivity* is used to refer to the entire range of attention disorders. Other times, the term is intended to describe only the specific characteristic of over-arousal. You should keep these different uses in mind as you think about your own students and try to determine whether some of them might have a form of ADHD.

Impulsive Hyperactivity

"I stopped taking Adam shopping or out in public months ago," said one parent of an ADHD child. "I spent all my time pacing the aisles looking for him, getting him down off anything climbable, and telling him to take his hands off the merchandise. He's always going ninety miles an hour. With only myself to look after him, I never accomplished much of anything."

Adam is impulsive and hyperactive. Such children can behave in a bizarre and aggressive manner. They often seem to feel no guilt, have little self-control, are explosive, and perform poorly at school.

One day I was interviewing a five-year-old girl who was suspected of being hyperactive and impulsive. I asked what her name was, and she replied, "Sally No." I knew her last name wasn't *No,* so I inquired further. I discovered that Sally had been reprimanded and told "Sally, no—don't do that" so often that she thought *No* was her real last name. Imagine the pain and heartache of her mom, who was at her wit's end in trying to parent this difficult child!

Inattention Distractibility

Amy is quite different from Adam and Sally. She daydreams constantly. She's seldom in trouble at school for disobedience or talking too much. She's a bright and talented young artist, yet she consistently gets low grades because she doesn't complete or turn in her homework. Her father said, "Recently I spent several hours struggling with Amy to get her homework done. At first she told me she didn't have any homework. I checked her notebook and found her assignment sheet, which showed she had several pages of math and language arts work to complete. Amy cried off and on for the entire two hours. You would have thought I was asking the impossible from her. Yet we finally got the work done.

"Imagine my frustration the next afternoon when Amy's teacher called to say that Amy had not turned in any assignments for the week. She'd forgotten! This included the math and language arts worksheets we had labored over so hard the night before."

There has been some debate about putting children like Amy into a subtype. Prior to the publication of DSM-III in 1980, little attention was given to children who may have significant problems with attention but without concomitant overactivity and impulsivity. Some have argued the combined and inattentive types are different enough to constitute distinct and unrelated disorders (Milich, Balentine, and Lynam 2001, 2002).

Executive Functioning and ADHD

The idea of ADHD as an impairment of executive functions has emerged as a useful way of understanding the puzzling nature of ADHD impairments. While there is no consensus for a definition of executive function, most researchers would follow Thomas Brown's description of it: the "wide variety of functions within the brain that activate, organize, integrate and manage other functions to allow the individual to function effectively" (Brown 2000).

To describe an executive function, some have used the metaphor of a conductor activating and organizing an orchestra so that all the musicians are playing their respective parts of the same score in a unified and integrated manner. Having someone to coordinate and direct the individual parts results in beautiful music. But the absence of this executive function results in disharmony and poor music.

As part of the discussion of ADHD as an impairment of executive function, there is disagreement about whether hyperactivity and impulsivity are essential to validate a diagnosis of ADHD. Russell Barkley, in developing a new theory of ADHD, describes it as developmental impairments of executive functions in which the primary problem is impairment in the capacity to inhibit behavior. Barkley's model identifies these four functions as nonverbal working memory, verbal working memory, self-regulation of affect/motivation/arousal, and reconstitution (Barkley 1997). He believes they are subordinate to behavioral inhibition.

Thomas Brown has argued with the idea of establishing the executive function of inhibition as primary while subordinating other executive functions to it. Brown has organized his assessment tools into five clusters: organizing and activating to work, sustaining attention and concentration, sustaining energy and effort, managing affective interference, and using working memory and accessing recall (Brown 1996, 1999).

Brown proposes an alternative to Barkley's theory. First, he asserts that impairment of one aspect of executive function, that of behavioral inhibition, is the core problem in the hyperactive-impulsive type of ADHD but not in the predominantly inattentive type (which Brown calls ADD). Second, other aspects of executive function, such as verbal working memory and self-regulation of affect, are impaired in the inattention symptoms, whether these symptoms appear in the combined type or in the type that is only inattentive (2000).

In Brown's formulation, people with the combined type of ADHD would likely have impairments in a wider range of executive functions. These would include functions that modulate behavioral inhibition and those that modulate the wide variety of cognitive impairments currently listed as inattentive symptoms of ADD. Meanwhile, those with the predominantly inattentive type of ADD would be seen as having impairments in executive functions related to the various aspects of inattention.

The term *attention deficit disorder* would be used to describe the inattentive type, and *hyperactivity impulsivity disorder* would be used for those with hyperactive impulsive symptoms as currently described in

DSM-IV. People could be diagnosed as having both disorders as long as the criteria for both impairments were met (Brown 2000).

Future Directions for ADHD

Eventually, we may find there are more than just three subtypes of ADHD. Using Single Photon Emission Computed Tomography imaging (SPECT scans), Daniel Amen and others around the country have been able to correlate the functions of various brain parts to certain behavior in patients and thus to determine how abnormal brain patterns cause specific mental and emotional problems. Amen has identified the following six types of attention deficit on the basis of these brain imaging results:

- *Classic ADD:* hyperactivity, restlessness, distractibility, and impulsiveness
- *Inattentive ADD:* tendency to be space cadets, daydreamers, and couch potatoes
- *Overfocused ADD:* trouble shifting attention; tendency to be stuck, obsessive, argumentative
- *Temporal Lobe ADD:* aggression, memory problems, headaches, dark thoughts
- *Limbic ADD:* depression, negativity, a negative internal filter
- *Ring of Fire ADD:* anger, over-sensitivity, moodiness, and opposition
                    (Amen 1997, 1999; Amen and Carmichael 1997)

While these ADD types are not yet part of the official diagnostic protocol, the research is very interesting, with promise for both diagnosis and treatment.

Because of all the research being conducted, some changes in the terminology about ADHD will undoubtedly be contained in DSM-V. Currently DSM-IV is the official guide, but you should be aware of the significant debate now going on in the field.

The major implications we can draw from this discussion are twofold. The first is that educators should be well aware of the large numbers of children and adults who exhibit the inattentive features. While these people do not have obvious features of hyperactivity or impulsivity, they can certainly have impairments in their ability to attend or concentrate under demanding conditions. The second implication is that as we come to understand the specific neurological underpinnings of these disorders, we may find that there are multiple manifestations or distinctly different types of what we now call ADHD.

Incidence of ADHD

Attention-deficit/hyperactivity disorder is one of the most common reasons that children are referred to mental health professionals. It may be one of the most prevalent problems of childhood. The consensus of professionals is that approximately 3 to 5 percent of children have ADHD. This statistic translates to as many as two million school-age children.

Most of the research on ADHD has been done in the United States and Canada. However, Thomas Brown reports that there are increasing data indicating that ADHD occurs at significant levels in countries as diverse as New Zealand, Germany, Italy, China, Japan, India, and Puerto Rico (2000).

The American Academy of Pediatrics (AAP) undertook a review of the research literature regarding the prevalence of ADHD and co-occurring conditions in children from primary care settings and the general population. Examination of the data revealed that prevalence rates of ADHD generally range from 4 to 12 percent of the elementary school population when applying the information in the DSM-III, DSM-III-R, or DSM-IV. Higher rates of the disorder were found among males and in school settings over those in community settings (AAP 2001).

ADHD affects both boys and girls. Females certainly share the primary features of inattention, impulsivity, and hyperactivity with their male counterparts. Rates of school failure, of similar comorbidity, and of mood, anxiety, and learning disorders are much the same in ADHD girls and boys. Some earlier studies suggest that the prevalence of ADHD is greater in boys than girls. However, because many girls have the inattentive form of ADHD, they have gone undiagnosed and thus may have been underrepresented in the incidence figures. When all forms of ADHD are included, the occurrence may be quite evenly distributed between the genders. In general, ADHD females manifest fewer primary symptoms and externalizing problems than males. In contrast, females are more likely to have comorbid conditions such as depression and anxiety than are ADHD males (Gaub and Carlson 1997; Gershon 2002a, 2002b).

Other studies have shown that girls with ADHD evidenced greater social impairment than girls without ADHD. In addition, girls showed impairments comparable to those of boys with ADHD except that girls have more problems in spare-time activities and less impairment in behavior at school (Greene et al. 2001).

If girls are under-identified, there are significant clinical and educational implications. Such an error would cause girls to be deprived of appropriate treatment and intervention (Wilens, Biederman, and Spencer 2002).

ADHD and Coexisting Disorders

ADHD does not often occur alone. Teachers should be well aware of this fact. Studies of the comorbidity of ADHD have found very high rates of its co-occurrence with many other disorders. Among children with ADHD, anxiety disorders have been found in approximately 25 percent. Similarly, elevated incidences of major depressive disorder, oppositional defiant disorder, conduct disorder, learning disorders, bipolar disorder, Tourette's syndrome, substance abuse, and other psychiatric diagnoses have been reported in children with ADHD (Biederman, Faraone, and Lapey 1992; Jensen 2000).

Data from the National Institute of Mental Health Multimodal Treatment Study of Children with ADHD indicate that as many as 69 percent of ADHD students have coexisting conditions that warrant treatment and intervention (MTA Cooperative Group 1999). In as many as 50 percent of the cases, ADHD children also have learning disabilities. Language difficulties; auditory, visual, or motor processing dysfunctions; and short- or long-term memory problems are examples of LDs to look for in the differential diagnosis of those with ADHD.

Because of this evidence of high comorbidity, adequate assessment and treatment of ADHD requires that the assessment process take into account the unique features of both ADHD and the accompanying disorders. We will examine this consideration further as we discuss the diagnostic process.

Causes of ADHD

Even though ADHD is one of the most thoroughly studied conditions of childhood, its exact cause still isn't known. Research suggests a biological basis. Many ADHD children seem to arrive in the world with temperaments that make them difficult to manage. More study is needed, but it seems likely that some type of inherited genetic predisposition that significantly alters the normal functioning of the brain is the source of ADHD.

Peter Jensen summarizes current research on pathophysiology and a brain basis for ADHD. He identifies five categories of factors that have been implicated as possible causes: (1) family and genetic factors, (2) prenatal or perinatal factors, (3) chemical "toxins," (4) psychosocial stressors and combined factors, and (5) brain structure and function abnormalities, which could result from the first four categories (2000).

The emerging neuropsychological and neuroimaging literature points to abnormalities in frontal and/or frontostriatal networks of the brain. Reviews of a number of brain structural and functional imaging studies have demonstrated differences between children with ADHD and matched groups (Zametkin and Liotta 1998). Structural magnetic resonance imaging studies have shown reduced volumes in various parts of the brain in those with ADHD (Castellanos et al. 2001). Earlier studies have shown reduced global metabolism in adolescent girls (Ernst et al. 1994).

Most neurological studies find that as a group, those with ADHD show less brain electrical activity and less reactivity to stimulation in one or more regions of the brain. Neuroimaging studies of those with ADHD also demonstrate relatively smaller areas of brain matter and less metabolic activity of this brain matter than non-ADHD subjects (Barkley 2002b; Wilens, Biederman, and Spencer 2002). SPECT scans have also been used to identify increased binding at the dopamine transporter protein (Dougherty et al 1999).

Daniel Amen has generated a large database of SPECT scans for a variety of psychiatric conditions, including ADHD. He has created a significant amount of data regarding the understanding of distinct brain function and ADHD (Amen 1999, 2001; Amen and Carmichael 1997).

ADHD is among the most recognized genetics-based disorders in psychiatry (McGuffin, Riley, and Plomin 2001). For example, family studies of ADHD have shown that relatives of ADHD children are at high risk for ADHD and other related problems. Additional lines of evidence from twin, adoption, and segregation analysis studies suggest that there is a substantial genetic component. Twin studies, for example, suggest that the heritability of ADHD ranges from 0.88 to 1.0, indicating a substantial role of genetic factors in its cause (Wilens, Biederman, and Spencer 2002). The genetic contribution to these traits, which is 70 to 95 percent of trait variation in the population, is found routinely to be among the highest for any psychiatric disorder, nearly approaching the genetic contribution to human height (Barkley 2002b).

Molecular genetic studies have implicated the dopamine D4 and the dopamine transporter as candidate genes. Of these candidate genes, multiple groups have reported independently on associations between ADHD and the postsynaptic D4 receptor in both children and adults with ADHD (Faraone et al. 2001). The occurrence of the postsynaptic D4 polymorphism in ADHD youth is higher than would be expected by chance. In addition, ADHD youth with the polymorphism have more severe symptomatology and impairment than those without it (Faraone et al. 2001).

A recent report from a United States and United Kingdom research team identified a specific region of chromosome 16 as contributing to ADHD susceptibility. The findings, based on 203 families in which at least two siblings had ADHD, suggest that a currently unidentified gene within this chromosome region is a major ADHD risk factor. This region overlaps a region also implicated in autism and suggests that variations in a gene on 16p13 may contribute to deficits common to ADHD and autism (Smalley et al. 2002).

Summary of Causes and Sources of Attention Disorders

With our present knowledge, we can conclude that attention disorders result because of a system dysfunction that causes a barrier. That barrier results in behavioral disinhibition and diminished sensitivity to behavioral rules or consequences. In short, because of a chemical deficiency or imbalance in the brain, children with ADHD are not as able as others to pay attention, tune out distractions, or learn from their mistakes. Children without this genetic predisposition can develop attention disorder through illness or injury, but that scenario seems to represent a minority of cases.

Some people claim ADHD is caused by food additives, sugar, yeast, vitamin deficiency, lead poisoning, fluorescent lighting, or faulty parenting. However, there is no reliable evidence to support those assertions.

Environmental conditions can play some role in attention problems, but the effects of factors such as diet show up on an individual basis more than in large numbers. For example, sugar has not been shown to be a consistent source of overactive behavior, yet there are definitely children who have dramatic negative reactions to excessive sugar. Poor parenting or inadequate teaching are also not significant causes of ADHD. Parental frustration, negative reactions, and unsympathetic teachers can aggravate the problem, but they don't actually cause ADHD.

Emotional Barriers to Learning

Cheryl was not learning at school. Her grades had fallen drastically over the past six months. She seemed moody and distractible. Her enthusiasm for learning was gone, and she was having an increasing number of conflicts with her classmates. The teacher couldn't figure out what was wrong. Cheryl had always been a good student.

At conference time, the teacher asked Cheryl's mother if anything had changed at home. "Yes," the mother reluctantly reported. "Her father and I haven't been getting along very well. There has been a lot of fighting and harsh words, so we're trying a trial separation. Right now her father is living outside the home. We tried to be open and honest with Cheryl and her brother, but I guess the whole thing is taking a larger toll than we thought."

That's a common type of family stress that can become a barrier to learning. A good student with no prior diagnosis of learning disabilities begins suddenly to deteriorate in school. Some outside event or change is most likely responsible, and in this case the negative influence is easy to identify. It may not be easy to overcome because so many dynamics are present. However, we can be fairly certain we know why Cheryl's grades have plummeted.

Let's take another example. Connie, a fifth grader, had been previously diagnosed with learning disabilities. Since the second grade, she had been receiving resource-room help and tutoring. Individualized education programs (IEPs) had been implemented for the past two and a half years. Her progress had been moderate, but she had been moving along well. She was well liked by other students and had seldom acted out unless she was extremely frustrated with a particular situation. Recently, however, Connie was much more temperamental. She cried easily and sometimes seemed apathetic. She went about her daily class activities like a robot. It was as if all her joy had been removed.

At the parent-teacher conference, Connie's parents were asked about changes in the home. "No," they responded, "nothing different has taken place in the home." They had also noticed changes in their daughter but had written most of them off as signs of normal pre-adolescence. The conference discussion provided no answers and few leads to explore further. However, Connie's parents did agree to consult with a counselor.

The cause in the first case is obvious, but in the second it isn't as clear. The line between an emotionally based learning problem and a cognitively based one is not always distinct. The behavioral symptoms common to both include disruptive behavior, indifference, anger, sloppy work, distractibility, missed assignments, and emotional outbursts.

There is a two-way balance between students' emotions and their academic performance. Emotional difficulties can lower classroom learning, and learning problems can cause students to react emotionally. Because of this overlap, distinguishing the learning-disabled student from one who has emotional problems can be tough. Likewise, it's difficult to identify the child who has both learning problems and emotional difficulties.

The window to children's inner emotions is their behavior. Certain behavioral patterns suggest emotional causes. A cry of agony reflects physical or emotional pain. Sorrow and remorse can serve as barometers for loss or wrongdoing. Some children may act out anger in the form of hostility or degrading comments about others, sometimes becoming teasers or bullies. Other children may express anger with passive aggression—never being on time, refusing to comply with instructions, or avoiding responsibility.

The signs of emotions are easy to see, but their meanings aren't quite so clear. If we determine a child has a learning disability, the course of treatment is to initiate accommodation and remediation strategies. If we know the source of a child's emotional problems, we can try to treat them with counseling, family therapy, or environmental changes. However, if we are uncertain about the source of the disturbance, we have to spend time sorting and diagnosing the issues. That's the case with Connie, our fifth grader. We know that something is affecting her learning. It's the job of her teachers, parents, and mental health professionals to try to figure out what that something is.

Stress and Its Relationship to Learning Problems

Stress is our body's physical, mental, emotional, and spiritual reaction to circumstances or stressors that frighten, excite, confuse, endanger, or irritate us. Children deal with their own versions of stress. It occurs in many forms and can be short-term, such as on the first day of school, or can persist for months, as in the case of parental conflicts. (For a comprehensive checklist of stress indicators, see page 73.)

There are three sources of stress for children. The first source is everyday living frustrations—the impending test or the term paper due the next day, relationship tensions, disagreeable siblings, or the competition of trying out for the ball team or musical group. These are ordinary tensions brought about because children live in an imperfect world where expectations aren't always met.

The second source of stress is developmental. It includes the stress of learning to walk, entering school, having a baby sibling come into the family, becoming a teenager, and taking on the responsibility of a part-time job, to name only a few. These are normal milestones, but they can cause some degree of inner tension as children learn to cope. The effectiveness of children's coping methods dictates how they will handle future situations. The more realistic and effective their coping methods, the better will be their emotional state.

The third source of stress is traumatic events that children cannot control—for example, parental divorce, domestic violence, sexual abuse, the death of a loved one, a natural disaster, or a major catastrophe. In each case, there is little that children can do to remove or avoid the event. The crisis comes, and they must find some way to cope.

Burnout results when the demands of a stressor exceed a person's coping abilities and resources. Stressors are impossible to avoid—but that's all right. Stress can build character and perseverance, and it can prepare children to handle unfamiliar events. Burnout, on the other hand, results when the magnitude of a particular event or the accumulation of events overloads the system. The children don't have the resources to deal with the single traumatic event, or they can't deal with the series of frustrations and unmet expectations. We usually apply the term *burnout* to adults, but it also explain the behavior of overloaded children.

There are many indicators of childhood stress. Children may not respond to the nurturing invitations or comments of parents or teachers. They may appear sullen or be overly sensitive to mild criticism. Overstressed children can become highly demanding of adults, clinging to their caregivers or continually displaying a "vacant expression." Additional signs of stress will be given in chapter 3 as we discuss how teachers can screen students for emotional barriers to learning.

Childhood Depression and Learning Problems

Paul had been an excellent student as well as a strong competitor on the school soccer team. Over the past several months, however, he had become a different child. Previously, he had usually awakened bright-eyed and ready to take on the world. Now he seemed constantly miserable, and he made everybody around him miserable. He got into frequent fights with his sister and brother. Previously, classmates would call and come to his house all the time; now none did. He spent most of his time in his room, listening to music of a kind that concerned his parents.

Paul would sleep around the clock if his parents let him. His school-work was suffering. His teacher reported that much of his work was incomplete, not turned in, or done carelessly. When his parents asked about his feelings or school performance, he responded with angry words, or he refused to talk and stalked off to his room. A couple of times, Paul said he wished he were dead and everybody would be better off without him.

Paul was displaying many of the critical signs of depression. In adults, depression can produce tears and sadness. Paul was irritable, angry, and uninterested in life. Something was out of balance, and Paul's parents needed help to find out what was responsible.

Depression can affect people at any age. It can take away their joy when they should be relatively carefree. Sleep patterns can change, ranging from sleeping too much to experiencing insomnia. And when depressed children do sleep, they can sleep fitfully and have night-mares. Depressed kids can also eat too much or experience a significant loss of appetite, gaining or losing weight without intending to. Depression takes away their energy as well so that they no longer want to do the things that used to bring them pleasure.

Self-esteem usually deteriorates in depressed children. They don't want to do anything, they no longer find friends fulfilling, they think school is boring, and they alienate their family. As a result, they become more despondent and think about running away or even about dying.

Depression is a puzzling malady. Is the child depressed because of some outside event, too many stressors, or a medical problem? Or is poor school achievement causing the child to feel like a failure, resulting in depression? It can go both ways. Depression is often symptomatic. Some combination of factors—whether emotional, physical, spiritual, or social—produces a negative view of the past, the present, the future, oneself, and others.

Before we go further, let me point out that no one is immune to depression. Even Christians may experience it. Depression is not a sin. Some Christians believe that a truly obedient follower of God would never get depressed. Some believe that depression means that we have failed to live up to God's expectations. It is true that depression can follow disobedience and the resulting feelings of remorse, as we can see, for example, in 1 Samuel 18 and Jonah 4. But depression itself is not a sin.

If depression were a sin, Jesus Christ sinned. For example, He was distraught in the garden of Gethsemane, saying, "My soul is overwhelmed with sorrow to the point of death" (Matthew 26:38). His words clearly reflected depression. Since we know He was without sin (1 Peter 2:22), it must be possible to experience depression without having sinned.

Depression can be a very natural response to grief, loss, confusion, competition, or stress. We should pay attention to this signal in ourselves and in children. It can be an indication that a person needs to slow down and relax. It can also come from periods of trauma, such as the death of a loved one. Improper diet, inadequate sleep, drugs, infections, and glandular disorders can also contribute. Whatever the source, depression tells us that something in the person's system needs attention before the consequences become more serious.

The causes of depression are far from ideally understood. Many cases are triggered by stressful life events, yet not every student becomes depressed under such circumstances. The intensity and duration of these events, as well as each individual's genetic endowment, coping skills and reaction, and social support network contribute to the likelihood of depression. That is why depression is broadly described as the product of a complex interaction between biological and psychosocial factors. The relative importance of biological and psychosocial factors may vary across individuals and across different types of depression. Because of the multiple possible causes of depression, a complete treatment must involve medical as well as emotional, social, and spiritual sources of help and intervention.

Children of Divorce and Learning Problems

Currently, 50 percent of all first marriages end in divorce (CDC 2002). Estimates are that 60 percent of all children in the United States will spend some part of their lives in single-parent homes.

Unfortunately, divorce and separation affect Christian homes as well as secular ones. Children always suffer from these events, for they are major stressors. Millions of children in classrooms across America are desperately trying to adjust to the personal tragedy of divorce. Even in the best of situations, divorce is painful for everyone involved. Part of the problem is that just when children are most in need of parental love, assurance, and support, their parents are the least able emotionally to provide it.

A recent large-scale study from Sweden tracked for ten years about one million children who grew up in single-parent families. The study found that these children are twice as likely to develop serious psychiatric illnesses, attempt suicide, experience injury, and develop addictions later in life (Weitoft et al. 2003). Studies of families in the United States also show negative consequences for children raised in single-parent homes (Lipman et al. 2002).

In addition, couples often separate or divorce during their children's first eight years. That's a time when many children don't have the language skills to process their pain, so their recovery is delayed until they become more skilled. And children whose parents have remarried and who end up with step-parents and step-siblings face another set of issues in their struggle to regain emotional balance (Frieman 1993).

Divorce is a double-duty stressor. First, it's a major emotional trauma. It signifies the collapse of the family support and protection system children need. As a result, children's trust in people and permanency is shaken, and these children face doubt and uncertainty instead.

Second, divorce is a cumulative experience. It can last for months or years. Usually, the turmoil doesn't stop after the divorce papers are signed. Parental hostility and bitterness may escalate through the years and continue to cause the children pain, suffering, and damage.

Children of divorce must also endure the transition from the status quo to single-parent living. Often they have to change schools, economic standing, living arrangements, and daily routines. Most children are given neither an adequate explanation nor an assurance of continued care, and the lack of these makes the perception of events all the more traumatic.

When children learn about their parents' impending divorce, they often respond with shock, apprehension, and anger. Even knowing their parents have been fighting and might separate doesn't reduce the impact of the announcement, for most children hope against hope that things will work out and their parents will stay together. Because many parents give only a single pronouncement, younger children may postpone their response out of disbelief. Inside they must believe that no news is good news, denying their awareness of any observable movement of their parents toward the separation or divorce.

One study of children of divorce cited a number of symptoms that they may experience. Behaviors in the classroom can include anxiety, depression, regression, asthma, allergies, tantrums, daydreaming, over-aggressive behavior, withdrawal from relationships, poor academic performance, frequent crying, absence of emotion, and difficulty in communicating feelings (Wallerstein and Kelly 1980).

Effects of Family Violence on Learning

Another source of stress, depression, and related emotional problems is abuse and family violence. Abused children can manifest their feelings in many ways. Screams of fright and muffled cries may sound from distant bedrooms. Terrifying nightmares, anxiety, and panic attacks are additional consequences. Lifelong emotional scars, such as an inability to trust, can also indicate pain in victimized children. These manifestations can result whether the violence is inflicted on the children themselves or on others in the home.

Do you remember Connie, the puzzling student described earlier in this chapter? Her parents took her to a counselor, who eventually determined that she had been sexually abused by a trusted relative. In spite of her parents' attempts to be cautious, an uncle had taken liberties with Connie. Of course, he told her not to tell anybody because it was their "own little secret."

So she and her family then had to deal with the effects of child sexual abuse in addition to the challenges of a learning disability. The counselor said that the combination of circumstances was less harmful than some, so Connie ought to make a full recovery. For about six months she would need counseling, and she would face the stress of participating in the prosecution of the perpetrator. However, because the family believed what Connie told them and provided strong support, she would be able to overcome her trauma.

Abused children are found at all socioeconomic levels, and the overall incidence rates are similar for city, suburban, and rural communities. Children are victimized in every community regardless of the status of their parents or caretakers. The Christian community, unfortunately, is not immune to the presence of child sexual abuse and spousal abuse. It's a horrible fact, but the reality is that family violence may be a real reason why a child isn't learning (Martin 1987, 1992).

Underachievement

We have seen that learning disabilities and attention deficits are conditions that can cause problems with learning. In contrast, underachievement is a by-product of some condition or situation, and it is a symptom that a student is either unable or unwilling to achieve at the expected level. Underachievement is a particular type of problem common in our schools, and we might ask, What can we do to help an underachieving student?

There is perhaps no situation more frustrating for parents than living with children who don't perform up to their academic potential. These children are labeled "underachievers," yet few people agree on exactly what the term means. At what point does underachievement end and achievement begin? Is a capable student who is failing mathematics while doing superior work in reading an underachiever? Does underachievement begin suddenly, or is it better described as a series of poor performances over an extended period?

The lack of consensus on how best to define and measure underachievement—qualitative or quantitative, amount of discrepancy, nature and extent of discrepancy—all make it difficult to estimate the number of gifted students who are underachieving. The estimates of gifted students who underachieve have ranged from 20 to 50 percent (Ford and Thomas 1997).

But the problem isn't limited to gifted students. Many other students don't work up to their potential. Parents and educators have struggled for years to determine how to motivate such students most effectively. Both this discussion of underachievement and the material in chapter 10 on working with underachieving students apply to students having a range of abilities, from average to gifted.

Besides underachieving academically, children may also underperform artistically, athletically, or musically. I've seen young people with tremendous athletic or musical talent who for some reason were not consistently motivated to apply or cultivate their potential. They seldom practiced, relying on natural ability to get them through the actual game or concert.

To find a solution to the problem of underachievement, we need to examine it closely. Underachievement, first and foremost, is a behavior, and as such it can change over time. Underachievement is often seen as a problem of attitude or work habits. However, neither habits nor attitude can be modified as directly as behaviors. Thus, when we refer to underachieving behaviors, we pinpoint those parts of children's lives that they're most able to alter.

This learning problem is specific to situations and subject areas. Many capable children who don't succeed in school are successful in outside activities such as sports, social occasions, and after-school jobs. Even a child who does poorly in most school subjects may display a talent or interest in at least one activity. Thus, labeling a child as an underachiever disregards any positive outcomes or behaviors the child displays. It's better to label the behaviors than the child. For example, we might say that a child is underachieving in math and language arts rather than that he or she is an underachieving student.

A judgment of underachievement can vary from one observer to another. For some students, teachers, and parents, as long as a student attains passing grades, there's no underachievement. "After all," this group would say, "a C is an average grade." To others, a grade of B+ constitutes underachievement if the student is expected to get an A. Recognizing what defines success and failure is the first step toward understanding underachieving behaviors.

Lack of achievement is tied closely to self-concept. Children who learn to see themselves in terms of failure eventually begin to place self-imposed limits on what is possible for them. They think that their academic successes are flukes, while their low grades reinforce negative self-perceptions. This self-deprecating attitude often results in comments such as "Why should I even try? I'm just going to fail anyway" or "Even if I do succeed, people will say it's because I cheated." When children have this mind-set, their initiative to change or to accept a challenge diminishes (Delisle and Berger 1990).

Underachievement can have many sources. One way to describe them is to identify environmental, personal, and family or emotional factors.

The two major environmental sources of problems are in the school and the peer group. The high-risk school environment for a capable student could include an anti-intellectual or anti-achievement atmosphere that sets a high priority on social status but not on intellectual attainment; athletic, musical, or artistic excellence; or preparation for post–high school education. An antigifted atmosphere might also pose a high risk. In such an environment, gifted programming is considered elitist, and the emphasis is on the importance of all students' being well adjusted and "fitting into a mold" (Rimm 1990).

Some capable students value social acceptance far more than high achievement. Such students may reject opportunities to participate in a more challenging academic program, or they may deliberately underachieve to avoid the psychological conflict created by peer rejection. In the eyes of capable but socially conscious students, advanced courses may take too much time, limiting their social activities.

Another environmental feature may be "too easy" curricula that are boring and unsatisfying. Talented students then escape into daydreaming or talking as more rewarding alternatives. An apathetic attitude, a critical approach to life, and indifferent performance may result when talented children aren't challenged in at least some aspect of their ability.

Other elements in underachievement can involve neurological and personal features. The neurological contribution can stem from some types of learning disabilities or at least from distinct learning-style differences. Researchers have found in gifted underachievers several peculiar patterns that suggest learning disabilities. One such pattern is high scores in vocabulary, abstract reasoning, spatial relations, and mathematical analysis coupled with low scores in tasks that require sequencing. Such a pattern indicates a spatial learning style and perhaps an auditory sequential-processing deficit (Silverman 1989).

One researcher found significant learning-style differences in junior high school underachievers. They weren't able to do as well on analytical tasks that were detailed or computational, or on convergent problem-solving tasks requiring precise and analytic information processing. Yet on tests of more holistic skills such as reading comprehension and vocabulary, the gifted underachievers were equal to the achievers (Redding 1990).

The education of gifted students with learning disabilities has only recently emerged as a focus of educational concern. Estimates are that at least 2 percent of children with learning disabilities may be gifted. We must keep on the lookout for possible disabilities or major learning-style deviations as possible sources of underachievement in capable students.

A multitude of family and emotional dynamics can also result in underachievement. Family dysfunction and conflict, parental divorce, abuse, relationship problems, lack of self-confidence, inability to persevere, inadequate goals, emotional problems, and cultural differences can all contribute to the problem. Researchers have found that under-achieving students tend to be inferior to achievers in emotional maturity, self-image, and school motivation (Gallagher 1991).

Family factors have been shown to affect normal-ability underachievers. One study found that four variables distinguished the families of achievers from those of underachievers: (1) they emphasized moral or religious values and ideals; (2) they modeled and affirmed the importance of realistic achievement; (3) they practiced family cohesiveness; and (4) they encouraged their adolescents to develop appropriate autonomy (Wood 1988). A recent study found that under-involved and non-encouraging parents and teachers, negative parental attitudes toward work, family conflict, lack of career direction, and family transitions were associated with underachievement (Peterson 2001).

Underachievement has drawn a great deal of attention from educators over the years. No easy answers exist. However, in chapter 10 I'll try to identify some tactics and interventions that have benefited many underachieving students.

We have concluded our overview of the four major barriers to learning. In the next two chapters, we turn to the process of screening for struggling students and of obtaining a specific diagnosis.

References

AAP. *See* American Academy of Pediatrics.

Amen, D. G. 1997. *Images into the mind.* Fairfield, CA: Mindworks Press.

———. 1999. Brain SPECT imaging and ADD. In *Understanding, diagnosing, and treating AD/HD in children and adolescents: An integrative approach.* J. A. Incorvaia, B. S. Mark-Goldstein, and D. Tessmer, eds. Northvale, NJ: Jason Aronson.

———. 2001. Why don't psychiatrists look at the brain: The case for the greater use of SPECT imaging in neuropsychiatry. *Neuropsychiatry Review* 2, no. 1:1, 19–21.

Amen, D. G., and B. D. Carmichael. 1997. High-resolution SPECT imaging in ADHD. *Annals of Clinical Psychiatry* 9, no. 2:81–86.

American Academy of Pediatrics. 2001. Prevalence and assessment of attention-deficit/hyperactivity disorder in primary care settings. *Pediatrics* 107, no. 3:e43.

American Psychiatric Association. 1994. *Diagnostic and statistical manual of mental disorders.* 4th ed. Washington, DC: American Psychiatric Association.

———. 2001. *Diagnostic and statistical manual of mental disorders.* 4th ed. Text rev. Washington, DC: American Psychiatric Association.

Barkley, R. A. 1997. *ADHD and the nature of self-control.* New York: Guilford Press.

———. 1998. *Attention-deficit hyperactivity disorder: A handbook for diagnosis and treatment.* 2nd ed. New York: Guilford Press.

———. 2002a. ADHD and accident proneness. *The ADHD Report* 10, no. 2:2–4.

———. 2002b. International consensus statement on ADHD. *Clinical Child and Family Psychology Review* 5, no. 2:89–111.

Baumgaertel, A., L. Copeland, and M. L. Wolraich. 1996. Attention deficit-hyperactivity disorder. In *Disorders of development and learning: A practical guide to assessment and management.* 2nd ed. St. Louis, MO: Mosby Yearbook.

Biederman, J., S. V. Faraone, K. Keenan, J. Benjamin, B. Krifcher, C. Moore, S. Sprich, K. Ugaglia, M. S. Jellinek, R. Steingard, T.

Spencer, D. Norman, R. Kolodny, I. Kraus, J. Perrin, M. B. Keller, and M. T. Tsuang. 1992. Further evidence for family-genetic risk factors in attention deficit hyperactivity disorder (ADHD): Patterns of comorbidity in probands and relatives in psychiatrically and pediatrically referred samples. *Archives of General Psychiatry* 49, no. 9:728–38.

Biederman, J., S. V. Faraone, and K. Lapey. 1992. Comorbidity of diagnosis in attention deficit disorder. In *Attention-deficit hyperactivity disorder.* G. Weiss, ed. Philadelphia, PA: WB Saunders.

Bradley, R., L. Danielson, and D. P. Hallahan, eds. 2002. *Identification of learning disabilities.* Mahwah, NJ: Lawrence Erlbaum Associates, Inc.

Brown, T. E. 1996. *Brown attention deficit disorder scales.* San Antonio, TX: Psychological Corporation.

———. 1999. Does ADHD diagnosis require impulsivity-hyperactivity? A response to Gordon and Barkley. *The ADHD Report* 7, no. 6:1–7.

———, ed. 2000. *Attention-deficit disorders and comorbidities in children, adolescents and adults.* Washington, DC: American Psychiatric Press.

Castellanos, F. X., et al. 2001. Quantitative brain magnetic resonance imaging in girls with ADHD. *Archives of General Psychiatry* 58:289–95.

CDC. *See* Centers for Disease Control and Prevention.

Centers for Disease Control and Prevention (CDC). 2002. Births, marriages, divorces, and deaths: Provisional data for 2001. *National Vital Statistics Reports* 50, no. 13:1–2.

Curry, L. 1990. A critique of the research on learning styles. *Educational Leadership* 48:50–56.

Delisle, J., and S. L. Berger. 1990. Underachieving gifted students. ERIC Clearinghouse on Disabilities and Gifted Education. ERIC EC Digest #E478. http://www.ericec.org/digests/e478.html.

Dougherty, D. D., A. A. Bonab, T. J. Spencer, S. L. Rauch, B. K. Madras, and A. J. Fischman. 1999. Dopamine transporter density in patients with attention deficit hyperactivity disorder. *The Lancet* 354: 2132–3.

Ellis, A. K., and J. T. Fouts. 1993. *Research on educational innovations.* Princeton Junction, NJ: Eye on Education.

Ernst, M., L. Liebenauer, A. King, G. A. Firtzgerald, P. M. Cohen, and A. J. Zametkin. 1994. Reduced brain metabolism in hyperactive girls. *Journal of the American Academy of Child and Adolescent Psychiatry* 33:858–68.

Faraone, S. V., A. Doyle, E. Mick, and J. Biederman. 2001. Meta-analysis of the association between the 7-repeat allele of the dopamine D4 receptor gene and ADHD. *American Journal of Psychiatry* 158:1052–7.

Ford, D. Y., and A. Thomas. 1997. Underachievement among gifted minority students: Problems and promises. ERIC Clearinghouse on Disabilities and Gifted Education. ERIC EC Digest #E544. http://www.ericec.org/digests/e544.html.

Frieman, B. B. 1993. Separation and divorce: Children want their teachers to know. *Young Children* (September): 58–63.

Gallagher, J. J. 1991. Personal patterns of underachievement. *Journal for the Education of the Gifted* 14:221–33.

Gaub, S., and C. L. Carlson. 1997. Gender differences in ADHD: A meta-analysis and critical review. *Journal of the American Academy of Child and Adolescent Psychiatry* 36, no. 8:1036–45.

Gershon, J. 2002a. Gender differences in ADHD. *The ADHD Report* 10, no. 4:1–16.

———. 2002b. A meta-analytic review of gender differences in ADHD. *Journal of Attention Disorders* 5, no. 3:143–54.

Goldman, L. S., M. Genel, R. J. Bezman, and P. J. Slanetz. 1998. Diagnosis and treatment of attention-deficit/hyperactivity disorder in children and adolescents. *Journal of the American Medical Association* 279: 1000–1007.

Gorski, P. A. 2002. Racing cain. *Journal of Developmental and Behavioral Pediatrics* 23, no. 2:95.

Greene, R. W., J. Biederman, S. V. Faraone, et al. 2001. Social impairment in girls with ADHD: Patterns, gender comparisons, and correlates. *Journal of the American Academy of Child and Adolescent Psychiatry* 40:704–10.

Grenz, Stanley. 1996. *A primer on postmodernism*. Grand Rapids, MI: Eerdmans.

Jensen, P. S. 2000. ADHD: Current concepts on etiology, pathophysiology and neurobiology. *Child and Adolescent Psychiatric Clinics of North America* 9, no. 3:557–72.

Leonard, C. M. 2001. Imaging brain structure in children: Differentiating language disability and reading disability. *Learning Disability Quarterly* 24, no. 3:158–76.

Lipman, E. L., M. H. Boyle, M. D. Doley, and D. R. Offord. 2002. Child well-being in single-mother families. *Journal of the American Academy of Child and Adolescent Psychiatry* 41, no. 1:75–82.

Lyon, G. R., J. M. Fletcher, S. E. Shaywitz, et al. 2001. Rethinking learning disabilities. In *Rethinking special education for a new century.* C. E. Finn Jr., A. J. Rotherham, and C. R. Hokanson Jr., eds. Washington, DC: Thomas B. Fordham. http://www.edexcellence.net/library/special_ed/special_ed_ch12.pdf.

Martin, G. L. 1987. *Counseling in cases of family violence and abuse.* Vol. 6. Dallas, TX: Word.

———. 1992. *Critical problems in children and youth: Counseling techniques for problems resulting from attention deficit disorder, sexual abuse, custody battles, and related issues.* Dallas, TX: Word.

McCallum, Dennis, ed. 1996. *The death of truth: What's wrong with multiculturalism, the rejection of reason and the new postmodern diversity.* Bloomington, MN: Bethany House.

McGuffin, P., B. Riley, and R. Plomin. 2001. Toward behavioral genomics. *Science* 291:1232–49.

Milich, R., A. C. Balentine, and D. R. Lynam. 2001. ADHD/combined type and ADHD/predominantly inattentive type are distinct and unrelated disorders. *Clinical Psychology: Science and Practice* 8:463–88.

———. 2002. The predominately inattentive subtype—not a subtype of ADHD. *The ADHD Report* 10, no. 1:1–6.

MTA Cooperative Group. 1999. A 14-month randomized clinical trial of treatment strategies for Attention-Deficit/Hyperactivity Disorder. *Archives of General Psychiatry* 56 (December): 1073–86.

National Joint Committee on Learning Disabilities (NJCLD). 1994. *Collective perspectives on issues affecting learning disabilities: Position papers and statements.* Austin, TX: Pro-Ed.

———. 1998. Operationalizing the NJCLD definition of learning disabilities for ongoing assessment in schools. ASHA *2002 Desk Reference* 3:535–42. http://www.asha.org/NR/rdonlyres/B3904ACD-DF17-4B39-85F6-6B34C19137FB/0/19137_1.pdf.

NJCLD. *See* National Joint Committee on Learning Disabilities.

Pastor, P. N., and C. A. Rueben. 2002. Attention deficit disorder and learning disability: United States, 1997–98. National Center for Health Statistics. *Vital and Health Statistics* 10, no. 206. http:// www.cdc.gov/nchs/data/series/sr_10/sr10_206.pdf.

Peterson, J. S. 2001. Successful adults who were once adolescent underachievers. *Gifted Child Quarterly* 45, no. 4:236–50.

Raskind, W. H. 2001. Current understanding of the genetic basis of reading and spelling disability. *Learning Disability Quarterly* 24, no. 3:141–57.

Redding, R. 1990. Learning preferences and skill patterns among underachieving gifted adolescents. *Gifted Child Quarterly* 34:72–75.

Richards, T. L. 2001. Functional magnetic resonance imaging and spectroscopic imaging of the brain: Application of fMRI and fMRS to reading disabilities and education. *Learning Disability Quarterly* 24, no. 3:189–203.

Rimm, S. 1990. Underachievement and superachievement: Flip sides of the same psychological coin. In *Handbook of gifted education.* N. C. G. Davis, ed. Boston: Allyn and Bacon.

Silverman, L. 1989. The visual-spatial learner. *Preventing School Failure* 34:15–20.

Smalley, S. L., V. Kustanovich, S. L. Minassian, et al. 2002. Genetic linkage of attention-deficit/hyperactivity disorder on chromosome 16p13 in a region implicated in autism. *American Journal of Human Genetics* 71:959–63.

U.S. Congress. 1997. *Individuals with Disabilities Education Act Amendments of 1997.* http://www.ideapractices.org/law/law/index.php.

U.S. Department of Education. 2001. OSERS twenty-third annual report to Congress on the implementation of the IDEA. http://www.ed.gov/about/reports/annual/osep/2001/index.html.

Wallerstein, J. S., and J. B. Kelly. 1980. *Surviving the breakup.* New York: Basic Books.

Weitoft, G. R., A. Hjern, B. Haglund, and M. Rosen. 2003. Mortality, severe morbidity, and injury in children living with single parents in Sweden: A population-based study. *The Lancet* 361, no. 9354:289–95.

Wilens, T. E., J. Biederman, and T. Spencer. 2002. attention deficit/hyperactivity disorder across the lifespan. *Annual Review of Medicine* 53:113–31.

Wood, J. 1988. Family environment and its relationship to underachievement. *Adolescence* 23:283–90.

Zametkin, A., and W. Liotta. 1998. The neurobiology of attention-deficit/hyperactivity disorder. *Journal of Clinical Psychiatry* 59:17–23.

CHAPTER 3

How to Identify the Learning Problem
Initial Classroom Screening

W e will now consider methods of identifying the reasons behind a student's struggles in the classroom. The process can be complicated because learning is an intricate and sometimes perplexing endeavor. Yet we must do our best to understand why a particular student is having so much trouble with learning. Once we know what's wrong, we can bring the most appropriate resources to bear on helping that student achieve more success. Remember that our mandate is to help all children reach the full level of the potential for which God designed them. Diagnosis is the first step.

This step begins with observations. You're asking if there's a possibility that your student has the symptoms of a learning problem. You decide by comparing what you've learned about the signs and symptoms of learning problems with what you know about the particular student. The checklists and descriptions in this chapter will help you make that comparison. You'll probably need additional information from the family and others who are familiar with your student's learning characteristics.

It is important that you not jump to conclusions, reserving judgment until the evidence seems reasonably clear and there has been a professional evaluation. The next step—and the subject of chapter 4—is how to make an evaluation. Your impressions as a teacher are important. Sometimes your own assessment will lead to changes in the classroom and improvements in the student's ability to learn. At other times, you will need competent professional input to delineate the exact nature of your student's problems and the probable causes. If clarity does not result from the data, if the symptoms aren't extreme, or if others who know the child aren't overly concerned, you may want to wait awhile to get a better grasp of the situation. Just the fact that a few of the symptoms from the checklists apply to a given student doesn't mean you have to launch a detailed diagnostic workup immediately. Quite a few symptoms need to be present, along with definite problems in some aspect of learning.

Determining Whether a Student Has a Learning Problem

I've prepared a series of general queries that can help both educators and parents begin to think through the nature of a student's problem and how they might begin the diagnostic or intervention process. First, we'll examine questions for both the school and home environments. Then we'll consider how to determine the specific problem the student might have.

School-Related Questions

❑ What has been tried so far? What was the rationale for each attempt?

❑ Which methods seemed to work, and which did not?

❑ What data or measures of progress are available to document these attempts?

❑ In what learning conditions does the student appear to respond best? What are examples of the most unfavorable conditions?

❑ What kind of evaluation will determine the specific educational needs of the student? How can such an evaluation be obtained?

❑ What school resources can be brought forward to help remediate the problem? What's the procedure for gaining access to those resources?

❑ What is the student's unique learning style, and how does it relate to the problem?

❑ How does the teacher's predominant learning style compare with the student's? How does the teacher adjust to meet the student's needs?

❑ What strengths can the student use to accommodate or compensate? For example, can the student use strong visual learning skills in the homework process to compensate for poor auditory learning skills?

❑ How does the student's progress in the problem area compare with his or her progress in other areas of schooling? In other words, how does the problem area relate to the big picture?

❑ Are other students having similar problems? If so, what are the implications?

❑ What kind of consultation has the teacher done to attempt to find help for the student?

❑ If the student has problems with reading, what approach or approaches to instruction are being used (whole language, language experience, basal reader, sight, or phonics)? What approach or approaches seem best for meeting the student's needs? Is a combined approach more appropriate than a one-dimensional strategy?

Home-Related Questions

❏ How is the student's homework routine organized? What changes might make the time spent on homework more efficient and productive?

❏ Could lifestyle factors be affecting the student's school performance? For example, is the student getting enough sleep, eating well, living in safe conditions, following an appropriate daily schedule, and not watching too much television or playing too many video games?

❏ Are there medical or other physical problems that could be affecting the student's schoolwork?

❏ Have the student's vision and hearing been examined? Could there be infections, chronic illnesses, chemical imbalances, or allergies?

❏ Are there emotional or family problems? Is there alcoholism, drug abuse, family violence, divorce, or a recent death? Have there been major changes such as a job loss, financial problems, or a new family member?

❏ How can you as a teacher assist the parents in remediation, accommodation, or compensation?

❏ Are the parents willing to follow through with the educational recommendations?

❏ What adjustments at home will be necessary to carry out those recommendations?

These questions will get you started. The idea is to be as comprehensive and thorough as possible in identifying your student's needs. You should also be as systematic as possible in considering the options for helping and selecting the best approach for the particular student. You need to take the time to evaluate all possible causes of your student's problems, realizing that there can often be several components to learning difficulties. Consistent and competent implementation of the components of the intervention plan can follow the steps given below.

Checklists for Identifying Common Symptoms of Learning Disabilities

If a student of yours is having learning problems, you begin the process of diagnosis with some preliminary observations about the kind of difficulties the child is experiencing. What follows is a checklist of the most common symptoms of learning disabilities. As we saw earlier, learning disabilities are believed to arise from dysfunctions in the brain. Students with learning disabilities have significant difficulties in perceiving information (input), processing and remembering information (integration), expressing information (output), or in some combination of these. Outward manifestations of any of these difficulties indicate a learning disability. These warning signs are grouped according to age in the following checklists to help you more easily identify symptoms in your students.

Although growth patterns vary among children and within individual children, uneven development or significant delays in development can signal the presence of LDs. It is important to keep in mind that the behaviors listed below must persist over time to be considered warning signs. Any child may occasionally exhibit one or two of these behaviors in the course of normal development.

Warning Signs for LDs in Preschool Children

Language
- ❏ Slow development in speaking words or sentences
- ❏ Pronunciation problems
- ❏ Difficulty learning new words
- ❏ Difficulty following simple directions
- ❏ Difficulty understanding questions
- ❏ Difficulty expressing wants and desires
- ❏ Difficulty rhyming words
- ❏ Lack of interest in storytelling

Motor Skills
- ❏ Clumsiness
- ❏ Poor balance
- ❏ Difficulty manipulating small objects
- ❏ Awkwardness in running, jumping, or climbing
- ❏ Difficulty learning to tie shoes, button shirts, or perform other self-help activities
- ❏ Avoidance of drawing or tracing

Cognition
- ❏ Trouble memorizing the alphabet or the days of the week
- ❏ Poor memory for what should be routine, or everyday, procedures
- ❏ Difficulty with cause and effect, sequencing, and counting
- ❏ Difficulty with basic concepts such as size, shape, and color

Attention
- ❏ High distractibility
- ❏ Impulsive behavior
- ❏ Unusual restlessness, or hyperactivity
- ❏ Difficulty staying on task
- ❏ Difficulty changing activities
- ❏ Constant repetition of an idea, or inability to move on to a new idea (perseveration)

Social Behavior

❑ Trouble interacting with others; choosing to play alone to an abnormal degree

❑ Tendency to have sudden and extreme mood changes

❑ Tendency to become easily frustrated

❑ Tendency to be difficult to manage and proneness to have temper tantrums

(Begert 2000)

Warning Signs for LDs in Elementary School Children

Warning signs for this age group may include any of those listed above for preschool children in addition to the following:

Language/Mathematics

❑ Slow learning of sound-to-letter correspondences

❑ Consistent errors in reading or spelling

❑ Difficulty remembering basic sight words

❑ Inability to retell a story in sequence

❑ Trouble learning to tell time or count money

❑ Confusion of math signs such as +, −, x, /, and =

❑ Transposition of number sequences

❑ Trouble memorizing math facts

❑ Trouble with place value

❑ Difficulty remembering the steps of mathematics operations, such as long division

Motor Skills

❑ Poor coordination, or awkwardness

❑ Difficulty copying from chalkboard

❑ Difficulty aligning columns in math

❑ Poor handwriting

Attention/Organization
❑ Difficulty concentrating or focusing on a task
❑ Difficulty finishing work on time
❑ Inability to follow multiple directions
❑ Unusual sloppiness or carelessness
❑ Poor concept of direction such as left and right
❑ Rejection of new concepts or changes in routine

Social Behavior
❑ Difficulty understanding facial expressions or gestures
❑ Difficulty understanding social situations
❑ Tendency to misinterpret behavior of peers, adults, or both
❑ Apparent lack of common sense

(Begert 2000)

Warning Signs for LDs in Secondary School Students

Warning signs of learning disabilities in secondary students include the following. To be considered warning signs, these must occur as a consistent pattern of behaviors to a significant degree over a period of weeks or months:

Language/Mathematics/Social Studies
❑ Avoidance of reading and writing
❑ Tendency to misread information
❑ Difficulty summarizing
❑ Poor reading comprehension
❑ Difficulty understanding subject-area textbooks
❑ Trouble with open-ended questions
❑ Continued poor spelling
❑ Poor grasp of abstract concepts
❑ Poor skills in writing essays
❑ Difficulty in learning foreign languages
❑ Poor ability to apply math skills

Attention/Organization
❑ Difficulty staying organized
❑ Trouble with test formats such as multiple choice
❑ Slow work pace in class and in testing situations
❑ Poor note-taking skills
❑ Poor ability to proofread or double-check work

Social Behavior
❑ Difficulty accepting criticism
❑ Difficulty seeking or giving feedback
❑ Problems negotiating or advocating for oneself
❑ Difficulty resisting peer pressure
❑ Difficulty understanding another person's perspectives

(Begert 2000)

Do any of the previous items apply to a student of yours? The presence of two or three probably doesn't indicate a learning disability. If five or more are present, further investigation is warranted. The following overview of the learning process and of the possible effects of LDs on a student's ability to learn will help explain some of the terms and concerns in these checklists.

Description of the Learning Process

We can describe learning as a sequence of operations illustrated in the following diagram, which shows the information-processing model of learning. This model identifies the flow of information during the learning process. It starts with the initial reception of information, moves through the processing function, and concludes with some action. The four steps shown in the illustration describe how the brain functions as it seeks to understand information. Since these thinking and doing processes are crucial to learning, if a problem occurs at any point in the sequence, a learning disability is probably present.

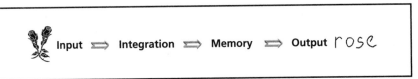

Figure 1. Sequence for Processing Information in the Brain

In this example, a student is taking a spelling test. The teacher says the word and uses it in a sentence: "The word is *rose*. The yellow rose looked beautiful in the garden." The student hears this verbalization. The sound waves have gone from the teacher to the ears of the student and have registered in the brain. That's the ***input*** part of the sequence. Input can come through any of the senses, such as hearing, seeing, or touching. At this initial point the brain begins to decode, or record and identify, incoming information. If there are any problems with this initial perceiving of information, the student will obviously have difficulty with learning. For example, a student who has difficulty with visual perception may have problems with identifying an object's shape or position. If there are problems with auditory perception, the student may have difficulty distinguishing subtle differences in sounds or letter combinations in words and thus may hear, for example, *grows* instead of *rose*.

After the initial perceiving, or input step, the student begins to ***integrate,*** or make sense of, the information. The student recognizes the word *rose* as the one she is supposed to spell out of all the words the teacher used in the sentence. The student has decoded the information and understands what is being taught or requested.

Integration can involve sequencing, abstracting, and organizing. In this case the student must translate the sound patterns into a recognizable form and separate the target word from the other spoken words. The integration process is how the brain interprets information.

Various other cognitive processes take place in this phase, such as making associations and decisions. Students who have problems with sequencing, abstracting, or organizing can have trouble understanding jokes or puns, or using pieces of information to make sense of a concept. Sequencing problems can result in confusing the order of events in a story or reversing letters or numbers.

The next step of the learning process is **memory,** the process the brain uses to store information. In our illustration, the student begins to search her memory for the right sequence of letters to spell *rose*. She has previously stored the correct spelling in her memory.

The storage and retrieval process can consist of either short-term (working) memory or long-term memory. In this case, the student uses long-term memory to recall the letter formation and eye-hand coordination necessary to write out the word. A student with problems of memory may often ask for questions or requests to be repeated, or may not be able to retain information without frequent repetitions or some type of visual or physical reminder.

The final step is the **output.** This is the encoding process in which the student uses or applies the information in some fashion. Information comes out of the brain by means of language or through muscle activity, such as writing or throwing a ball. In our example, this process occurs as the brain sends messages to the nerves and muscles, resulting in a fine-motor response of writing the letters that make up the correct spelling of *rose*. If all goes well, the word is correctly spelled, and the process has worked without a hitch. Students with output problems may act clumsily, speak haltingly, or struggle with either their speed or the quality of their handwriting.

This example, though relatively simple, illustrates the major stepping-stones in the pathway to learning. A student with a learning disability doesn't function well in one or more of those steps as compared with his or her ability in other areas (Lerner 2003; Silver 2001).

The preceding description is just one way to explain learning disabilities. The learning process is complex, and no one understands completely the intricate workings of the brain. However, this model provides a general understanding of how your students learn and where problems may exist. All students have their own combination of learning strengths and weaknesses. The goal is to arrive at a profile that best describes your student who is having trouble.

Screening for ADHD

Earlier, we saw that an attention-deficit student could be primarily inattentive, primarily impulsive-hyperactive, or a combination of both. The following checklist is taken from the fourth edition of the *Diagnostic and Statistical Manual of Mental Disorders*. To be considered as exhibiting any item in the checklist, a student must have a minimum number of specific symptoms that have persisted for at least six months. These symptoms also need to occur to a degree that is maladaptive and inconsistent with the child's developmental level (American Psychiatric Association 1994).

DSM-IV Diagnostic Criteria for ADHD

Symptoms of Inattention
- ❏ Often fails to give close attention to details or makes careless mistakes in schoolwork, work, or other activities
- ❏ Often has difficulty sustaining attention in tasks or play activities
- ❏ Often does not seem to listen when spoken to directly
- ❏ Often does not follow through on instructions and fails to finish schoolwork, chores, or duties in the workplace, but not because of oppositional behavior or failure to understand instructions
- ❏ Often has difficulty organizing tasks and activities

❑ Often avoids, dislikes, or is reluctant to engage in tasks that require sustained mental effort, such as in schoolwork or homework

❑ Often loses objects such as toys, school assignments, pencils, books, or tools that are necessary for tasks or activities

❑ Is often easily distracted by extraneous stimuli

❑ Is often forgetful in daily activities

A1: _____ out of 9 criteria met

Symptoms of Hyperactivity-Impulsivity

Hyperactivity

❑ Often fidgets with hands or feet, or squirms in seat

❑ Often leaves seat in classroom or in other situations in which remaining seated is expected

❑ Often runs about or climbs excessively in situations in which it is inappropriate (in adolescents or adults, this symptom may be limited to subjective feelings of restlessness)

❑ Often has difficulty playing or engaging in leisure activities quietly

❑ Is often "on the go" or acts as if "driven by a motor"

❑ Often talks excessively

Impulsivity

❑ Often blurts out answers before questions have been completed

❑ Often has difficulty waiting turn

❑ Often interrupts or intrudes on others: for example, into conversations or games

A2: _____ out of 9 criteria met

_____ 314.01 ADHD, Combined Type

_____ 314.00 ADHD, Predominantly Inattentive Type

_____ 314.01 ADHD, Predominantly Hyperactive-Impulsive Type

Note the numbers of items you checked in A1 and A2. Six or more in A1 may indicate that your student has the inattentive type of ADHD. Six or more in A2 may indicate the hyperactive-impulsive type. If you checked at least six items on the entire chart, your student may have the combined type of ADHD.

Besides the fact that six or more of the symptoms within each category must have persisted for six months or longer to be considered warning signs, these ADHD symptoms must be evident before age seven. There also must be some impairment evident in two or more settings, such as school and home. There must be clear evidence of clinically significant impairment in social, academic, or occupational functioning, and the symptoms must not be a result of other conditions such as mental illness, moodiness, or anxiety disorder. Additionally, it is important to remember that while hyperactivity used to be the primary descriptive feature in attention disorders, it actually occurs in fewer than 30 percent of children who have an attention disorder. If the student you are observing has at least five or six behaviors in either the inattentive or the impulsive-hyperactive category, you need to obtain a professional opinion.

Screening for Stress

Children give various indications that they are overly stressed. I've tried to compile as many of those red-flag behaviors as possible to give you a comprehensive reference. Because each person experiences his or her stress in unique ways, no one list can guarantee to mention everything a student might display. However, this list provides a good start. These same symptoms can indicate other emotional problems. No single symptom is in itself an indicator of stress or underlying emotional disturbance. You as a parent or teacher must look instead for clusters of these symptoms that tend to endure for extended periods. Teachers may not see many of these symptoms at school, but you may get some indications from talking with the parents or other caretakers.

Indications of Stress in Children

Emotional Signs

- ❏ Appears worked up and excited
- ❏ Is worried and anxious
- ❏ Has crying spells
- ❏ Grinds teeth or clenches jaws
- ❏ Feels at loose ends
- ❏ Is forgetful and confused
- ❏ Has memory losses or lapses
- ❏ Has difficulty concentrating and is inattentive or distractible
- ❏ Sleeps too much or can't sleep; has nightmares or fitful sleep
- ❏ Overeats or undereats
- ❏ Snacks excessively
- ❏ Is depressed and apathetic
- ❏ Does not respond to nurturing efforts or comments
- ❏ Has persistent fatigue
- ❏ Shows lowered level of achievement or performance
- ❏ Complains of being dizzy and disoriented
- ❏ Is often grouchy and irritable
- ❏ Makes excessive demands
- ❏ Wets the bed or struggles with daytime wetting or soiling
- ❏ Seems nervous
- ❏ Paces about and can't sit still
- ❏ Has excessive or irrational fear
- ❏ Panics or has anxiety
- ❏ Is clingy or overdependent on caregiver
- ❏ Exhibits obsessive, repetitive, or ritualistic behavior
- ❏ Taps fingers, feet, or pencil or has leg tremors
- ❏ Frowns or scowls continually
- ❏ Has anger outbursts, temper tantrums; acts out aggressively

Internal Signs

❑ Has an upset stomach, nausea, or a churning sensation

❑ Has heartburn or acid indigestion

❑ Has intestinal upset or cramps

❑ Reports fast or irregular heartbeat

❑ Has clammy, cold, or clenched hands

❑ Feels light-headed or faint

❑ Has hot or cold spells

❑ Has elevated blood pressure

❑ Has loss of breath or an uneven breathing pattern

❑ Feels "tight" all over

❑ Feels tingling sensations on skin

❑ Has cold sores in mouth or lips

❑ Complains of feeling sick but has no observable symptoms

Bodily Signs

❑ Has headaches

❑ Has backaches or other muscular aches

❑ Has low-grade infections

❑ Feels generalized body pain

❑ Has hives

❑ Has a rash or acne

❑ Has an increase of asthma or allergies

❑ Has constipation or diarrhea

❑ Exhibits habitual coughing, throat clearing, or vocalizations

❑ Has a dry mouth or throat

❑ Has tight and stiff muscles

❑ Has certain muscles that twitch or has facial tics

❑ Stutters or stammers

❑ Is unable to stand still or stay in one place

❑ Has shaky hands

❑ Exhibits the onset of poor vision

❑ Perspires to an abnormally high degree

If students demonstrate more than three or four of these signs with a frequency of once a week or so, there's a strong possibility that they are experiencing high stress levels. Emotional problems could be part of the reason as well. If these symptoms persist in class, you as the teacher should talk to the parents about your concerns. If the parents report that there are possible social, emotional, or family stressors, suggest that they consult with a mental health professional to locate the source of the stress.

Determining Whether a Student Is Depressed

A combination of certain behavior changes and disturbances in mood can suggest a depressive disorder. To be indicators of depression, the symptoms need to last for at least two weeks and must represent a departure from the way the student usually acts. The following nine categories can help you to recognize these symptoms in your students. If five or more of them describe the way a student is behaving, depression is possibly the cause.

Symptoms of Depression

❑ Has a restless, depressed, sulky, or irritable mood most of the time
❑ Has a persistently sad, anxious, or "empty" mood
❑ Has lost interest or pleasure in activities once enjoyed
❑ Has changed significantly in appetite or body weight
❑ Exhibits insomnia, early-morning awakening, or oversleeping
❑ Has an increased or decreased activity level
❑ Has fatigue or a loss of energy
❑ Has inappropriate guilt or feelings of worthlessness

❑ Has thinking or concentration problems

❑ Has recurrent thoughts of death or suicide

❑ Makes frequent vague, nonspecific physical complaints, such as of headaches, muscle aches, stomachaches, or tiredness

❑ Is frequently absent from school or performs poorly when there

❑ Refuses to go to school

❑ Clings to parent

❑ Worries that parent or other family member may die

❑ Talks about running away from home, or tries to do so

❑ Has outbursts of shouting, complaining, unexplained irritability, or crying

❑ Exhibits boredom

❑ Lacks interest in playing with friends

❑ Exhibits alcohol or substance abuse

❑ Exhibits social isolation or poor communication

❑ Has an abnormal fear of death

❑ Has extreme sensitivity to rejection or failure

❑ Has increased irritability, anger, or hostility

❑ Exhibits reckless behavior

❑ Has difficulty with relationships

(National Institute of Mental Health 2000)

When to Be Suspicious of Depression

Many situations can lead to depression in a child. The separation or divorce of parents or even of a close friend or relative can be devastating. The death of a loved one, such as a grandparent or even a pet, can have a strong impact. A move from one town to another or a change in schools can be significant. Academic failure can be traumatic. Being informed of a diagnosis of a physical or learning problem can also have a negative impact, as can the experience of an illness or injury.

The common element in these experiences is a sense of loss. The child's expectations aren't met. Goals and dreams are crushed. Familiar and comfortable routines change. Embarrassment and shame may result. These feelings can lead to depression, an outcome that is particularly likely when children are not able to express their feelings or obtain loving support.

Sometimes the symptoms of depression are present, but no predisposing events are evident to the family. The loss may be only in the eyes of the child. An event that seems insignificant to the parents can have devastating meaning to the child.

I've had adults tell me of classroom experiences in which a teacher made fun of them, made a critical comment, or called them "stupid" or "ugly." The parents never knew the incident happened, and the child never told anybody. Yet the child internalized that experience, and it had lifelong implications. Children who are carrying the secret of abuse provide another example of a traumatic event unknown to others.

As a teacher, you may not be able to relate your student's symptoms of depression to specific events. In that case, you should talk with the parents. If they can't identify a trigger for the depression, it may be crucial to get the help of a mental health professional, a medical practitioner, or both.

Consequences and Symptoms of Abuse

It was the end of a long, depressing day, and I was close to tears. I had finished my third initial interview with parents of abused children. The first case involved the sexual abuse of a four-year-old by a relative who had babysat the child. The next case concerned a church member who battered his wife, committed adultery without remorse, and beat his second son with a belt buckle until the boy bled. During the final interview of that day, the parents offered significant evidence to suggest that the grandparents of a young boy and girl had systematically involved the children in group sexual ceremonies in the basement of their home.

Why would anybody—let alone those who claim to be Christian—subject a loved one to that kind of pain and humiliation? It just doesn't make sense. But then, abuse never does make sense until you consider both the current knowledge about the cycle of violence and the fact that the human heart is deceitful above all things (Jeremiah 17:9) and corrupted by its deceitful desires (Ephesians 4:22).

There are two main types of victimization. The first is common: the case of a child who is abused directly. The second has not received much attention but is crucial nonetheless: the case of a child who lives in a home where domestic violence or spousal abuse is occurring.

Impact of Direct Abuse on Children

The injury and trauma stemming from abuse undoubtedly influence the physical development of children. For example, such children tend to develop a greater vulnerability to illness. A growing concern for victims of sexual abuse is susceptibility to sexually transmitted diseases. Abused children also commonly become anemic, exhibiting apathy, poor learning ability, listlessness, and exhaustion.

Children's intellectual development is also influenced by abuse. Research suggests that neglected and abused children perform poorly on standardized tests, receive lower grades, are more likely to repeat a grade, and have more discipline referrals than other children (Eckenrode 1993). Poor language skills can result from chronic or severe abuse. I've worked with several children who have spent their early years with incompetent parents, and they showed developmental delays in language and other cognitive abilities. The good news is that a nurturing environment put those same children on track for normal development.

There is strong evidence that victimization has significant effects on children's mental health. For example, sexually abused children have a nearly fourfold lifetime risk for psychiatric disorders and a threefold lifetime risk for substance abuse (MacFarlane and Waterman 1986).

To help you make an initial determination of whether your student or others you know have suffered abuse, a comprehensive listing of symptoms often seen in children who are abused—sexually abused in particular—follows below.

Symptoms of Sexual Abuse

A trauma such as child sexual abuse always results in symptoms. Usually, there are no clear physical signs, so the child is the best and sometimes only source of warning signals. These behavioral signs will vary according to the age of the child:

- ❑ Indirect hints or open statements about abuse
- ❑ Difficulty in peer relationships and violence against younger children
- ❑ Less verbalization; withdrawal, depression, or apathy
- ❑ Abrupt and drastic personality changes
- ❑ Self-mutilation
- ❑ Preoccupation with death, guilt, heaven, or hell
- ❑ Retreat to fantasy world; dissociative reactions: loss of memory, imaginary playmates, or use of more than one name
- ❑ Unexplained acquisition of toys, money, or clothes
- ❑ Fear, tendency to cling to parent, need for reassurance
- ❑ Unwillingness to participate in physical or recreational activities
- ❑ Refusal to undress for physical education class at school
- ❑ Sudden increase in modesty
- ❑ Fear of bathrooms and showers

❑ Self-consciousness about use of bathroom; severe reaction if intruded upon

❑ Anger, acting out, disobedience

❑ Refusal to be left with potential offender or caretaker

❑ Discomfort around persons they used to trust

❑ Lack of trust

❑ Active hostility and anger toward formerly trusted person

❑ Runaway behavior

❑ Refusal to go home or stated desire to live elsewhere

❑ Extreme fear or repulsion when touched by an adult of either sex

❑ Tendency to be touchy-feely to abnormally high levels

❑ Inappropriate dress; use of clothing to reverse roles: resemblance to a sophisticated adult or a mother

❑ Onset of poor personal hygiene; attempts to make self appear unattractive

❑ Sophisticated sexual knowledge

❑ Precocious, provocative sexual behavior

❑ Seductive, indiscriminate display of affection

❑ Pseudo-maturity: for example, acting like a small parent

❑ Regression to earlier, infantile behavior, such as bed-wetting or thumb-sucking

❑ Sleep disturbances, nightmares

❑ Change in sleep habits, such as staying up late; constant tiredness

❑ Continual, unexplained fear, anxiety, or panic

❑ Onset of eating disorders, such as anorexia, bulimia, or compulsive eating

❑ Inability to concentrate in school; hyperactivity

❑ Sudden drop in school performance

❑ Extreme compliance

❑ Compulsivity in actions

❑ Early arrival or late leaving at school; few if any absences

❏ Excessive masturbation

❏ Combination of violence and sexuality in artwork, written schoolwork, language, and play

❏ Hysterical seizures

❏ Attempts to establish boundaries, such as wearing clothing to bed

❏ Total denial of problem with total lack of expression of feeling

(Martin 1992)

Impact of Domestic Violence on Children

What are the effects on children who live in homes where there is domestic violence? The children may not be direct victims of beating, but seeing their mother suffer at the hands of her husband or partner will still have a drastic impact. Pain will continue to be their constant companion.

I talked with a ten-year-old boy who had watched his father beat his mother numerous times. "How did you feel when this happened?" I asked.

"I was scared, but I didn't know what to do," he said. "So I ran and hid in the closet. When I heard Dad slam the door and leave the house, I knew it was okay to go see if Mom was all right. It happened so often, I sorta got used to it. But then I got mad. I hated my father for hurting her. I wanted to see him dead. But now that he's gone, I miss him. Do you think I'm crazy?"

That story is typical of the 10 to 30 percent of children who live in violent homes. These children appear to have significantly greater emotional problems, more somatic symptoms, lower cognitive skills, and more difficulty with social interactions. They feel powerless and out of control.

Another finding has been that both boys and girls act out and are disobedient when they suffer from depression and anxiety at the same time. In other contexts, when children exhibit behavior problems, boys tend to be disobedient and girls tend to be anxious and depressed. However, living in a home where battering occurs seems to merge these patterns (Adler 1991).

Following are some of the major effects on children who live in homes where there is domestic violence. This summary can be used to help diagnose abusive situations as well as to help identify victimized children and direct the intervention and treatment process:

Symptoms of Children Who Live with Family Violence

Emotional Effects
- ❏ Feel guilt for the abuse and for not being able to stop it
- ❏ Feel grief and remorse for family and personal losses
- ❏ Feel confused and ambivalent about conflicting feelings toward parents
- ❏ Experience fear of abandonment, of expressing emotions, of the unknown, and of physical danger and injury
- ❏ Feel angry about the violence and chaos in their lives
- ❏ Feel depressed, helpless, and powerless
- ❏ Feel embarrassed about the effects of the abuse and the dynamics at home

Cognitive Effects
- ❏ Blame others for their own behavior
- ❏ Believe it's acceptable to hit people they care for in order to get what they want, to express their anger, to feel powerful, or to get others to meet their needs
- ❏ Have a low self-concept resulting from a sense of family powerlessness
- ❏ Don't ask for what they need, let alone for what they want

---

❑ Don't trust

❑ Develop the belief that to feel angry is bad because people get hurt

❑ Develop rigid stereotypes: to be a boy means …; to be a girl means …; to be a man, woman, husband, wife means …

Behavioral Effects

❑ Often show opposite extremes and act opposite to previous patterns

❑ Act out rather than withdrawing

❑ Are aggressive rather than passive

❑ Overachieve instead of underachieve

❑ Refuse to go to school

❑ Take on a caretaking role, act more concerned for others than self, become parent substitutes

❑ Develop rigid defenses: aloofness, sarcasm, defensiveness, polarized thinking

❑ Show excessive attention-seeking behavior, often using extreme behaviors

❑ Often wet the bed and have nightmares

❑ Are out of control, are not able to set own limits or follow directions, and may appear to have ADHD

Social Effects

❑ Isolate themselves from friends and relatives; are sometimes controlled by parent

❑ Frequently have stormy relationships that start intensely and end abruptly

❑ Have difficulty trusting, especially adults

❑ Have poor anger-management and problem-solving skills

❑ May engage in excessive social involvement to avoid home life

❑ May be passive with peers, or may bully or be aggressive

❑ May engage in exploitative relationships, either as perpetrator or as victim

❑ Engage in exceedingly rough childhood play

Physical Effects

❑ Develop various somatic complaints, such as headaches or stomachaches

❑ Appear nervous or anxious, or have short attention spans

❑ Seem chronically tired and lethargic

❑ Suffer frequently from illnesses

❑ Practice poor personal hygiene

❑ May show evidences of regression in development, such as bed-wetting or thumb-sucking

❑ May seem insensitive to pain

❑ May engage in high-risk play activities

❑ May exhibit self-abuse, such as self-mutilation

(Mitchell 1994)

Underachievement

The symptoms of underachievement are reasonably easy to detect. The following checklist identifies the most common indicators:

Symptoms of Underachievement

❑ Consistently does incomplete work, seems disorganized

❑ Is not a self-starter; does not display appropriate sense of urgency; misses deadlines

❑ Makes poor grades compared with known ability or potential

❑ Performs below expectations or ability

❑ Does well on achievement or intelligence tests, but performs at levels far short of abilities

---

- ❑ Can do well but is erratic; needs excessive supervision
- ❑ Starts enthusiastically but quickly fades; promises to do better in the future
- ❑ Receives low evaluations by teachers or coaches
- ❑ Exhibits inadequate motivation
- ❑ Is apathetic or depressed, unable to enjoy own success
- ❑ Cannot seem to function as a group member
- ❑ Has social problems or maladjustments
- ❑ Seldom accepts responsibility for personal failure, tends to blame others
- ❑ Has an apparent fear of failure or success
- ❑ Has a preoccupation with activities unrelated to academics or other areas of concern to caregivers
- ❑ Shows irritation, anger, or defiance when confronted with lack of effort
- ❑ Denies existence of homework when asked
- ❑ Has low self-esteem or a sense of inferiority
- ❑ Has a self-deprecating attitude; for example, not wanting to try because expects to fail
- ❑ Shows a lack of initiative to change or try new solutions, doesn't find new ideas challenging
- ❑ Has phobias about test-taking or working in areas of difficulty
- ❑ Refuses to pursue more challenging courses, skills, or competition
- ❑ Seems unable to persevere
- ❑ Lacks personal, academic, physical, or spiritual goals
- ❑ Is emotionally immature
- ❑ Appears easily distracted when needing to do work; displays selective attention and memory
- ❑ Minimizes future consequences
- ❑ Fakes happiness; for example, by saying he or she is happy but really isn't
- ❑ Does not perform better as a result of punishment, reward, logic, tutoring, training, or the absence of any typical motivation

Though easier to identify than other learning obstacles, underachievement is not an easy problem to solve. Often there are combinations of reasons why students are not motivated to work up to their capacity. A thorough evaluation like those implemented for suspected learning disabilities, attention deficits, or emotional problems may be needed. Once a teacher and parent have observed three to five of the above symptoms, movement to the next level of evaluation is advised.

Conclusion

We've looked at some screening tools you can use to decide whether any of your students have a particular learning problem or are suffering from some type of stress or abuse. If any of the checklists or descriptions seemed to apply to a significant degree, the next step is to initiate a thorough diagnosis of the problem. The next chapter will tell you how to obtain the necessary information by working with students and their familires.

References

Adler, T. 1991. Abuse within families emerging from closet. *APA Monitor* (16 December).

American Psychiatric Association. 1994. *Diagnostic and statistical manual of mental disorders.* 4th ed. Washington, DC: American Psychiatric Association.

Begert, S. 2000. The warning signs of learning disabilities. ERIC Clearinghouse on Disabilities and Gifted Education. ERIC EC Digest #E603. http://www.ericec.org/digests/e603.html.

Eckenrode, J. 1993. School performance and disciplinary problems among abused and neglected children. *Developmental Psychology* 29:53–62.

Lerner, J. W. 2003. *Learning disabilities: Theories, diagnosis, and teaching strategies.* New York: Houghton Mifflin.

MacFarlane, K., and J. Waterman. 1986. *Sexual abuse of young children.* New York: Guilford Press.

Martin, G. L. 1992. *Critical problems in children and youth: Counseling techniques for problems resulting from attention deficit disorder, sexual abuse, custody battles, and related issues.* Dallas, TX: Word.

Mitchell, A. 1994. *Domestic/dating violence: An information and resource handbook.* Seattle, WA: Metropolitan King County Council.

National Institute of Mental Health. 2000. Depression in children and adolescents. Bethesda, MD: National Institute of Mental Health. http://www.nimh.nih.gov/publicat/depchildresfact.cfm.

Silver, L. B. 2001. What are learning disabilities? *LD Online* (November). http://www.ldonline.org/ld_indepth/general_info/what _are_ld _silver.html.

CHAPTER 4

How to Identify the Learning Problem
Obtaining a Formal Diagnosis

You've now learned about various reasons why students may have trouble in school. You've read the descriptions of the barriers to learning. One or more checklists have aroused your suspicions, and you've decided that a certain student may have some type of learning difficulty. Now it seems appropriate to take the next step. You're going to recommend that the family pursue a formal evaluation.

The following pages will describe the steps in obtaining a comprehensive evaluation of a student. I will highlight components of LD and ADHD evaluations specifically, but regardless of a student's learning problems, the process of diagnosis follows the same general pattern. The evaluation personnel will alter the tests and procedures according to the child's needs and the suspected source of the learning difficulties.

Process of Classroom Screening and Making a Referral

You have identified a student who appears to have a learning problem. Now you can take the following steps to recommend that the child be evaluated. You may find variations, depending on your school's resources and policies, but the suggestions will serve as general guidelines if sufficient directions have not already been established.

Make classroom observations of the student. Chapter 3 explained this process and included checklists to help you discover the nature and significance of the student's learning problem. If your school has developed screening instruments, use them when appropriate. The goal here is to further clarify the exact nature of the problem. Could it be ADHD, a learning disability, stress, depression, or some combination of these? What has been tried so far to help the student? Is there anything else you could try before initiating a formal evaluation? Review the school-related questions in the previous chapter to help you think through what else might be tried. Should you consult with someone to help you decide what you might do next? The last question takes us to the next step—but first we need to consider how to report abuse.

A major deviation from the process of obtaining a formal diagnosis is necessary when students show signs of abuse. By law, if you suspect some kind of abuse, you must report it to your local version of child protection services. This requirement often presents a major dilemma—whether to involve the family before making a report. If you suspect abuse, the laws in every state mandate that you must report it, and in such a case, you should not contact the family before making the report. Instead, you need to talk to the child services caseworker about your concern and let that person follow up on your report. If you doubt the appropriateness of a report, you can consult informally with the children's services intake worker or law enforcement personnel.

You can report to a local law enforcement agency by telephone, in writing, or in person; the department of social and health services; or child protective services. Be sure to take time to find out the proper procedures in your locality.

The report will consist of the name, address, and age of the child; the name and address of the adult having custody; and the nature and extent of the injury, neglect, or sexual abuse. Also included should be any other information that would help to establish the cause of the abuse and the possible identity of the perpetrator.

All fifty states mandate the reporting of all types of abuse, including sexual abuse. For most social service, medical, and educational personnel, failure to report suspected child abuse is a misdemeanor. In most areas the responsibility for identifying and reporting abuse belongs to those people who have direct contact with children as part of their job or profession. Although any citizen may report, most states name medical personnel, mental health workers, educators, and clergy as those responsible to report abuse. Those who do so generally receive immunity from liability and can remain anonymous as long as the report was made in good faith. A report of suspected child abuse, sexual or otherwise, should be based on concern for the health and safety of the child, not on a desire to punish the child's caretakers.

The second step in obtaining a formal diagnosis is to consult with your colleagues and administration. Talk with other teachers about your concerns, asking whether any of them have had similar experience with the student. Do they know anything that would help you reach the student? Perhaps others in your school have had better success in getting the student to perform in their class. What are those teachers doing that you may be able to adapt to your class?

A word of caution is necessary at this point. Don't be a gossip. Limit your discussions to classroom performance and possible solutions. Don't spread rumors or unsubstantiated hearsay about students or their families. Yes, if the parents are going through a divorce or the father is out of a job, the situation is likely to have an impact on the children. Those are facts that may be relevant and common knowledge in your school and community. However, if there are other personal issues that you suspect but that are not common knowledge, be very careful about discussing them. Keep them confidential, and respect students' privacy.

Another consideration is whether the severity of the problems jeopardizes a student's ability to remain in your school. Sometimes the situation reaches that point. If you have to consider such an outcome, make sure you have the backing of your administration and try to gain their participation. Always keep the focus on finding solutions that benefit the student rather than on describing the problem.

Acquire information on the process of obtaining an evaluation and on where to refer. Talk with your school administrator about school policies for initiating a recommendation to seek a formal evaluation. Consult your procedural manual, if you have one, to help guide you through this process. Some larger schools may have a specialist designated to help you. However, most private schools have limited resources, so you may be on your own in this step. You may need to complete certain forms or documentation that must be itemized to make sure you have a valid reason for making this kind of recommendation. Some schools may have their own questionnaires to be completed with certain cut-off scores established in order to have sufficient justification for bringing such a recommendation to the family.

The next major challenge is to have some resources in mind to discuss with the parents. Some schools may have staff that can do some academic or achievement evaluation. Maybe your school has contracted with a local mental health or medical professional who provides formal evaluations. The public school in your area can provide educational evaluations. Find out the process for obtaining an evaluation through the public school. You should be able to give this information to the parents when you talk with them. You can also consider such resources as private psychologists, other professionals, mental health centers, or universities. Talk with your administration and colleagues about who would be a good referral for this particular student. This chapter will provide more details about using community resources and choosing a professional. For now, your goal is to be as informed as possible about where to refer.

Meet with parents and make recommendations. Now you are ready to schedule a parent meeting and present your concerns to the family. You could discuss your concerns as part of your regularly scheduled parent-teacher conference held in the fall or spring. In many cases, you will need a separate meeting in order to have enough time to explore your concerns and options with the parents. Perhaps someone else from the staff would also need to be present. Follow the procedure laid out by your administration.

Present your concerns in an organized and concise fashion. Tell the parents you are concerned but unsure how to work best with their child. Explain that you believe a formal evaluation will enable everybody to do a better job of helping their child learn. Highlight the student's strengths that you see at school. Share the informal observations and checklist summaries you have gathered.

Be prepared for denial by the parents, especially fathers. Many dads have a hard time admitting that their child could have any kind of problem, so they might greet your suggestion with emotions ranging from apathy to anger. Let them vent their frustrations. Some parents will need to go home and think about the information before they proceed.

Make sure they have a list of resources with phone numbers, and set a time to conference with the parents about their intentions. Also let them know that you are available to answer any questions they have after they get home and discuss the situation.

Remain supportive and open to accommodations and interventions. This last step is the most important. Be encouraging and supportive as the parents proceed with the evaluation. Let them know how other students have benefited from this process. Then, once you learn about the results and recommendations, be ready to implement as many of the suggestions as you can. Sometimes you may disagree with the findings. That's all right. Discuss your concerns with the evaluator or the family. Try to obtain clarification about the points that have generated differences of opinion. Above all, look for ways to implement the findings of the assessment so that the student will learn more effectively. The balance of this book will focus on more details about translating the assessment into teaching practices. Now we will look at the actual assessment process in more detail.

How to Pursue a Diagnosis

Obtain a medical exam. One of the first steps in the evaluation process is to rule out any medical problems that could be affecting a student's learning. It is always wise for the student to have a complete physical exam as well as thorough vision and hearing evaluations. If problems exist with the initial input of data because of poor hearing or vision, we want to identify that source. Sometimes we can eliminate learning problems by correcting physical impairments.

When the exam takes place, make sure the parents tell the physician that you and they are concerned about the child's learning process. The usual physical exams required for school may not show anything if the child is otherwise healthy. Provide descriptions for the parents to give to the doctor so that a complete evaluation can take place. Explain the nature of the student's school problems. If the child has had many ear infections or often doesn't seem to listen, make sure his or her ears are examined. Learning disabilities aren't usually the result of obvious medical problems, so don't expect this examination to turn up significant previously unidentified problems. Yet it's a necessary first step.

Screening for neurological problems may also be necessary. I would not recommend this specific evaluation unless a doctor recommends it or unless later psychological testing produces a number of significant "soft sign" indicators of neurological dysfunction. Even sophisticated procedures such as computerized axial tomography (CAT) or positron emission tomography (PET) scans may not provide any clear definition of brain-function problems. So make sure there are reasonable indicators before spending the time and money for a neurological evaluation. Keep in mind that such an evaluation can involve primarily medical procedures such as clinical exams and various scans of the brain, as well as neuropsychological tests.

Neuropsychological testing can sometimes help to identify which brain functions are weaker than others, and it can also point to brain-function strengths that can be emphasized for compensation. The Reitan-Indiana Neuropsychological Test Battery (for children ages five to eight) or the Halstead-Reitan Neuropsychological Test Battery for Children (ages nine to fourteen) are examples of the kind of testing that a neurologist, who is an M.D., or a neuropsychologist with a Ph.D. can do.

Obtain a psychological evaluation. Screening for emotional problems is also important. However, it is difficult to distinguish between the chicken and the egg. Did emotional factors cause the learning problems, or did the learning difficulties cause the emotional problems? Most children with learning disabilities will struggle with self-esteem issues, for example. There will be times when they're unhappy or depressed. Has their failure in the classroom caused the depression, or have other factors such as parental divorce, the death of a loved one, or undisclosed abuse caused the black cloud of gloom? A mental health professional such as a child psychiatrist or psychologist, as well as social workers and child therapists, can evaluate whether emotional problems are contributing to learning difficulties.

A number of years ago, a four-year-old boy named Marty was brought to my attention because of suspected sexual abuse by a family member. The abuse was confirmed, and I worked with the boy and his family. In the first grade, Marty began to have trouble with reading. I evaluated him for learning disabilities and found severe problems. The school district personnel later indicated that he was the most severely reading- and learning-disabled child they had observed.

While everyone worked hard to improve the child's reading skills, the boy was still not making much progress. He had trouble with attention, distractibility, and concentration. However, he wasn't hyperactive. Some of his symptoms were apparent early on, but they seemed related more to his abuse and were consistent with a diagnosis of post-traumatic stress disorder. Yet when Marty reached the fourth grade, his attention problems persisted even though he was no longer struggling with abuse issues. So I evaluated him for ADHD and found that it was also present.

Here was a likable young boy with a tremendously unfair combination of abuse, learning disabilities, and ADHD. Sorting out the various components of the learning problems in such a case is difficult. However, over the years, Marty's resource team—teachers, tutors, a psychologist, a physician, and a parent—tried to treat each problem area in as comprehensive a way as they knew how. Marty made good emotional progress, his attention difficulties were helped by medication, and his reading skills gradually improved. My last contact with him and his mother was to encourage an increased effort in one component of his reading and to begin negotiating with the school to place him in a transition or prevocational program in order to give him some career skills that would not draw heavily on reading.

Marty's situation illustrates a complex combination of disorders and experiences. We can make several significant points regarding this case. First, the evaluation isn't necessarily completed all at once. It may evolve over several years as various features receive attention and other symptoms become easier to identify. We must be prepared to understand a student's problems one portion at a time. It may take everyone quite a while to put the puzzle together.

Another point is to be prepared for difficulties in identifying precisely all the causes of a student's learning problems. Emotions, brain function, learning style, and environment interact in wonderfully complex ways, and we professionals aren't smart enough to figure everything out in all cases.

The final point is the importance of understanding a student's emotions as they relate to school problems. The attitudes formed in the early school years will likely shape a person's entire life. We want that time to be as successful and beneficial as possible. Don't neglect the countless opportunities to encourage and nurture all your students as much as you possibly can. In spite of any problems in the classroom, highlight their areas of success, and give them every opportunity to develop their areas of strength and competency.

Who Does the Evaluation?

Public School Resources for Private and Homeschooled Students

Even though you teach in a private school, your students have access to the services of the public school for the assessment. The same level of services is supposed to be available to everyone. The Individuals with Disabilities Education Act of 1997 (IDEA) stipulates that local school districts must make the same effort to identify private school students with disabilities that they make to find public school students with special needs. The IDEA regulations also mandate that local educational agencies (LEAs) have a responsibility to locate, identify, and evaluate children who may have a disability and may be in need of special education services, whether they are enrolled in a public school or a private one. The process of locating such children is called "child find," and the LEA must consult with appropriate private school representatives about how to carry out child find activities for private school students.

The child find activities in which LEA engages for private school children must be comparable to the activities it uses to evaluate students in the public school. Therefore, parents are entitled to the procedural safeguards that apply. These include the right to participate in evaluation and eligibility meetings, to receive a copy of the evaluation report and eligibility determination, to receive prior written notice of proposed or refused actions, and to be given the opportunity to provide informed written consent for the initial evaluation. In addition, parents have the right to request a due process hearing to challenge the results pertaining to the identification and evaluation of their child. The determination that a private school student has a disability and needs special education services, however, does not result in an entitlement to individualized education plan (IEP) services unless the student then enrolls in the public schools (Cernosia 2002).

In most public schools, a child find, or "focus-of-concern," process is used to evaluate a student and determine eligibility for services. A parent can initiate a focus-of-concern process, and each district is supposed to have the process spelled out so that parents know exactly what will take place and what the schedule will be. The parents should go to the local school that their child would ordinarily attend and fill out the focus-of-concern request. It is the responsibility of the public school staff to make a decision about the appropriateness of the referral and then to move ahead if there seems to be a legitimate reason for the assessment. The public school will need to get some basic performance information from the private school teacher, but the process is supposed to be the same as it would be if the student were a part of the public school.

The process consists basically of identifying the concerns on some type of referral form. Then the various school personnel—for example, a nurse, communication-disorder specialist, classroom teacher, school psychologist, learning specialist, and the administrators—collect data on the student's academic, medical, social, emotional, and intellectual characteristics. The spiritual category is missing, but that's understandable in a secular setting. A Christian teacher will keep a sensitive eye on spiritual issues that might affect the child's learning.

The school district has a specified number of days, usually fifteen to twenty, to act on the referral and make a determination of whether there's good reason to believe the student is a candidate for assessment. If the school concludes that there is reason to complete the evaluation, the parent is informed in writing and asked to give permission for the process to continue. After the parent gives permission, the assessment takes place. The assessment is supposed to be completed in a certain amount of time, usually thirty-five to forty-five days, after receipt of parental consent. If the school does not believe an assessment is justified, the parent can use an appeal process (CAPE and ILIAD 2003).

Parents have the right to demand a complete evaluation as mandated by Public Law 94-142, the *Education for All Handicapped Children Act*. However, this right doesn't mean that the private school student is guaranteed public school services, even if the assessment turns out to be positive. We'll explore this issue more in the next chapter. The point is that you should be aware of how the process works in your area so that if parents wish to obtain at least part of the evaluation through the school district, you will know how to get them started.

Some public schools have a private school liaison staff person who helps coordinate services for private school students with special needs. Find out whether there is such a person in your area so that you can direct parents to that office. And remember, honey catches more flies than vinegar. While families have a legal entitlement to assessment services, they are encouraged to be tactful and pleasant in their dealings with the public school personnel. Someone from your own school might want to take on the task of developing positive working relationships with the appropriate local school district staff in order to make the whole process work more efficiently.

Private Resources for Evaluation

Sometimes the public school evaluation may not seem adequate. School personnel may be so overburdened and understaffed that the evaluation process is minimal or incompetent. Some parents don't want to go through all the paperwork and administrative hassles to get an evaluation completed through the public schools. Sometimes parents believe the school doesn't want to identify special-needs students because it doesn't have, or doesn't want to spend, the money for students from private schools.

I've had many parents come to me because they wanted to make sure a Christian psychologist would be involved in assessing their child. Some also need a second opinion. Sometimes, after evaluating the results of the school assessment, parents want an elaboration or confirmation by an independent source.

Any of these reasons may prompt a family to seek an evaluation with a private clinician or organization. It's very important to work with a professional who has the necessary credentials and experience. Parents will often ask you for recommendations. Rather than recommending just one person, you should give the parents a list of several professionals who specialize in evaluating children with learning problems.

How do you learn about good resources? Find other parents who have already been through the evaluation process, and ask them what resources they used and whether they were satisfied. Contact a local branch of the Learning Disabilities Association of America or Children and Adults with Attention-Deficit/Hyperactivity Disorder (CHADD) for a list of clinicians. (The resource section at the end of this book includes these organizations.)

Call a local Christian counseling center and ask whether it has anyone specializing in learning problems. Check with your local university or college and ask whether it offers services of this type. Sometimes you can get an excellent evaluation at a lower cost through a university if the university is permitted to use your student's case for training purposes. Below is a checklist you can use to guide your selection of a professional who will make the evaluation and perhaps help direct the intervention efforts:

Checklist for Selecting a Learning Specialist

❑ Has appropriate professional degree and licensing, such as Ph.D., Ed.D., M.D., M.S., or M.S.W.

❑ Has experience working with children who have learning problems

❑ Has specific training in assessment and treatment of depression, other emotional problems, learning disabilities, and ADHD

❑ Is able to manage a multidisciplinary approach to assessment and treatment

❑ Is able and willing to work closely with the family and school

❑ Seems to appreciate the complex nature of learning problems and is able to draw on many community resources to help the child

❑ Has a balanced perspective on learning problems; recognizes the long-term nature of the problem but is encouraging about the amount of help available

❑ Makes no promises of instant cures and doesn't propose unorthodox procedures

❑ Was recommended by a satisfied client or some other professional familiar with his or her work

❑ Has a sensitivity and an ability to deal with spiritual issues and is a Christian who can relate faith and practice to the needs of the situation

Before you refer a family, know about the person's qualifications for and experience in evaluating for learning problems. The person should have at least a master's degree in a related field, and the more experience the person has in dealing with learning problems, the better.

A basic evaluation will cost several hundred dollars, with $500 to $1,000 being common. Complicated cases requiring extensive specialized equipment and expertise may cost several thousand dollars. The parents should be told what services are covered, including school visits, phone conferences, testing supplies, report preparation, and summary conferences. Most clinicians simply charge for the time spent working on the case, with an hourly charge for all services provided. Encourage parents to ask about reduced fees and scholarship or grant programs. They may have to complete a financial disclosure statement, but doing so may allow them to qualify for various forms of financial aid.

It's important for the family to inquire whether their insurance carrier will cover the testing and, specifically, whether insurance will pay for a diagnosis of learning disabilities or ADHD. Some policies exclude certain kinds of learning problems. For example, it's common for insurance companies to refuse to pay for any evaluation for learning disabilities, claiming that the public schools can do the assessment. This explanation is not appropriate and doesn't make sense, but that assessment is still a frequently excluded coverage. Assessments for ADHD and various emotional conditions usually qualify for insurance coverage.

The parents may also inquire whether the school district can pay for an independent evaluation. If the parents have had an evaluation completed by the school but aren't satisfied, it might be possible for the school to pay for a second opinion or an independent educational evaluation (IEE). The school may have a specific list of people it wants the family to use if it is going to pay for the whole evaluation. The school may pay only a portion of the total fee if the parents choose someone outside the school's network. The school district may contest the parents' request for an IEE and ask for a due process hearing to show that its evaluation was appropriate. If the final decision is that the school's evaluation is appropriate, the parents still have the right to an IEE, but not at public expense. In any case, it may be worthwhile for them to check the options before assuming that they will have to pay the entire cost of an independent evaluation.

Specific Evaluation for Learning Disabilities

To give you a general idea of what to expect, I'll describe briefly the typical components of an evaluation for learning disabilities. Remember that evaluators will have their own battery of preferred tests and procedures. They differ from one another in the various combinations of tests they use to arrive at a diagnosis. Children usually take an intelligence test, which provides an estimate of general ability. Then the evaluators can make a determination of the discrepancy between general intelligence and performance in one or more of these categories: oral expression, listening comprehension, written expression, basic reading skill, reading comprehension, math calculations, and math reasoning. The United States Office of Education has identified these categories, and most states use them to determine eligibility for special education services.

If a learning disability is suspected, the battery of tests is likely to include tests of intelligence such as the Wechsler Intelligence Scale for Children–III or IV (WISC-III or -IV), Tests of Cognitive Abilities from the Woodcock-Johnson III (WJ-III), the Kaufman Assessment Battery for Children (K-ABC), or the Stanford-Binet Intelligence Scale (SB4 or SB5). Any general ability test addresses to some degree the areas of verbal, performance, and perceptual-motor abilities. The WISC-III includes a number of subtests grouped into verbal and performance domains, and results in verbal, performance, and full-scale IQ scores. The comparison of the verbal and performance IQ scores can be a part of the determination of a learning disability, and the general measure of academic potential from the WISC-III is useful.

The SB4 provides measures of verbal reasoning, quantitative reasoning, abstract/visual reasoning, and short-term memory. A fifth edition of the Stanford-Binet, which was released in 2003, has nonverbal and verbal domains with five factors of fluid reasoning, knowledge, quantitative reasoning, visual-spatial processing, and working memory for each of the domains (Roid 2002).

I prefer to use the WJ-III Tests of Cognitive Abilities. I find that it has greater prescriptive utility than do the other instruments. The broadest score is the general intellectual ability (GIA), which is a measure of the ability required for academic or occupational success.

The WJ-III identifies three broad cognitive clusters: verbal ability, thinking ability, and cognitive efficiency. Verbal ability is a broad category of language-based acquired knowledge and the ability to communicate that knowledge. Thinking ability includes long-term retrieval, visual-spatial thinking, auditory processing, and fluid reasoning. The cluster represents an aggregate of the abilities that allow a person to process information that has been placed in short-term memory but that cannot be processed automatically. Cognitive efficiency is a broad cluster of skills that sample automatic cognitive processing, processing speed, and short-term memory. Cognitive efficiency represents the capacity of the student's cognitive system to process information automatically (Woodcock, McGrew, and Mather 2000).

Other tests of specific learning functions such as perceptual and motor-skill tests might include the Developmental Test of Visual-Motor Integration, the Bender-Gestalt Test, the Bruinicks-Oseretsky Test of Motor Proficiency, or the Wepman's Auditory Discrimination Test. Speech and language tests could include the Illinois Test of Psycholinguistic Abilities, Third Edition, or the Peabody Picture Vocabulary Test. Since a learning disability results in a discrepancy between potential and actual performance, assessments usually include some type of academic achievement test. This testing can include the Woodcock-Johnson III Tests of Achievement, the Wechsler Individual Achievement Test, or the Wide Range Achievement Test 3.

Remember that the most common method of determining eligibility for classifying a student as having a learning disability is to use some type of IQ-achievement discrepancy formula. Often a child's standard score on an IQ test is compared with the child's standard score on an achievement test. If the difference is greater than one or two standard deviations, the child is classified as having a learning disability and is eligible for special education services in the public schools. One significant problem with this method is that it doesn't identify learning disabilities in young children. We have to wait a couple of years for the student to fall far enough behind in order to qualify for services. Yet we know that early intervention in kindergarten and first grade is the most effective instruction (Foorman et al. 1998).

There have been several proposed alternatives such as assessing discrepancies among academic or cognitive skills. My own preference is to look for significant variation within the pattern of cognitive skills as found on a test such as the WJ-III Tests of Cognitive Abilities. A student who has average general intellectual ability and good reasoning ability but has very low auditory processing, for example, would be said to have a learning disability. This student's suspected area of deficit is in the ability to analyze, synthesize, and discriminate auditory stimuli.

Evaluators also use various rating scales; educational, family, and personal history forms; parent and teacher observation forms; and specific tests that explore emotional factors. Examples of rating scales that screen for learning disabilities are the Learning Disabilities Diagnostic Inventory, the Pupil Rating Scale (Revised): Screening for Learning Disabilities, and the Devereaux Elementary School Behavior Rating Scale.

The goal is to determine the extent of the student's learning disability and to identify exactly where the problem lies. Is it visual, auditory, oral, or motor; or does it involve one or more of the input, integration, memory, or output parts of the learning process? We also want to know the affected academic areas, such as reading comprehension, written language, listening skills, or math abilities.

Specific Assessment of ADHD

There is no simple test or medical marker that tells us a child has an attention disorder. Diagnosis is a complicated process. It requires a skilled medical or mental health professional such as a psychologist, psychiatrist, pediatrician, or pediatric neurologist.

An important point to be made here is that the public schools will not make an ADHD diagnosis, which is considered a medical diagnosis and outside the purview of the schools. Therefore, if you are recommending that a student be evaluated for ADHD, someone other than the public schools will have to do the evaluation. This could be the family physician or one of the other professionals described earlier in this chapter.

An evaluation should be comprehensive. A good evaluation is important because we need to determine accurately why a child is having trouble with inattentiveness, impulsiveness, and overarousal. Treatment varies because it depends on the underlying problem. Several problems can masquerade as ADHD. For example, an anxious or even depressed child can be inattentive and fidgety in the classroom. An abused child can be very distractible and disorganized. Students with learning disabilities can appear inattentive when their underlying problem is difficulty with language processing. The treatments for these problems differ significantly from one another.

A proper diagnosis orients the child, parents, and caregivers to the general nature of the child's difficulties and, in doing so, provides information about strengths and weaknesses. It helps identify which situations are particularly troublesome for the child and which are more comfortable. The assessment should also identify particular academic strengths and weaknesses so that the educational program can achieve the best possible results.

A thorough evaluation is important for another reason as well. The severity of ADHD itself is not the crucial predictor of long-term adjustment. Rather, the presence or absence of coexisting problems such as learning disabilities, conduct disorder, poor peer relationships, and disruptive family relationships plays a key role in determining future health. A comprehensive assessment will determine whether any of those additional factors are present along with the ADHD. The student will need treatment, as appropriate, for each problem area.

A proper diagnosis of attention disorder must include observations and data representing all aspects of a child's life. The coordinating clinician obtains detailed information from the parents. This information includes both current descriptions of the problem and developmental information about the child and family. The clinician also needs both objective observations provided by the child's teacher(s) and a physician's medical evaluation. Finally, there will be a clinical interview of the child and formal diagnostic testing (Martin 1993, 1995).

A great deal of work has gone into the formulation of diagnostic procedures for the assessment of ADHD. Several major efforts at establishing scientifically based diagnostic procedures have been published. For example, the Committee on Quality Improvement of the American Academy of Pediatrics (AAP) has prepared clinical practice guidelines for the diagnosis and evaluation of ADHD. These guidelines are designed to assist primary care clinicians by providing a framework for diagnostic decision making. The AAP guidelines include six recommendations:

1. If a child who is six to twelve years old displays inattention, hyperactivity, impulsivity, academic underachievement, or behavior problems, the primary care clinicians should initiate an evaluation for ADHD.

2. The diagnosis of ADHD requires that a child meet the criteria in the fourth edition of the *Diagnostic and Statistical Manual of Mental Disorders*.

3. The assessment of ADHD requires evidence obtained directly from parents or caregivers regarding the core symptoms of ADHD in various settings, the age of onset, the duration of symptoms, and the degree of functional impairment.

4. The assessment of ADHD requires evidence directly obtained from the classroom teacher or other school professional regarding the core symptoms of ADHD, the duration of symptoms, the degree of functional impairment, and the associated conditions.

5. Evaluation of a child with ADHD should include assessment for associated (coexisting) conditions.

6. Other diagnostic tests are not routinely indicated to establish the diagnosis of ADHD but may be used for the assessment of other coexisting conditions, such as learning disabilities and mental retardation.

(AAP 2000; Harrerias, Perrin, and Stein 2001)

While these guidelines should help primary care physicians evaluate children with ADHD, some limitations exist. The guidelines do not recommend to pediatricians that complex cases with possible comorbid conditions be referred to other mental health professionals who have training in making differential diagnoses. Consultation and interdisciplinary cooperation on differential diagnosis and complex treatment planning should also be a part of a primary care physician's approach to the diagnosis and treatment of ADHD. Nevertheless, these guidelines do help add rigor and accuracy to the diagnostic process.

Meeting the criteria for ADHD described in the previous chapter is only the beginning of a comprehensive evaluation. A thorough diagnostic examination will include the following additional information:

- The child must score significantly high on one or more of the rating scales completed by the parents and teacher(s). Examples of frequently used scales include the Behavioral Assessment System for Children, the Conners' Parent and Teacher Rating Scales, and the Achenbach Child Behavior Checklist. Additional rating scales that zero in on specific ADHD features include the ADHD

Rating Scale-IV, the McCarney Evaluation Scales, and the Brown ADD Scales. Usually, significant scores will be seen on forms describing the child's behavior at home as well as at school. If there isn't consistency between parent and teacher observations, some explanation should be found.

- The objective tests that the mental health professional administers should show deficits in specific areas such as reflection, vigilance, persistence, auditory memory, impulsivity, and visual concentration. No single test can accurately screen for ADHD. However, there are several batteries of tests, each sensitive to various features that can help us arrive at a clear description of the child's deficit areas.

- The child should be found to have problems with attention, concentration, hyperactivity, or impulsivity across numerous situations such as at home, at church, in the store, in the presence of either parent, in the classroom, and at recess. This evaluation component helps define whether the most consistent feature of the child is his or her apparent inconsistency.

- The clinician must gather sufficient historical, behavioral, and assessment data to rule out or identify the contribution of such accompanying conditions as medical problems, language or learning deficits, and psychological problems that could contribute to attention-disorder symptoms.

Studies of the comorbidity of ADHD have found very high rates of co-occurrence between ADHD and many other disorders. For example, among children with ADHD, the observed rate of anxiety disorders is approximately 25 percent. Similarly elevated incidences of major depression disorder, oppositional defiant disorder, conduct disorder, learning disorders, bipolar disorder, Tourette's syndrome, substance abuse, and other psychiatric diagnoses have been reported for children with ADHD (Biederman, Faraone, and Lapey 1992; Jensen 2000). Data from the National Institute of Mental Health Multimodal Treatment Study of Children with ADHD indicate that as many as 69 percent of comorbid conditions are found with ADHD (MTA Cooperative Group 1999).

In 50 percent of the cases, ADHD children also have learning disabilities (Pastor and Rueben 2002). With this statistic in mind, the clinician must carefully evaluate the learning characteristics of the student in order to make the most appropriate recommendations for educational intervention. Language difficulties; auditory, visual, or motor-processing dysfunction; short- or long-term memory problems; and various learning-style features are examples of the kinds of considerations to use in the differential diagnosis for ADHD and learning disabilities. Therefore, even if ADHD is suspected, a psycho-educational assessment should discriminate between features that are ADHD-related and those that are learning disability–related (Martin in press).

The overlap of ADHD and bipolar disorder (BPD) is currently one of the most active areas of research and professional dialogue. Previous studies of children and adolescents found rates of ADHD ranging from 57 to 98 percent in children with BPD. Yet despite emerging literatures from convergent sources, much controversy continues regarding the validity of the concurrent diagnoses of ADHD and BPD (Wilens, Biederman, and Spencer 2002).

The two disorders share many characteristics. Both can include impulsivity, inattention, hyperactivity, abnormally high physical energy, talkativeness, and behavioral and emotional liability. Also, conduct disorder, oppositional-defiant disorder, and learning problems frequently coexist. Motor restlessness during sleep occurs in both, although children who are bipolar may have little physical motion during sleep when they are depressed or "low." Family histories in both conditions often include mood disorder. In view of the similarities, it is not surprising that distinguishing between these disorders is difficult (Geller et al. 1998; Geller and Williams 1998; Geller et al. 2000).

More research is needed to establish the nature of these coexisting disorders and to provide guidelines for therapeutic management. Because of the emerging research, it is all the more important that the person doing the evaluation have the necessary training and experience to determine the most precise diagnosis and treatment plan.

Children and adolescents with ADHD often have common features in their developmental history. From the parent interview and childhood history, the clinician should look for evidence of similar problems with inattention, distractibility, and impulsivity in either of the parents or in immediate family members. The incidence of ADHD is 20 to 40 percent in adopted children.

Other notable features are irritability or unwillingness to be cuddled as an infant, eating or sleeping problems, allergies, or frequent ear infections. Parents tend to report more sleep problems in ADHD children than in non-ADHD children, though research results are inconsistent regarding sleep issues. Many ADHD children are also reported to be finicky or picky eaters.

Parents also often describe their child with ADHD as being constantly into things, excessively curious, unable to play with toys for any length of time, prone to accidents and injuries, and tending to experience difficulty with both large- and fine-motor coordination.

These children seem bright, but their parents note that they frequently forget, lose things, daydream, display messiness and disorganization, and sometimes appear to be in a fog. Parents report a pattern of excessive temper outbursts followed by immediate remorse and repentance. The children don't seem to learn from their mistakes, discipline seems ineffective, and some parents observe that their child even wears out shoes faster than do other children.

Many of these children also have a history of not handling changes in plans or schedules well. They often make big deals out of minor frustrations. And some are hypersensitive to texture, sound, light, or touch. I often ask parents whether their child has made a fuss about stockings, and many report their child would get extremely upset if his or her socks weren't adjusted in a certain way. At this time there isn't any standardized way to summarize these features, but most clinicians will have some way of obtaining this important developmental information.

What to Tell the Child About the Testing

Honesty and a calm presentation are the key ingredients in communicating to school-age children about the prospect of testing. I tell parents to inform their child that he or she and the doctor are going to do some activities to help the family and the teacher determine how to make it easier for the student to learn. Parents should acknowledge with their child the trouble he or she has in a particular area such as reading or math. Since the student is struggling in that area, the information won't come as a surprise.

Students need to know that they won't be graded on these tests and that other children won't see any of the results. The purpose of the evaluation is to help make the students' schooling more successful by finding out how they learn. Students benefit from having some idea of the kinds of changes they might expect as a result of the test information. For example, the approach to homework might be different, or students might receive extra help to strengthen their weak areas in the learning process. Above all, parents should emphasize their unconditional love and support for their children.

Parents' and teachers' attitudes will set the stage. If you're calm and optimistic about the process, your student will probably mirror the same attitude. Since parents won't likely be allowed in the same room once the formal testing starts, inform your student that the examiner will be very nice, most of the activities are fun, and there will be bathroom breaks. Also, be clear that this kind of doctor doesn't give shots or pull teeth.

Tell the parents to make sure their child has a good night's rest before testing, and inform the evaluator if there has been any trauma or major change in recent days that might affect the child's performance. For example, I was scheduled to evaluate a young boy who was suspected of having ADHD. However, he had come down with a bad cold and an ear infection. The mother had given him some medicine that morning, and by the time they arrived at my office, he was sound asleep. I tried to talk to the child, but he was barely able to walk down the hall, let alone produce accurate results in a testing situation. We rescheduled the evaluation for a time when the lad was feeling better.

The child should have a good breakfast or lunch and avoid any foods that have a negative effect on performance. The parents shouldn't ask their child too many questions about how the testing went. The student may not have been given specific feedback about the results and thus might not know how the test went. A general inquiry is understandable, but parents shouldn't probe, and nor should teachers.

How Test Results Are Translated into a Plan

Determining Eligibility for Public School Services

The following discussion applies if the family is using local school district resources to evaluate the child. If they are using an independent evaluator, this detailed process may not apply. It is only when state or federal funds are being used to provide special services that the focus-of-concern or child find process must be followed. However, even for private school students, most of the following process of translating test results into program recommendations will apply. I am describing the public school process because parents will frequently use this resource rather than incurring the expense of a private evaluation.

Once the testing is completed, the psychologist, child study team, or both will evaluate the results. In the public school process, an eligibility committee must meet and review the evaluation to determine whether the student is to be classified as *handicapped* and in need of special education, related services, or both. The public school must provide special services only after the child is deemed "handicapped and in need of special-education and/or related services." You may not like the heavy sound of the word *handicapped,* but the legislation that mandates and provides funds for the child to receive extra help uses such terms. Therefore, the terms and their definitions must be used in this process.

To qualify a student for help within the learning-disabled category, the eligibility committee must see from the evaluation evidence that there is a severe discrepancy between the student's intellectual ability and academic achievement in one or more of the categories we've mentioned. Your state regulations may specify similar but different categories for learning disabilities. Other eligibility criteria exist for each special-needs category.

Parents and private-school teachers may not automatically be a part of the eligibility committee meeting. After the evaluation process has been completed, parents have a right to review the information, obtain copies of the evaluation, and receive an explanation of it. Parents may also request that they be allowed to attend the eligibility committee meeting.

These steps all take place before the IEP meeting because the eligibility committee may determine that the student does not meet the criteria for a particular learning problem and therefore does not qualify for special services. For instance, the committee may conclude that the child's scores on any of the achievement categories are not low enough to meet the criteria. The student may have problems in, for example, written expression, but he or she is only one-and-a-half grade levels behind and not two. Since two levels below expectations is the cutoff score, the child isn't eligible for services.

The eligibility committee must make this kind of deliberation, and they have to follow fairly rigid criteria established by your state office of public instruction. If the child is found not to be eligible for services, the IEP does not take place. That's why parents may want to ask to attend the eligibility committee meeting. It includes a crucial decision point in the total process, and the parents may want to advocate strongly for their child's best interests. In the meeting, parents may disagree with the findings and ask for another evaluation if they believe the results do not accurately reflect their child's abilities and needs.

I must emphasize that these procedures are necessary if special education services are provided in the public schools or if public school personnel complete the evaluation. If a private clinician does the evaluation, the implementation activities will take place in your school, through other community resources, or both. It's also important to remember that even when students have been identified by the public school process as having significant learning deficiencies, they may still not be able to obtain public school services. The next chapter explains this possibility.

Preparation of an IEP

It's now time to formulate a plan of action. What intervention, accommodation, and remediation will help the student? According to federal law, a meeting must take place within thirty days of the time the student has been found to qualify for special-education and related services. The purpose of this meeting is to formulate and review the IEP appropriate to the child's needs. The same timeline would apply whether the local school district or an independent evaluator did the evaluation. The clock would start ticking once the district had received the test results and the eligibility committee had confirmed that the child had a learning disability or other health impairment such as ADHD, as defined by your state guidelines.

If the family used an independent evaluator outside the public school process, a summary session would ordinarily take place with that person shortly after the testing was completed. In this session the evaluator would explain the entire testing process, describe specific test results, and give a summary of the implications for that child. As the child's teacher, you want to know the student's strengths and weaknesses, areas of learning disability, and what methods of instruction are likely to be of most value. The content would be similar to what the local school district meeting would provide. If the family expects to use the services of the public school, the results of the evaluation must be forwarded to the district, and the eligibility process would still have to be completed. If all services are going to be provided by your school, the public school probably won't be involved in any of the educational deliberation and implementation.

Federal guidelines require that the local school district use a multidisciplinary team to interpret the evaluation data and contribute to placement and instructional recommendations. This team will include the child's classroom teacher and at least one person, such as a school psychologist, qualified to conduct individual diagnostic examinations of children. Often other people such as a nurse, a speech and language specialist, a learning disorder specialist, and an administrator will be involved. This team is supposed to draw on information from a variety of sources to make its recommendations. The data can include aptitude and achievement test results, teacher recommendations, physical or medical conditions, social or cultural background, and adaptive behavior.

The information obtained from all these sources should be documented and carefully considered. A group of people, including those who are knowledgeable about the student, will make the placement decision. In doing so, the group should consider all placement options and make use of the least restrictive environment. All these steps culminate in an IEP for the child.

Private School Planning

What happens if the evaluation does not involve the public school? The expectation is that everything will take place within your school or through private resources. Your school will have its own process for determining eligibility into special programs. However, there must still be some process for taking the assessment information and translating the recommendations into an educational plan for your student. Your school may have another name for the planning process, but the goal is still to arrive at specific ways to help the student.

Components of an IEP

I'm going to draw on some of the components of an IEP as described in the IDEA legislation. You may not be bound by law to include all these elements, but most of them help make an educational plan more effective. An IEP serves as a management instrument that describes what's going to be done for your student. It also functions as a monitoring tool to make sure the program unfolds as promised. And finally, an IEP provides a basis for evaluating the effectiveness of the student's program. It makes sense, then, to make sure the IEP is clear, accurate, and comprehensive.

A well-executed IEP contains certain components. Though various schools might use different forms, a comprehensive IEP includes the following information:

1. A statement of the child's present levels of educational performance
2. A statement of annual goals, including short-term instructional objectives
3. A statement of specific educational services to be provided
4. A statement of the extent to which the child will be able to participate in regular educational programs
5. A statement of whether modifications in the administration of standardized schoolwide tests should be made for the child
6. The projected dates for initiating services, and the anticipated duration of those services

7. A statement of whether any transition or prevocational skills and services are needed after the child turns fourteen

8. Appropriate criteria and evaluation procedures for determining, at least annually, whether the instructional objectives are being achieved

Now let's look at these components in more detail.

1. An IEP presents up-to-date information on test results in basic academic, vocational, and social skills, or a combination of those skills. An IEP lists the names of the tests, the dates when they were administered, and the results. Most important are the data that identify the weakness or special needs of the student. This basic information drives the entire process. On the basis of this description of deficits, the programming can be developed.

2. Annual goals and short-term instructional objectives specify the general intent and direction of the services provided from year to year. Every area of need documented under "present levels of educational performance" in item 1 should result in goal statements. Each goal should also generate short-term instructional objectives that map out a systematic sequence of skills needed to achieve the goal.

3. The next component of an IEP is a presentation of the services the student is to receive. This description includes the type of special program (such as a remedial program for reading comprehension) and the particular model of service delivery. An IEP also identifies the number of hours per day the student will participate in special classes. Types of classroom accommodations are also identified, such as oral testing, computer access, or taped books. In addition, an IEP describes any related services, such as counseling, physical therapy, and tutoring. The next chapter will explore these components extensively.

4. An IEP specifies the amount of time the student will participate in regular educational programs, including the extent of the student's participation in such activities as physical education. If the student is unable to participate in the regular physical education program, for example, an IEP gives a description of the specially designed alternate program.

5. Most public and private schools give some type of districtwide or schoolwide standardized achievement tests. An IEP states what test modifications should take place, such as allowing extended time or providing a distraction-free room for testing.

6. An IEP contains the dates when the services are to begin as well as their anticipated duration.

7. An IEP addresses the post–high school goals of the student in its explanation of any needs for transition service. This coordinated set of activities promotes movement from school to post-school adult living activities. An example would be prevocational classes in high school that would prepare the student to enter a full-time program of vocational-technical training. The plan would include a list of any agencies, in addition to the school, responsible for services.

8. The final component contains a description of objective criteria and evaluation procedures for determining progress toward the goals. Each goal and objective generates a statement that identifies the level of mastery required and how to evaluate the level. The need is to be able to monitor the student's growth and to evaluate the effectiveness of the IEP. The plan specifies a date and method of annual review. The IEP committee should meet at least once each school year to evaluate the IEP, the student's progress, and the achievement of the instructional objectives.

An IEP of secondary students can also include statements about whether the student is working toward graduation and a diploma, and what accommodations if any the student needs. Some school systems award handicapped students a "certificate of attendance," which signifies completion of four years of attendance rather than graduation from high school. Therefore, an IEP should state the type of certificate or diploma the student is working to achieve.

In signing an IEP, parents are giving permission for their child to receive the services outlined in that document. Only those services outlined on the IEP are required, in addition to the basic regular educational services. This fact is more of a legal concern for families who are receiving special education services from a local school district. In that case, the parents need to make sure everything discussed is actually included in the final form of the IEP. In the private school situation, no legal mandate exists for an IEP. However, if parents spend several thousand dollars to have their child participate in a special program, a formal IEP or contract would seem advisable.

Questions to Ask About a Student's IEP

Since the IEP document is so crucial in identifying all the services that are going to be provided for the student, teachers and parents should make sure the IEP is as comprehensive and accurate as possible. The following questions can help parents and teachers evaluate the IEP. You can check off the boxes for yes if the question can be answered in the positive, and for no if you believe the IEP does not fulfill that particular element of a question. Finally, you can mark the boxes under the question mark when you feel uncertain and need more information.

Questions to Help Evaluate a Student's IEP

Yes	No	?	
❏	❏	❏	Was the evaluation comprehensive, nondiscriminatory, and multidisciplinary?
❏	❏	❏	Does the evaluation describe a full range of the child's strengths and weaknesses, including learning styles and possible disabilities?
❏	❏	❏	Does the IEP accurately and fully describe the child's present level of educational performance in all relevant developmental areas?
❏	❏	❏	Do you agree with the assessment results?

Yes	No	?	
❑	❑	❑	Is more information needed to present a fair and accurate picture of the child's learning status?
❑	❑	❑	Do the goals included in the IEP accurately and adequately describe the skills, behavior, and understanding you wish the student to acquire in the next year?
❑	❑	❑	Do the goals represent all aspects of the educational experience and draw from the intellectual, social, emotional, physical, and spiritual domains that you believe are crucial for the child?
❑	❑	❑	Are the goals listed in order of priority from most to least important?
❑	❑	❑	Are the goals written in such a way that they will build on the child's strengths and present level of performance?
❑	❑	❑	Do the goals specify what service is to be provided, who will provide the service, how and where the service will be delivered, how often and how much service will be provided, and when the service will start?
❑	❑	❑	Do all the professionals who know and will work with the student agree with the components of the IEP?
❑	❑	❑	Does the IEP clearly outline the balance of time the child will spend in regular- and special-education programs?
❑	❑	❑	Is there at least one annual goal and short-term objective for each type of service the child will receive?
❑	❑	❑	Are all goals and objectives written in under-standable, positive, and measurable terms?

Yes	No	?	
❏	❏	❏	Does the IEP include clearly defined methods for systematically—at least annually, if not more often—evaluating the child's progress toward each goal and objective?
❏	❏	❏	Given all the contents of the IEP, do you agree?

These questions have several purposes. We want to ensure that the IEP reflects the student's needs accurately. It also needs to be comprehensive and designed to do everything possible to help the student achieve more success in school.

Conclusion

This chapter has described how to obtain a formal evaluation and arrive at intervention and treatment decisions. In the next chapters, we'll look at specific and valuable ways to accommodate and remediate the deficiencies identified in the formal assessment.

References

AAP. *See* American Academy of Pediatrics.

American Academy of Pediatrics (AAP). 2000. Clinical practice guideline: Diagnosis and evaluation of the child with attention-deficit/hyperactivity disorder. *Pediatrics* 105, no. 5:1158–70.

Biederman, J., S. V. Faraone, and K. Lapey. 1992. Comorbidity of diagnosis in attention deficit disorder. In *Attention-deficit hyperactivity disorder.* G. Weiss, ed. Philadelphia, PA: WB Saunders.

CAPE and ILIAD. *See* Council for American Private Education (CAPE) and IDEA Local Implementation by Local Administrators Partnership (ILIAD).

Cernosia, A. 2002. Parentally-placed students with disabilities. Council for Exceptional Children. http://www.ideapractices.org/ resources/files/parentallyPlaced.pdf.

Council for American Private Education (CAPE) and IDEA Local Implementation by Local Administrators Partnership (ILIAD). 2003. Children with disabilities placed by their parents in private schools: An IDEA practices toolkit. http://www.ideapractices.org/resources/files/CAPE_Final.pdf.

Foorman, B. R., D. J. Francis, J. M. Fletcher, C. Schatschneider, and P. Mehta. 1998. The role of instruction in learning to read: Preventing reading failure in at-risk children. *Journal of Educational Psychology* 90:1–15.

Geller, B., K. Warner, M. Williams, and B. Zimmerman. 1998. Prepubertal and young adolescent bipolarity versus ADHD: Assessment and validity using the WASH-U-KSADS, CBCL and TRF. *Journal of Affective Disorders* 51, no. 2:93–100.

Geller, B., and M. Williams. 1998. Prepubertal and early adolescent bipolarity differentiated from AD/HD by manic symptoms, grandiose delusions, ultra-rapid or ultradian cycling. *Journal of Affective Disorders* 51:81–91.

Geller, B., B. Zimmerman, M. Williams, et al. 2000. Diagnostic characteristics of ninety-three cases of a prepubertal and early adolescent bipolar disorder phenotype by gender, puberty and comorbid attention deficit hyperactivity disorder. *Journal of Child and Adolescent Psychopharmocology* 10, no. 3:157–64.

Harrerias, C. T., J. A. Perrin, and M. T. Stein. 2001. The child with ADHD: Using the AAP clinical practice guideline. *American Family Physician* 63, no. 9:1803–10.

Jensen, P. S. 2000. ADHD: Current concepts on etiology, pathophysiology and neurobiology. *Child and Adolescent Psychiatric Clinics of North America* 9, no. 3:557–72.

Martin, G. L. 1993. Assessment procedures for attention deficit disorders in children. *Journal of Psychology and Christianity* 12, no. 4:357–74.

——. 1995. *Help! My child isn't learning.* Colorado Springs, CO: Focus on the Family.

——. In press. Current developments in the assessment of attention-deficit /hyperactivity disorder. *Marriage and Family: A Christian Journal.*

MTA Cooperative Group. 1999. A fourteen-month randomized clinical trial of treatment strategies for attention-deficit/hyperactivity disorder. *Archives of General Psychiatry* 56 (December): 1073–86.

Pastor, P. N., and C. A. Rueben. 2002. Attention deficit disorder and learning disability: United States, 1997–98. National Center for Health Statistics. *Vital and Health Statistics* 10, no. 206. http://www.cdc.gov/nchs/data/ series/sr_10/sr10_206.pdf.

Roid, G. 2002. Organization of the Stanford-Binet. 5th ed. Itasca, IL: Riverside Publishing. http://www.riverpub.com/products/clinical/sbis5/features.html.

Wilens, T. E., J. Biederman, and T. Spencer. 2002. Attention deficit/hyperactivity disorder across the lifespan. *Annual Review of Medicine* 53:113–31.

Woodcock, M. L., K. S. McGrew, and N. Mather. 2000. *Woodcock Johnson III complete battery.* Itasca, IL: Riverside Publishing.

PART II

Treatment of Learning Problems

CHAPTER 5

Accommodation of Learning Disabilities in the Classroom

We now turn our attention to the teaching process for students with learning disabilities. No single chapter can hope to address all the instructional strategies that might be used with LD students. My goal is to begin by giving you some proven and useful ideas for accommodating such students in the regular classroom. Then I will describe what research has identified as the key ingredients in remedial or instructional material and will give you some examples of remedial programs that could work in your school. I'll include references so that you can get more details about any of the programs mentioned.

In the next chapter I will share some detailed descriptions of instructional methods for a few specific types of learning disabilities such as auditory processing, learning strategies, and expressive writing. The goal is to achieve the best possible intervention strategy for your LD student.

A complete program for an LD student will include strategies for both accommodation and remediation. The student may be receiving help from the resource-room teacher to remediate some basic deficits.

However, it takes a long time, often one to three years, to bring deficit areas up to a functional level. In the meantime, we want to see the child experience as much success as possible in the regular classroom. Achieving that level of success may require some modifications in the way the student receives instruction and completes assignments.

Accommodation

Accommodation is the adjustment of materials such as textbooks and worksheets, as well as of assignments and classroom routines. The intent is to help LD students work around their specific disability so that they can be more successful. Accommodations provide ways for teachers to maintain the standards of their class while altering the environment or providing assistance to allow LD students to meet the class requirements. We want the student to participate in as many classroom activities as possible and to benefit from them.

In the following section I have included a broad selection of accommodations that can be appropriate for an LD student. They are organized according to learning environment, materials, interactive instruction, motivational techniques, organization, classroom behavior, parent involvement, and teacher attitudes. Some overlap will always occur between accommodations for LD and for ADHD students. I have tried to separate them to some degree and will include the list for ADHD students in chapter 8.

These ideas have not been matched to each specific category of learning-disabled students. The accommodations tend to be generic, and this chapter includes them as a menu of options for you to use as you empower students to become more successful in your classroom. As one teacher/author has said, "If students are not learning the way you are teaching them, find and use a more appropriate method so you can teach them the way they learn" (Winebrenner 1996). These accommodations should help you do just that.

Provide These Students with Low-Distraction Work Areas

- Have a quiet, distraction-free area for these students to study and take tests. The teacher has the responsibility of "sending" them discreetly—without drawing peer attention to them—to a quiet, distraction-free room or area for each testing session. Once they begin a task in such an environment, it is important to assure that no interruptions occur until they are finished.
- Always seat the students near the source of instruction or stand near the students when you give instructions in order to reduce barriers and distractions between them and the lesson.
- Encourage the students to sit near positive role models to reduce distractions.
- Make sure computers and other equipment with audio functions operated in the students' classroom or designated work areas are used with earphones to eliminate the broadcasting of the sound into the classroom or designated work areas.
- Avoid distracting stimuli, such as air conditioners and high-traffic areas. Instead, seat the students in a low-distraction work area in the classroom.
- Increase the distance between desks.

Prepare the Students for Transitions

- Tell the students in advance about upcoming changes in routine, such as field trips and transitions from one activity to another.
- Make sure there is planned supervision during transitions: for example, between subjects, classes, recess and classes, lunch and classes, and assemblies and classes.
- Help the students prepare for ending the day and going home: for example, check the student's book bag for items needed for homework.

Alter Test Procedures and Materials

- Do not give handwritten tests, and make sure all duplicated materials contain clear, large, dark, easy-to-read text.
- On tests, remove from the students' view any questions that they are not supposed to answer. The simpler and less distracting a page is, the better it is.
- Whenever possible, place the instructions next to the questions to which they relate, and make sure test questions stand out visually from the answers: for example, on multiple choice and matching tests.
- Assure that the test questions progress logically through the material being tested: for example, covering sections 1, 2, and 3 in that order and not skipping from section to section.
- Give frequent short quizzes and avoid long exams.
- Prior to a test or quiz, provide the students with specific information, in writing if necessary, about what materials it will cover.
- Provide the students with a practice test or quiz, called a pre-review, to study the day before the actual test or quiz.
- Because ADHD and LDs can impede students' information retrieval ability, help to eliminate their test anxiety by allowing them extra time to complete quizzes, exams, and tests—including standardized tests.
- Whenever LD students are unable to finish a test in the time provided to other students, allow them to write a note on the test to arrange for more time.
- Provide the students with various opportunities, methods, or test formats to demonstrate what they know.
- Allow the students to take tests or quizzes in a quiet place so that they have as few distractions as possible.
- Consider allowing these students to use a calculator when it is clear that they understand math calculation concepts.
- Give open-book exams.
- Give exams orally.
- Give take-home tests.

- Use a greater number of objective items and require fewer essay responses.
- Allow the students to give test answers on a tape recorder.
- Read test items to the students.
- Avoid placing the students under the pressure of time or competition.

Make Accommodations for Assignments and Other Materials

- Use a tape recorder. Students can listen more than once to directions, stories, and lessons recorded on tapes or CDs and thus can clarify their understanding of directions or concepts.
- Give extra time to complete tasks.
- Simplify complex written directions, and highlight significant parts of the directions.
- Hand worksheets or assignments out one at a time to help prevent students from being overwhelmed.
- Decrease the reading level of the assignments.
- Develop a reading guide that features periodic questions to help students focus on relevant content. You can create one that asks questions paragraph by paragraph, page by page, or section by section.
- Provide a glossary of terms for content areas.
- Require fewer correct responses to achieve grades, focusing on quality instead of quantity.
- Allow the students to tape-record assignments and homework.
- Provide a written description of the routine, including daily activities.
- Shorten assignments, breaking work into smaller segments.
- Allow the students to begin an assignment and then show it to the teacher after completing the first few problems to confirm that they are doing the assignment correctly and to offer gentle correction or praise.
- Encourage the use of books on tape to support students' reading assignments.
- Provide published book summaries, synopses, or digests of major reading assignments for the students to review before you teach the

related lessons. An example would be to provide CliffsNotes for literature studies.

- If needed, periodically modify classroom and homework assignments. For example, have the students do every second or third problem, or have them use a timer and draw a line across their homework page at the end of fifteen minutes of sustained work.
- Make a second set of books and materials available so that these students can keep a backup set at home.
- If necessary, allow typewritten or computer-printed assignments either prepared by the student or dictated by the student and recorded by someone else.
- Reduce the size or number of homework assignments.
- Do not grade handwriting.
- Do not penalize students for reversals and transpositions of letters and numbers. Instead, simply point these mistakes out for correction.
- Do not require lengthy outside reading assignments.
- Monitor the students' self-paced or long-term assignments. For instance, if a report is due in four weeks, check students' progress often—daily, weekly, biweekly.
- Make arrangements for homework assignments to reach the students' home with clear, concise directions.
- Recognize and give credit for the students' oral participation in class.

Make Accommodations That Involve Interactive Instruction

- Use explicit teaching procedures.
  - Present an advanced organizer.
  - Demonstrate the skill.
  - Provide guided practice.
  - Offer corrective feedback.
  - Set up independent practice.
  - Monitor practice.
  - Review.

(Simmons, Fuchs, and Fuchs 1991)

- Ask students who have difficulty following directions to repeat the directions in their own words.
- Ask the students to review key points orally.
- Maintain daily routines so students know what is expected.
- Provide a copy of lecture notes to students who have trouble taking notes.
- Provide a peer note-taker.
- Provide a graphic organizer, such as an outline, chart, or blank web.
- Use step-by-step instructions for students who need explicit or part-to-whole instruction.
- Provide visual aids, large print, and films.
- Combine verbal and visual information.
- Write key points or words on the chalkboard or an overhead.
- Make an effort to balance oral presentations with visual information and participatory activities.
- Teach by using various sensory modes, such as visual, auditory, kinesthetic, and olfactory.
- Create a balance among large-group, small-group, and individual activities.
- Use mnemonic devices to help students remember either key information or steps in a learning strategy.
- Emphasize a daily review of previous learning or lessons.
- Pair students so that they can check each other's work.
- Provide peer tutoring.
- Allow the students to tape-record lessons.
- Use computer-assisted instruction.
- Provide a model to help students, post the model, and refer to it often.
- Provide cross-age peer tutors who can help the students find the main idea: for example, by underlining, highlighting, and using cue cards.
- Break longer presentations into shorter segments.

Employ Effective Motivational Techniques

- Match students' needs and learning style with teachers who have the appropriate attributes in order to provide the students with the best education and support possible.
- Match the students with teachers who know how to create opportunities for academic and social success; who can increase the frequency of positive, constructive, supportive feedback; and who can identify, recognize, reinforce, and build on the students' strengths and interests.
- Recognize the students' efforts to reach a goal, and distinguish between the problems resulting from skill deficits and those from noncompliance.
- Look for positives. Provide immediate feedback to the students every time they accomplish desired behaviors and achievements— no matter how small the accomplishment.
- Create a nonthreatening learning environment in which students feel safe and comfortable asking questions, seeking extra help, and making mistakes.
- Provide an environment in which it is safe to learn—academically, emotionally, and socially.
- Praise in public whenever possible; reprimand in private when necessary.
- Encourage empathy and understanding from faculty, staff, and peers; and do not permit humiliation, teasing, or scapegoating.
- Provide clearly stated rules, consequences, and expectations that are consistently carried out for all students.

Provide Training and Guidance for Study Skills and Organizational Planning Skills

- Provide the students with a regular program in study skills, test-taking skills, organizational skills, and time management skills.

- Provide daily assistance/guidance in how to use a planner on a daily basis and for long-term assignments; help the students plan how to break larger assignments into smaller, more manageable tasks.
- Provide the students with a notebook for homework assignments.
- Help the students set up a system of organization that uses color coding by subject area, especially with materials that need to be stored in a school locker during the day.
- Teach the students how to identify key words, phases, operations signs in math, and sentences in instructions and in general reading.
- Teach the students how to scan a large text chapter for key information and how to highlight important selections.
- Teach the students efficient methods of proofreading their own work.
- Across all subject areas, display and support the use of mnemonic strategies to aid memory formation and retrieval.
- Allow alternate methods of outlining, such as mind mapping or clustering.

Provide Guidance and Support for Learning Skills

- Provide consistent coaching from all teachers to support the students' organizational skills, time management skills, study skills, and test-taking skills.
- Designate one teacher as the advisor/supervisor/coordinator/liaison for each of the students and for the implementation of a plan. This person will periodically review the student's organizational system, will listen to other staff members who have concerns about the student, and will act as the link between the school and the student's home.
- Permit the students to check in with their advisor as the first activity each week (Monday mornings) to plan/organize the week and as the last activity each week (Friday afternoons) to review the week and to plan/organize homework for the weekend.
- Encourage all students to form study groups that include LD students, encourage LD students to seek assistance from their peers, and encourage overall collaboration among students.

- Send daily/weekly progress reports to the students' parents.
- Develop a reward system for student work completed at school and at home.

Make Accommodations for Classroom Behavior

- Use timers with the students to facilitate task completion.
- Structure transitional and unstructured times, such as those involving recess, hallways, the lunchroom, the locker room, the library, assemblies, and field trips.
- Praise specific behaviors.
- Use self-monitoring strategies, such as self-charting.
- Give extra privileges and rewards for improved behavior.
- Keep classroom rules simple and clear.
- Make prudent use of negative consequences. Use positive approaches most often.
- Allow for short breaks between assignments.
- Cue the students to stay on task. Use verbal or nonverbal signals.
- Mark the students' correct answers, not their mistakes.
- Implement a classroom behavior management system.
- Allow the students time out of their seat to participate in such activities as running errands.
- Ignore inappropriate behaviors that are not drastically outside classroom limits.
- Allow legitimate movement.
- Contract with the students for specific improvements in behavior.
- Increase the immediacy of rewards.
- Implement time-out procedures.

Encourage Parental Involvement

- Make sure that teachers report to the parent any time one of these interventions or accommodations seems to be ineffective so that you can modify the plan as needed.

- Involve parents in the selection of the students' teachers.
- For daily communication with the parent, use the student's planner, the phone, or email.
- Make sure each teacher sends home the weekly communication sheet at the end of each school week.
- When special or long-term projects are assigned, use the weekly communication sheet to inform in advance the parent, advisor, or both.

Address Teacher Attitudes and Beliefs

- Accept characteristics of LDs, especially inconsistent performance.
- Recognize that students with LDs perform at their best in an environment that is safe—academically, emotionally, and socially. Always avoid using sarcasm, bringing attention to deficits, and allowing constant criticism. Children with LDs respond significantly better when they are encouraged and feel safe to make mistakes.
- Send the students' teachers to in-service workshops on LDs.
- Provide the students' teachers with reading material on LDs.
- Recognize that no two students with LDs are alike, that there are multiple approaches to working with each LD student, and that the approaches can and will be different from student to student.
- Be flexible when working with LD students.
- Accept poor handwriting and printing.
- Do not attribute the students' poor performance to poor motivation or character traits such as laziness.
- Recognize that an LD is a neurological problem that students do not choose to have. Yet recognize also that the diagnosis is intended to explain and not excuse.

(Chapman Booth 2002;
Fetal Alcohol Syndrome Community Resource Center 2003)

Treat these lists as a smorgasbord, and pick out the suggestions that make sense for your situation. Many of these accommodations simply describe good teaching techniques, so it shouldn't involve too much of a stretch for you to incorporate them into your daily teaching plan. Feel free to do some experimenting. Each LD student will need individualized adjustments. However, you should be able to find some methods that work for you more consistently than others.

I had a college student client who had both ADHD and learning disabilities. His first years of college had been a real struggle, resulting in mostly poor grades. I evaluated him and identified the attention-deficit component of his problem. He started on medication, and experienced beneficial results. Now he could concentrate and focus on his studies much more effectively. We did some counseling to help with several family and social relationship issues. Then I wrote a letter to the learning center at his university, explaining his disabilities. I also requested that he be allowed to take his exams orally. The university made the accommodation, his professors cooperated, and my client got straight A's the next quarter! I've had the same results with selected junior and senior high school students.

Remediation

Remediation is the process of using individualized instruction to improve specific skills, such as reading or language arts. It consists of first identifying the precise needs and deficits of the student. The teacher may draw on the formal evaluation completed earlier and will probably use certain in-class testing procedures to refine further where to begin instruction. Then a strategy for remedial intervention is developed. The teacher implements lesson plans that include the scope and sequence of the material that the student needs to learn. Ideally, the teacher allows the student's needs to dictate the curriculum rather than simply having the student work through a particular textbook because it seems to be a good program.

To be effective, remedial instruction must take place with a low teacher-student ratio. At the least that ratio means that the students will be in small groups of three to five, preferably with as much one-on-one teacher contact as possible.

Most remedial approaches use some type of task analysis, meaning that concepts and skills are broken down and taught in small, incremental steps. The information at each step should build on previous concepts so that the students can move through the material in an almost error-less fashion. This process reinforces the learning of students, building up their confidence and willingness to keep going.

Often the remediation process also employs a slower pace of instruction and frequent repetition. The deficit skills are presented and practiced multiple times in a variety of ways to help the students overlearn and thus master the material.

Effective teachers also match their instructional style to their students' learning styles. It is necessary to try a variety of instructional materials and methods in order to find the approach that best helps each student. No one method will work with all students. All teachers need to have a set of strategies that they use with most students, but when the initial methods do not work, the philosophy must be to try, try again.

I recall a public school situation that put this philosophy to the test. Danny, a student with severe learning disabilities, was placed in a self-contained classroom after resource-room contact proved to be insufficient. He also had outside tutorial help in reading twice a week. The LD teacher tried numerous techniques to get his reading skills to move past first-grade level. Nothing seemed to help.

The school sent the teacher to several other schools to find some other method to try. She went to LD workshops and researched the professional literature. The school paid for Danny to go to a summer reading institute at a nearby university. He still didn't seem to make any real progress in reading. Meanwhile, Danny's attitude deteriorated. He hated reading and was beginning to hate school, although he liked his teacher and knew she was trying her best to help him.

Finally, a unique program was found in a special-reading clinic in another city, and it was tried with Danny. The program was expensive to implement, but the school went ahead with it, and it worked. His progress was slow, but his reading did improve. Most important, his attitude improved. He liked the program and looked forward to participating. At last, after several years of effort, the teachers felt encouraged. Hats off to the teacher and special-education personnel who wouldn't give up on this difficult case. This illustration brings us back to the question of if and how private school students may access services from their local school district.

Availability of Public School Resources to Private School Students

The law and practices regarding the provision of special education and related services to students with disabilities whose parents have placed them in private schools have developed over the past several years as a result of court cases and administrative policy interpretive guidance. Until the 1997 amendments to the Individuals with Disabilities Education Act (IDEA), neither the federal statute nor the applicable federal regulations addressed this issue in detail. Keep in mind that Congress is considering the IDEA legislation as this material is being written, so there may well be changes that will impact private or parentally placed students.

As we saw in the last chapter, the IDEA regulations underscore the fact that local educational associations (LEAs) maintain the responsibility to engage in child find activities that locate, identify, and evaluate children who are legal residents in the area under their purview. Their child find activities for children in private schools must be comparable to those for public school children.

The determination that a private school student has a disability and needs special education services, however, does not result in an entitlement to IEP services. Under the IDEA statute and regulations, a student with a disability who is placed by his or her parents in a private school has no individual legal entitlement to receive some or all of the special education and related services that this student would receive if enrolled in a public school.

Under recent policy guidelines of the Office of Special Education Programs, if a determination is made that a private school student is eligible for special education services, the rule is that the LEA must convene an IEP team to develop an IEP for the student. The IEP provides the parents with specific information regarding what a free appropriate public education (FAPE) would be for their child. Then they can decide whether to maintain the private school placement or to enroll their child in the public school to receive IEP services. The exception to this requirement would occur if the parents clearly indicate their intent to enroll or to maintain their child in the private school and are not interested in considering a public program or placement. In such a case, an IEP would not be necessary.

If the LEA places a student who has a disability in a private school as a means of fulfilling the school's obligation to provide a free appropriate public education, the student maintains an individual legal entitlement to services, and the parents have full access to all the procedural safeguards provided by the IDEA. In addition, when the parents have made a "unilateral placement" of their child in a private school when the provision of a free appropriate public education is an issue, the parents may seek full reimbursement for all costs associated with that placement from a hearing officer or a court. The parents may not get the costs of the private school paid for, but they can at least try.

Although IDEA provides significant assistance to public school children in need of special education, it has never provided the same scope and quality of services to children in private schools. Currently, no individual child in a private school is entitled to any services under IDEA. And collectively, children with special needs in private schools receive funding for only about one-seventh of the level of special education services available to their public school counterparts.

When Congress reauthorized IDEA in 1997, it required a given school district to provide to private school children with special needs only those services that could be purchased by a proportionate share of the federal funds available to the district under the statute. Thus, if 10 percent of students with disabilities in a school district are enrolled in private schools, the district must set aside only 10 percent of its IDEA funds to serve those children. And since IDEA funds cover only a small share of the total cost of special education services to begin with, the net effect is that children with special needs in religious and independent schools receive only a fraction of the services they would otherwise receive. Since IDEA does not provide any particular private school child the right to special education services, the proportionate spending rule applies to private school students as a whole. As a result, public school officials must ration the scarce resources available for private school students. They choose which students if any will be served, which disabilities will be addressed, and whether any direct services will be provided (Cernosia 2002; Council for American Private Education 2003; Office of Special Education Programs 2001).

The reader should also be aware that many states have state laws that provide for greater rights and legal entitlements than does the IDEA. For example, states such as Texas and Idaho have dual enrollment state statutes allowing students who attend private schools, including those with disabilities, to enroll also in the public schools to receive desired services, which may include special education. Therefore, you should also review your own state law and local school district policy.

You can find updated information on legislation as it impacts private schools at the website of the Council for American Private Education at http://www.capenet.org. Another resource is the website of the U.S.

Department of Education's Office of Non-Public Education at http://www.ed.gov/about/offices/list/oii/nonpublic/index.html. You can seek specific information about current developments surrounding IDEA legislation and implementation at www.ideapractices.org.

A resource entitled *Children with Disabilities Placed by Their Parents in Private Schools: An IDEA Practices Toolkit* has recently become available. The Council for American Private Education (CAPE) and the IDEA Local Implementation by Local Administrators (ILIAD) partnership developed it. You can obtain it free of charge from CAPE.

The purpose of this toolkit is to help parents, private school officials, and public school officials understand the IDEA provisions that relate to children with disabilities whose parents have placed them in private schools. Reviewed and funded by the U.S. Department of Education, the toolkit offers examples of effective practices, ideas for enhancing cooperation between the public and private sectors, and practical resources for delivering services under IDEA to children in private schools. You can download the toolkit from the CAPE website at http://www.capenet.org/pdf/IDEATool.pdf. The website contains the following extract:

> When this toolkit went to press, the U.S. House of Representatives had approved legislation to reauthorize the Individuals with Disabilities Education Act and the Senate was taking up its own version of the legislation. The House bill included significant changes in provisions relating to IDEA services to children placed by their parents in private schools, and those changes or others may make their way into the final law. To keep this toolkit up to date, any changes in the law, regulations, and U.S. Department of Education guidance relating to services for parentally placed children in private schools will be posted on the following website: http://www.capenet.org/IDEA.html.

The previous information applies if the parents of your LD student wish to try to obtain special education, or remedial, services from the local school district for their child. However, in many cases you and your school will be the primary or only source of help.

Additional Information on Remedial Instruction

Immediate reinforcement for correct responses is important in the remedial process. It's crucial for the students to experience success. Students can receive feedback through such ways as programmed and computer-aided instruction. In this format, the students see and/or hear a sequence of instructional information. The program then provides a practice item or question for the students to answer. If the answer is correct, the program gives some kind of visual and/or auditory feedback and moves to the next element in the sequence. If the answer is wrong, the program may repeat the question, provide the correct answer, or branch to an easier question or to another subroutine that clarifies the concept. Teachers can use an ever-increasing amount of computer technology and software to good effect in the classroom.

Rewards, progress charts, contracts, and various incentive systems can help a student stay on task and motivated. Most important is the relationship between the student and teacher. The teacher must be encouraging and positive about the student and the student's progress. Verbal praise and enthusiasm are more important than new textbooks or fancy computers.

Students in a remedial situation may also receive instruction about ways to work around their specific learning disabilities. Examples of accommodation were mentioned earlier, but I'm referring here to teaching the student to use self-management techniques rather than expecting the teacher to make all the adjustments. This instruction can include activities such as using mnemonic devices to help remember material for a test. As another example, the teacher can record a lecture and then have someone listen to the tape and critique the students' note-taking skills. The goal would be to improve the student's ability to listen and take good notes. However, it may be that the students will need to listen to the lecture several times for certain kinds of content. Audiotaping may then become a common practice for these students.

Still other students may find that if they translate lecture content into some kind of visual picture or collection of symbols and diagrams, the material makes more sense and recalling it is easier. In that case, students are using a visual strength to compensate for an auditory weakness.

Remedial classrooms are usually going to have a high degree of structure and organization, with the teacher clearly outlining student expectations. Students need to know exactly what is required as well as the consequences of appropriate and inappropriate behavior, and when various events and activities will take place. These children need a certain amount of predictability but not a regimented or harsh environment. The teachers have their own method for achieving structure in the classroom. If your students know what's happening throughout the day, seem comfortable with the sequence of events, and are making progress, the appropriate structure is probably in place.

The final component of a remedial effort for LD students is a close monitoring of their progress. They need some kind of continual evaluation, which can take the form of pretest-teach-posttest. In this process, students take a pretest on the skills and concepts that a particular unit will include. Instruction on the material then takes place. Finally, the students take a posttest that shows whether they have achieved success according to certain criteria. If the students do not demonstrate success on the posttest, instruction on the material takes place again until the students can pass the posttest.

Educators can also use continuous forms of measurement to determine student progress. This approach pinpoints specific academic targets and then charts students' performance daily. This close monitoring provides more clarity about the effects of various interventions or curriculum changes as they happen.

Effective Teaching Practices

Before we look at some specific programs for teaching LD students, let me summarize what research has revealed about the core elements of effective teaching practices and the key features of effective materials that can be used with these students. First, what are the most important procedures teachers must follow if they are going to have maximum impact on students with learning disabilities? The effective teaching studies are a collection of research investigations about effective schools and teachers. These studies suggest that the following procedures can help you in your effectiveness:

- Begin each lesson with a short review of previous learning.
- Begin each lesson with a short statement of goals.
- Present new material in small steps and provide time for students to practice after each step.
- Give clear explanations and detailed instructions.
- Provide a high level of active practice for all students.
- Ask many questions, check for student understanding, and obtain responses from all students.
- Guide students during the initial practice.
- Provide systematic feedback and corrections.
- Provide explicit instructions and practice for seatwork and exercises, and, when necessary, monitor students during seatwork.

(Rosenshine 1986, 1997)

Effective teachers of LD students also give explicit instructions, offer praise, use good management, provide individual attention, create a healthy emotional climate, provide opportunities for responding time, and use active learning strategies (Morsink, Soar, and Thomas 1986).

Explicit Instruction

Many students with learning disabilities need explicit, or direct, instruction. teachers clearly state what they are going to teach and explain what the students need to do. The following list provides a summary of the principles of explicit instruction:

- Provide students with an adequate range of examples to help them understand a concept or problem-solving strategy.
- Provide models of proficient performance, including either step-by-step strategies or broad generic questions and guidelines that focus attention and that prompt deep processing.
- Provide experiences in which students explain how and why they make decisions.
- Provide both frequent feedback on quality of performance and constant support so that students persist in performing activities.
- Provide both adequate practice and activities that are interesting and engaging.

(Gersten 1998)

Even though we could mention other effective teaching practices, these lists will benefit you significantly as you apply them in your work with LD students.

Effective Instructional Programs

The next issue concerns which features contribute the most to making a particular program or method most effective in teaching LD students. Researchers have attempted to identify the various forms of instruction that are intended to improve student learning.

One meta-analysis review looked at 272 studies that measured the outcome of using various instructional methods with LD students. The researcher concluded that the most effective method of teaching children with learning disabilities combined components of direct instruction (teacher-directed lecture, discussion, and learning from books) with components of strategy instruction (teaching ways to learn, such as memorization techniques and study skills).

The main instructional components of this combined model include the following:

- Control of task difficulty: for example, sequencing material from easy to difficult
- Instruction in small groups of five or fewer students
- Directed questioning and responses: for example, the teacher asks process or content questions for students to answer orally
- Sequencing: for example, breaking down the task and providing step-by-step prompts
- Drill-repetition-practice: for example, daily testing, repeated practice, and sequenced review
- Segmentation, or breaking skills into parts and then synthesizing the parts into a whole
- Use of technology: for example, computers and presentation media
- Teacher-modeled problem solving
- Strategy cues, such as reminders to use strategies and think-aloud models

Of these components, the one most linked to student achievement was control of task difficulty. In applying this component, for example, the teacher offers necessary assistance and uses tasks that are sequenced from easy to difficult. Another significantly influential component is the use of small interactive groups of five or fewer students. A third strongly influential component was the use of structured questioning and directed responses, involving, for instance, interactive questions and direction from the teacher for students to ask questions and summarize (Swanson 1999b).

Effective Methods for Problem Solving

Another analysis of outcome studies was done to focus on problem solving, or high-order processing, in adolescents with learning disabilities. The analysis included fifty-eight intervention studies that employed either direct instruction or strategy instruction in efforts to improve problem-solving skills. The results were very similar to those reported earlier. The author concluded that success did not depend on whether a particular method was used. Regardless of the overall model of instruction, only a few specific instructional components increased treatment effectiveness.

The conclusion was that drill-repetition-practice, sequencing, teacher modeling, systematic probing, and a clear orientation to task tend to supersede any particular method (Swanson 1999a). Keep these characteristics in mind as you evaluate the programs and materials that the following sections will describe.

Examples of Programs for Teaching LD Students

Some debate exists about whether learning disabilities can actually be corrected. Many professionals have looked at the countless research efforts to remediate LD problems and concluded that the basic disability doesn't really change. They have decided that intervention simply helps a student compensate for deficiencies. The core problem is considered a lifelong characteristic. As a consequence of this belief, the special-education field moved toward compensatory procedures that are designed to build on students' strengths rather than to address their weaknesses.

Other professionals would argue vigorously that deficits can be treated. They believe LD children can overcome many of their problem areas if they are given sufficient time and if the treatment concentrates on key areas of learning.

The following programs are all designed to remediate or build up the specific areas of weakness in an LD student. In reading about them, you will have enough information to evaluate the appropriateness of implementing them in your school. This list by no means encompasses all the remedial programs available to you. However, as I have visited numerous Christian schools, I most often hear about those that follow.

The Orton-Gillingham Approach

The Orton-Gillingham Approach is named after neurologist and pathologist Samuel Orton and psychologist and educator Anna Gillingham. As early as 1925, Dr. Orton identified the syndrome of dyslexia as an educational problem. Anna Gillingham had a superb mastery of the English language, and she worked with Dr. Orton to train teachers. Dr. Orton became known as the "Father of Dyslexia," making four major contributions to this field:

- Identified the syndrome of "specific language disability"
- Separated this group of disabled students from those with mental retardation, brain damage, and primary emotional disturbances
- Offered a neurophysiological explanation coupled with the conviction that diagnosis and treatment were possible
- Outlined and initiated remediation principles to help disabled readers overcome their handicaps

The Orton-Gillingham Approach is appropriate for teaching individuals, small groups, and classrooms of all age levels.

Specific Approaches/Strategies Used
- Language-based
- Multisensory
- Structured, sequential, and cumulative
- Cognitive
- Flexible
- Emotionally sound

To learn more about this program, use the following contact information:
Academy of Orton-Gillingham Practitioners and Educators
PO Box 234
Amenia, NY 12501
845-373-8919
info@ortonacademy.org
http://www.ortonacademy.org

The Alphabetic Phonics Program

The Alphabetic Phonics Program, based on the Orton-Gillingham Approach, was used and perfected at the Scottish Rite Learning Laboratory from 1965 to 1975 under the direction of Aylette Cox, a pediatrician, and Dr. Lucius Waites, a child development specialist, both in the pediatric neurology unit. Psychologists, neurologists, and speech therapists added sound neurological and speech techniques to the program. Alphabetic Phonics evolved directly from Orton-Gillingham because the latter was scientific, universally successful, and specific; and it combined the auditory, visual, and kinesthetic learning modalities. Approaches straight from Orton-Gillingham were implemented faithfully from 1960 to 1965 in the language lab under the close guidance of Sally Childs, Gillingham's professional heir.

Specific Approaches/Strategies Used
- Based on phonics
- Taught from simple to complex
- Taught in a structured way, using steps and procedures that lead to conscious thought-processing
- Multisensory, or taught through the simultaneous engagement of the visual, auditory, and kinesthetic senses
- Intensive
- Interactive and one-on-one

To learn more about this program, use the following contact information:
Vicki Fehr, Center Director
Hardin-Simmons University
Multisensory Language Training Center
PO Box 16158
Abilene, TX 79698
915-670-5842
vfehr@hsutx.edu
http://www.hsutx.edu/academics/education/mltc/alphabet.htm

The Association Method

In the 1920s and 1930s the late Mildred A. McGinnis, a teacher of deaf students at the Central Institute for the Deaf in St. Louis, developed the Association Method. She developed it originally to teach deaf children whose learning patterns were significantly different from and less successful than those of other deaf children in the school. The approach is multisensory and incremental.

Specific Approaches/Strategies Used
• Multisensory, including auditory, visual, tactile, and motor-kinesthetic cues
• Phonetically based
• Systematic
• Incremental
• Taught requiring precise articulation
• Taught using cursive writing for initial instruction
• Taught using color differentiation
• Taught using the Northampton Symbol System

To learn more about this program, use the following contact information:
Maureen K. Martin, Director
DuBard School for Language Disorders
The University of Southern Mississippi
PO Box 10035
Hattiesburg, MS 39406
601-266-5223
dubard@usm.edu
http://www.dubard.usm.edu/associat.html

Earobics

Earobics is a computerized program designed to improve auditory and phonological skills in a variety of skill areas, such as auditory attention, auditory discrimination, auditory figure-ground, and auditory memory.

Specific Approaches/Strategies Used
The program provides systematic, comprehensive phonological awareness and auditory processing training, which are important prereading skills. The software adapts to each student's skill level and progress. It targets skills such as the following:
- Blending
- Segmentation
- Phoneme identification
- Auditory discrimination
- Rhyming
- Sound-symbol correspondence
- Manipulation
- Auditory sequential memory

Several versions of Earobics are available, including home, school, and specialist editions. Four-year-olds through adults can benefit from this material.

To learn more about this program, use the following contact information:
Cognitive Concepts, Inc.
990 Grove St.
Evanston, IL 60201
888-328-8199
support@earobics.com
http://www.cogcon.com

Fast ForWord

The company Scientific Learning developed Fast ForWord, a family of computer-based training programs designed to improve core language and reading skills. These programs are the result of over twenty-five years of neuro-scientific research that proved the brain has a type of "plasticity" that enables us to continue to learn and develop throughout life. This research also proved our brains can be "rewired" through intensive training to improve the skills that are the basic to all learning.

Specific Approaches/Strategies Used
These intensive CD-ROM and Internet-based adaptive training exercises focus on language comprehension and phonological awareness skills by requiring children to listen actively and to make decisions about the sounds they hear. The key components of Fast ForWord include seven training exercises presented in a game-like environment. The exercises use five levels of acoustically modified speech. Sounds are stretched and emphasized in the lowest levels and progress to natural speech at the highest level. The exercise schedule is intense—100 minutes per day and five days per week, for four to eight weeks.

The second component of the program is an Internet-based performance review. At the end of each day, every student's training data are uploaded to the Internet. Teachers and parents can retrieve data and review each student's progress.

The program focuses on improving the following:
- Auditory word discrimination
- Ability to follow spoken directions
- Listening and speaking fundamentals
- Auditory processing speed
- Speech discrimination
- Language processing
- Grammatical comprehension
- Overall language comprehension

Versions of Fast ForWord are available for schools and families, and site licenses are for entire schools. Fast ForWord products include the following:
- Fast ForWord Language: develops the fundamental language skills that are building blocks for reading success
- Fast ForWord Language to Reading: builds rapidly the skills critical for learning to read or become a better reader
- Fast ForWord Reading: builds rapidly and systematically the reading skills that correlate with school curriculum standards

- Fast ForWord Middle and High School: improves thinking, listening, and reading skills; developed for adolescents and adults
- Reading Edge: measures the language and early reading skills that are necessary for success; developed by reading experts from Harvard, Stanford, and Johns Hopkins
- Fast ForWord Basics: improves the critical early learning skills that every child needs for success through skill-building exercises and assessment tools developed by leaders in brain research
- Fast ForWord Bookshelf: offers students a fun early reading adventure through an award-winning, multimedia reading kit of original storybooks and stories on CD

To learn more about this program, use the following contact information:
Scientific Learning
300 Frank H. Ogawa Plaza, Ste. 600
Oakland, CA 94612
888-665-9707
info@scilearn.com
http://www.scientificlearning.com

The Herman Method

During the years from 1964 to 1975, Renee Herman developed the Herman Method in Los Angeles, California. She designed the program to meet the needs of dyslexic students in the public school setting. Ms. Herman was encouraged and influenced by Samuel T. Orton's philosophy that dyslexic students can become proficient readers if taught according to their needs. She developed a sequence of instruction and a methodology that started students at their point of deficit and sequentially taught them mastery of each skill level. Students never received anything to read until they had mastered all the necessary skills. As a result, they experienced consistent success.

Specific Approaches/Strategies Used
- Multisensory
- Taught using multimedia

- Phonetic
- Sequential
- Systematic
- Cumulative
- Taught using spelling and writing components
- Individualized
- Meaning-based

To learn more about this program, use the following contact information:
The Herman Method
Lexia Learning Systems, Inc.
PO Box 466
2 Lewis St.
Lincoln, MA 01773
800-435-3942
781-259-8752
info@lexialearning.com
http://www.hermanmethod.com
http://www.lexialearning.com

Lindamood-Bell Learning Processes

During the 1960s and 1970s, Patricia Lindamood, a speech and language pathologist, and her late husband, Charles, began researching
the lack of phonemic awareness in poor readers. Their research led to
the Auditory Discrimination in Depth Program, first published in
1969. Patricia and her daughter, Phyllis, created the third edition, now
the LiPS Program, which became available in 1998. The Lindamood
Auditory Conceptualization (LAC) Test, designed to assess phonemic
awareness, was initially published in 1971.

Patricia Lindamood and reading specialist Nanci Bell cofounded a
company in 1986 and developed programs to help people with auditory, visual, and language processing. Lindamood and Bell believe that
when people have a deficit in one of these areas or when their auditory,
visual, and language processes work fine by themselves but don't work

together properly, these people will have trouble understanding certain material. Lindamood-Bell sensory-cognitive programs develop the underlying brain functions necessary for reading, spelling, language comprehension, math, and critical thinking.

Specific Approaches/Strategies Used
The Lindamood Phoneme Sequencing (LiPS) Program stimulates phonemic awareness. The assumption is that the primary cause of decoding and spelling problems is difficulty in judging sounds within words, or phonemic awareness. LiPS helps remedy and stimulate phonemic awareness. Students become aware of the mouth actions that produce speech sounds so that they can "feel" sounds within words. This awareness becomes the means of verifying sounds within words and enables people to become self-correcting in reading, spelling, and speech. The program can take people from training in consonants and vowels to training in multi-syllable words.

Seeing Stars is an integrated reading and spelling program that helps stabilize phonemic awareness and assists in the development of sight words and spelling. Specific steps of imaging letters for phonemes through multi-syllable words help establish reading and spelling in context.

The Nancibel Visualizing and Verbalizing for Language Comprehension and Thinking (V/V) Program stimulates concept imagery and helps students with language comprehension, reasoning, and expressive language skills. Students learn to develop mental pictures while listening or reading. A systematic way of describing the pictures uses words such as *color, size, shape, movement, number, background, mood, perspective,* and *sound* to stimulate detailed and vivid imagery. Students use the mental images to develop higher-order thinking skills regarding main idea, conclusion, inference, prediction, and evaluation.

A primary cause of math difficulties is an inability to imagine and verbalize the concepts underlying math processes. Many students attempt to memorize facts instead of trying to think, reason, and problem solve with numbers. The On Cloud Nine Math Program integrates concept imagery and numeral imagery with language, and then applies that processing to math computation and problem solving. The focus is on addition, subtraction, multiplication, and division, with some exposure to fractions, decimals, and percentages.

You can obtain instruction in sensory cognitive solutions through Lindamood-Bell centers located around the country. You can find information at http://www.lindamoodbell.com/learningcenters/clinicaldirectory.html. The program can include an hour a day of one-on-one regular instruction for four to six months. Intensive instruction is given for four hours a day and lasts six to eight weeks, and the program also offers group instruction. Schools can also implement programs that last for six hours a day. Teachers can receive training through Lindamood-Bell workshops as well as through third-party instructors.

To learn more about this program, use the following contact information:
Home Office
416 Higuera St.
San Luis Obispo, CA 93401
800-233-1819
805-541-3836
http://www.lindamoodbell.com

The National Institute for Learning Disabilities (NILD)

Deborah Zimmerman, a Christian nurse and educator, developed the NILD Educational Therapy model in the 1960s in conjunction with Drs. Archie Silver and Rosa Hagin at New York University. The first formal program was pioneered in 1973 in Norfolk Christian Schools to help children who learn differently. Under the direction of Grace Mutzbaugh, the National Institute for Learning Disabilities was formed in 1982 to make the program available to the Christian school community. The NILD program was specifically designed for Christian schools and those in the Christian community as a model of intervention to assist students who have average to superior intelligence and who have learning difficulties.

Specific Approaches/Strategies Used
- Taught using nontutorial intervention to develop underlying skills necessary for learning
- Integrative by developing perceptual and cognitive skills within the context of reading, writing, spelling, and math
- Intense and one-on-one in nature in that students participate both in two 80-minute sessions per week and in therapy for an average of three to four years
- Taught using interactive language and questioning
- Taught by stimulating areas that are deficient in perceiving and processing information
- Characteristic of providing needed structure and consistency by having parents work with their children at home for ongoing stimulation during the week
- All-age inclusive, taking into account that educational therapy can be effective even for adults

To learn more about this program, use the following contact information:
Kathy Hopkins, Executive Director
National Institute for Learning Disabilities
107 Seekel St.
Norfolk, VA 23505
877-661-6453
757-423-8646
info@nild.net
http://www.nild.net

PACE—Processing and Cognitive Enhancement

Over the course of fifteen years, Dr. Ken Gibson, a specialist in pediatric visual processing, and his brother, Dr. Keith Gibson, a clinical psychologist, developed PACE. The PACE program is an intense twelve-week one-on-one cognitive training program that corrects and enhances learning skills. Each week students receive six hours of help: three from a tutor and three from their parents.

Specific Approaches/Strategies Used
The students work with a trainer three times a week for an hour each session. PACE training includes thirty-three procedures. Each session may include four to eight procedures, depending on where the students are in their training schedule. Each procedure is a nonacademic mental exercise that focuses on one area needing improvement. PACE strengthens the following:

- Attention
- Simultaneous processing
- Sequential processing
- Planning
- Processing speed
- Short-term memory
- Long-term memory
- Auditory processing
- Visual processing

PACE also offers Master The Code (MTC), a reading and spelling program. MTC contains embedded procedures that pinpoint, evaluate, and develop advanced levels of required underlying mental skills for fast and efficient learning-to-read skills. These skills include memory, segmenting, blending, attention, visualization, processing speed and working memory, and auditory analysis.

To learn more about this program, use the following contact information:
Tanya Mitchell, Director of Client Services
5085 List Dr., Ste. 201
Colorado Springs, CO 80919
866-679-1569
tanya@pacetutoring.com
http://www.pacetutoring.com

Phono-Graphix

Dr. Diane McGuiness, a professor of psychology at University of South Florida, developed the Phono-Graphix approach to reading. Her son, Geoffrey McGuiness, and his wife, Carmen, have continued to develop her work. Carmen and others at the Read America clinic in Florida conducted the initial research on Phono-Graphix and published the results in a 1996 issue of the *Orton Annals of Dyslexia*. The next year, Simon and Schuster released the book *Reading Reflex*, making Phono-Graphix accessible to parents and teachers across the United States and Canada.

Specific Approaches/Strategies Used

Phono-Graphix is a phonics-based reading system that starts with the sounds and letters of the language. The written English language is a phonetic code, meaning that a symbol, or sound picture, represents each sound in a word. The teacher says each sound first and the children replicate the sound—as they hear it.

The Phono-Graphix method teaches children that groups of letters stand for sounds, treating letters as symbols of these sounds. English is broken down into forty-three of these sounds, each symbolized by one to four letters. The teacher shows the child a picture of an object, such as a dog. The child says the word for the picture and listens for the first sound, or /d/. This process continues until the child learns all sounds. Once students can identify the sounds that each letter symbolizes, they can work on the more complex words. They also learn to separate the phonemes in a word so that they can later blend them back into the right order.

Phono-Graphix is said to be effective for a person who is beginning to read or for a reader who has some reading problems. It is a phonetically based comprehensive approach that does the following:
- Teaches the English language code in a simple, logical fashion
- Teaches and applies strategy and logic, not the rhymes and rules that other phonetic methods teach

- Addresses phonemic awareness and auditory processing in a comprehensive manner
- Allows learners to apply these skills within the context of words, sentences, and stories, since people learn best through application

Phono-Graphix focuses on the following skills, which successful readers and spellers must master:
- Blending, the ability to push sounds together
- Segmenting, the ability to separate sounds in words
- Phoneme manipulation, the ability to "put in" or "take out" sounds in words

Phono-Graphix focuses on the following concepts:
- Letters are pictures of sounds: for example, in *cat* the sound /k/ is represented by the sound picture <c>.
- A sound picture can be made up of one or more letters: for example, the <sh> in *ship* or <igh> in *right.*
- There is more than one way to spell most sounds, giving variation in the code: for example, the sound /o/ in *note* is represented by the sound pictures <ow> in *slow,* <o> in *voting,* <oe> in *toe,* <ough> in *though,* and <oa> in *soap.*
- There is overlap between many of the sound pictures, and thus that one sound picture may make two different sounds: for example, the sound picture <ow> stands for /o/ in *flown* and /au/ in *brown.*

You can obtain Phono-Graphix instruction from certified therapists, and teacher training can take place through licensed trainers. You can find further information at the Read America website. Parents who wish to teach their children to read using this method can obtain the book *Reading Reflex: The Foolproof Phono-Graphix Method for Teaching Your Child to Read* (McGuinness and McGuinness 1999).

To learn more about this program, use the following contact information:
Read America
PO Box 1246
Mount Dora, FL 32756
800-732-3868
352-735-9292
RAchat@aol.com
http://www.readamerica.net

Powerline Programs

In 1967, Darwin and Myra Frye opened a remedial reading and learning disability clinic in Long Beach, California. Darwin's background was in linguistics, and Myra's was in speech therapy, special education, learning disabilities, and psychology. After three years of meticulous clinical research and experimentation with varied approaches to learning, they concluded that reading and spelling problems were perceptual problems, language problems, or both. They developed the Frye model of diagnosis that identifies problems in four major areas:

- Input
- Memory, or storage, and thought-processing
- Retrieval, as manifested in a motor response
- Feedback

The Reading Perception Diagnostic Test thoroughly examines these areas, which are emphasized in the approach taken in the remedial program Powerline.

Specific Approaches/Strategies Used
The Powerline Remedial Reading Program (PRRP) is a phonics-based program specifically designed to develop, use, and integrate the perceptual skills needed for reading, writing, and spelling. The PRRP uses a multisensory approach to meet the needs of students. The PRRP demands an immediate response in writing and speech (reading) to visual and auditory input so that the teacher can monitor each step of the learning process. The program is designed for teaching individuals or small groups.

This program has a major emphasis on auditory processing and memory training. The Powerline Reading Programs run on phonics as their main track. The main instructional tool comprises audiotape lessons with corresponding workbooks. The students can receive instruction five days a week with at least one tutorial session per week.

The sequential arrangement of the lessons in the PRRP reinforces and uses all previously learned concepts and provides positive daily success in students' reading, writing, spelling, listening, speaking, and language experience. The goal of the program is to provide information and training for students over the age of seven in order to improve the following:
- Memory
- Spelling
- Writing
- Reading accuracy
- Language development
- Reading comprehension

To learn more about this program, use the following contact information:
Don Olson, CEO
Powerline Programs Trust
700 E. Barrel Springs Rd.
Palmdale, CA 93550
800-876-7323
661-947-9192
powerlineprograms @earthlink.net
http://www.powerlinereading.com

The Slingerland Approach
Beth Slingerland grew up in California and received her degree in education from San Francisco State University. Her work in specific language disability began in 1935 when she first heard of the work of Dr. Samuel Orton and the teaching approach based on his research that was devised by Anna Gillingham and Bessie Stillman. Beth Slingerland observed Gillingham and Stillman as they taught individual students,

and they in turn observed her. Anna Gillingham gave her approval to the Slingerland Adaptation for Classroom Use, which came out of the Orton-Gillingham Approach for Specific Language Disability Children. The first Slingerland training course for teachers took place in 1960, and the Slingerland Institute was founded in 1977.

Specific Approaches/Strategies Used
- Uses simultaneous multisensory teaching strategies
- Preventive and remedial in nature
- Is used in group settings as well as in one-on-one settings
- Uses the alphabetic-phonic principle of beginning with a letter, the smallest unit of sight, sound, and feel
- Uses oral expression, decoding, reading comprehension, spelling, handwriting, and written expression

To learn more about this program, use the following contact information:
Slingerland Institute for Literacy
One Bellevue Center
411 108th Ave. NE
Bellevue, WA 98004
425-453-1190
mail@slingerland.org
http://www.slingerland.org

Positive Qualities of LD Students

As we conclude this chapter, which focuses on remediation of certain deficiencies in learning, I want to encourage you to remember that LD students always have some positive characteristics. No two people are alike, a fact that is particularly evident in LD students. Each one is a unique collection of gifts as well as of learning-disability features. When you feel discouraged about some of your students, remember their positive characteristics.

Many LD students can grasp concepts rapidly if the instruction presents those concepts to their strongest modality of learning. They may be sensitive to and aware of patterns, whether in music, other sounds, visual arts, numbers, or concepts. They can have boundless energy and a keen curiosity for such areas as science, mechanics, computers, nature, or history. Some children are able to concentrate within their area of strength for hours on end. Others have a fantastic long-term memory for dates, places, experiences, or information related to their hobby.

Children with learning disabilities can be quite empathetic because they know what it's like to be frustrated, embarrassed, and humiliated by others. They can also be quite open with their feelings and life experiences. They may carry their feelings on their sleeve, but you know exactly where they stand on an issue and how they feel about it.

I've also known LD children who have a special spiritual sensitivity. They love God and want other people to know about their faith. They like to sing songs, listen to Bible stories, and draw pictures relating to their understanding of God's love.

Recently, I reviewed a report card from a local Christian school that described the progress of a third-grade client. The teacher made the statement, "She also has an insatiable appetite for spiritual things." Isn't that great? This girl has both learning disabilities and ADHD, yet she thrives on learning about God. That same spiritual quality also helps her deal with the frustrations caused by her special needs, and it gives her hope when schoolwork seems too demanding.

LD students can have a high level of sensory awareness and perception. They can see, hear, feel, or sense things far better than can their peers. We're all familiar with how a visually or hearing-impaired person develops other senses to compensate. The same can happen for an LD child.

My father-in-law was extremely color-blind. When he served as a pastor, his wife had to supervise his dressing each Sunday to keep him from wearing outlandish combinations in the pulpit. He was also an erratic driver who enjoyed going fast. I was his passenger a few times in poor weather conditions, such as fog, and vowed never to repeat the experience.

In graduate school, however, I discovered that color-blind people typically compensate, with the result that in the fog they can actually see more clearly than a person with normal vision. In fact, color-blind soldiers have acted as forward scouts in foggy weather because of their ability to discriminate shapes in monochromatic conditions. After learning this, I questioned my father-in-law and discovered he could see better than others in gray conditions because of his "disability." He wasn't aware of his advantage until I started talking about it.

"Come to think of it," he said, "I've played golf a few times in the fog and could see the green or the flag pole on the green when no one else could. Maybe this explains it." We can liken his experience to that of LD children who develop their sensory or emotional awareness in specific areas to make up for deficiencies in other areas.

LD students can also have superior ability in divergent thinking. They can address a problem in ways others wouldn't consider, paving the way for unique solutions. They can be creative in a multitude of ways—constructing outrageous inventions or mechanical contraptions, concocting great recipes in the kitchen, putting electronic equipment together, assembling a computer system, or actually setting the timer on a VCR.

Some of these children have very directed or focused intelligence, which can involve any academic area or interest. Within that narrow field, they seem to have a Ph.D. level of knowledge. I've seen students who had special needs but knew as much about transportation systems, Washington State ferries, steam locomotives, sports figures and teams, or animals as any expert. Maybe they couldn't write it in a report, but they could describe their specialties orally in superb detail.

And finally, some LD students are gifted in music and the arts. I have pictures in my playroom drawn by LD children whose artwork is years ahead of their reading level. Others can pick up a tune with ease, learn instruments, and remember a melody far better than their peers can.

Conclusion

This chapter has identified many of the accommodations that can be made for LD students in the classroom, and it has summarized the characteristics of effective instructional methods. It has also provided you with a list of some of the effective programs that teach basic skills to students so that you can investigate them for possible use in your school. The next chapter contains some additional instructional strategies that have been found to work well with LD students.

References

Cernosia, A. 2002. Parentally-placed students with disabilities. Council for Exceptional Children. http://www.ideapractices.org/resources/files/parentallyPlaced.pdf.

Chapman Booth, R. 2002. List of appropriate school-based accommodations and interventions for a 504 plan or for adaptations and modifications section of an IEP. Oxnard School District. http://www.oxnardsd.org/pupils/list_504_accomodations.htm.

Council for American Private Education (CAPE). 2003. Reauthorization of IDEA. Council for American Private Education. See http://www.capenet.org/pubpol.html#anchor 1001400.

Fetal Alcohol Syndrome Community Resource Center. 2003. 504 accommodation checklist. Fetal Alcohol Syndrome Community Resource Center. http://www.come-over.to/FAS/IDEA504 .htm.

Gersten, R. 1998. Recent advances in instructional research with learning disabilities: An overview. *Learning Disabilities Research and Practice* 13, no. 13:162–70.

McGuinness, C., and G. McGuinness. 1999. *Reading reflex: The foolproof Phono-Graphix method for teaching your child to read.* New York: Simon & Schuster.

Morsink, C. V., R. S. Soar, and R. Thomas. 1986. Research on teaching: Opening the door to special education classrooms. *Exceptional Children* 53:32–40.

Office of Special Education Programs. 2001. Individuals with Disabilities Education Act (IDEA) 1997/Services to parentally placed private school students with disabilities. U.S. Department of Education, Office of Special Education and Rehabilitative Services. http://www.ed.gov/about/offices/list/oii/nonpublic/idea1.html.

Rosenshine, B. 1986. Synthesis of research on explicit teaching. *Educational Leadership* 43:60–69.

———. 1997. Advances in research on instruction. In *Issues in educating students with disabilities.* J. Lloyd, E. Kame'enui, and D. Chard, eds. Mahwah, NJ: Lawrence Erlbaum Associates, Inc.

Simmons, D. C., D. Fuchs, and L. S. Fuchs. 1991. Instructional and curricular requisites of main-streamed students with learning disabilities. *Learning Disability Quarterly* 24:354–60.

Swanson, H. L. 1999a. Intervention research for adolescents with learning disabilities: A meta-analysis of outcomes related to high-order processing. Paper presented at the Keys to Successful Learning, Washington, DC. http://www.ncld.org/research/ncld_high _order.cfm.

———. 1999b. Intervention research for students with learning disabilities: A meta-analysis of treatment outcomes. Paper presented at the Keys to Successful Learning, Washington, DC. http://www.ncld.org/ research/osep_swanson.cfm.

Winebrenner, S. 1996. *Teaching kids with learning difficulties in the regular classroom.* Minneapolis, MN: Free Spirit Publishing.

CHAPTER 6

Teaching Strategies for LD Students

Before we get into the specifics of teaching LD students, let's look at the big picture. In order to be an effective teacher, you must remember that these young people are not necessarily less capable than your other students. The latter are fortunate because they enjoy a good match between the way their brain works and the requirements of the typical classroom. Their brain can handle the skills required to be successful in an environment where typical instruction takes place.

Often, however, LD students do not do as well with standard teaching methods. While they are called "learning disabled," it might be more accurate to say they are "learning-strategy disabled." Most have not consistently been taught those learning strategies that are compatible with the way they think and learn. Once we teach them in ways that match their unique needs, their learning problems will decrease greatly. The goal is to find the strategies that best match their needs (Winebrenner 1996).

When we implement the right instructional methods, we don't have to water down the curriculum for LD students. When we find the right matches, these students can succeed. When that happens, we are actually achieving the mandate to help *all* students reach their full potential.

This chapter will describe several approaches to meeting the specific needs of LD students. First, we will examine research findings for improving reading comprehension and subsequent learning strategies. Next we will look at some useful ideas for teaching expressive writing skills to LD students. Finally, we will examine some general guidelines for managing homework for LD students.

Improving the Reading Comprehension of LD Students

Research on the effective teaching of reading comprehension to students with learning disabilities has identified the following:

- Successful reading comprehension correlates with oral reading fluency and vocabulary knowledge. However, interventions that focus on improving fluency or vocabulary do not necessarily improve reading comprehension, especially of long passages.
- Students with LDs often show signs of giving up too quickly when facing a difficult passage. Task persistence, a skill that all readers need, is especially important for the successful reading of expository text, such as history and science textbooks, newspapers, and voter pamphlets.
- Children with LDs who have a history of academic difficulties have documented gaps in grade-appropriate knowledge of history, geography, and other subjects. These knowledge gaps interfere with their understanding of material they encounter in new texts, compounding their problems with reading comprehension.

(Gersten and Baker 1999)

Gersten and Baker (1999) made the following recommendations for teaching reading comprehension, basing them on their review of the research:

- Students with LDs need to learn an array of strategies to enhance their understanding of the narrative and expository material they read.
- For expository text, reading instruction should emphasize a fluid approach to self-monitoring skills. Teachers should help students use an array of strategies flexibly rather than having them adhere rigidly to a text structure approach, as they might while reading a narrative or story.
- It appears that the more successful interventions teach multiple strategies, with the goal of having students internalize each one.
- Socially mediated instruction, of which peer-assisted learning strategies (PALS) is one example, seems to hold considerable promise. In these situations, students learn to process verbally with a peer or group of peers what they've read verbally. After reading a passage, for example, students, or a student and a teacher, discuss its content, ask each other questions about it, and in narrative texts predict what will happen next.
- Frequent, ongoing discussions about the meaning of the text, in which the teacher models the array of strategies and tools that good readers use to make sense of text, is a promising approach to reading comprehension instruction.
- Finding ways to help students generalize their newly acquired reading comprehension skills is essential.

The major point is that strategy instruction can be very useful in teaching LD students. It certainly can be valuable in teaching reading comprehension as identified above. However, teachers can also apply strategy instruction to any other subject matter. We will now explore how this method works as we consider its components.

Introduction to Learning Strategies

As students shift from the skills emphasis of the elementary grades to the content emphasis of the secondary grades, they face greater demands to read textbooks, take notes from lectures, work independently, and express understanding in written compositions and on pencil-and-paper tests. Students who have not acquired such important academic skills often fail at the task of mastering content. In response to this challenge, many students with such learning problems as LDs, ADHD, or both need to be able to acquire and use specific learning strategies in order to become successful despite their knowledge and skill deficits. For such students these strategies can prove to be a crucial part of their process of accommodation, or learning how to learn.

Because of the nature of their learning difficulties, students with learning challenges need to become strategic learners. We would hope that they would not just haphazardly use whatever learning strategies or techniques they have developed on their own. Our goal is for them to be consciously aware of strategies that might be useful in a given learning situation and capable of using them effectively.

What Is a Learning Strategy?

A learning strategy is a student's approach—a tool, plan, or method—to completing a task. Learning strategies are techniques, principles, or rules that facilitate the acquisition, manipulation, integration, storage, and retrieval of information across situations and settings. Strategies are efficient, effective, and organized steps or procedures that people use when learning, remembering, or performing.

Specifically, a learning strategy is a student's way of organizing and using a particular set of skills in order to learn content or to accomplish other tasks more effectively and efficiently in school as well as outside of school. Learning strategies are the tools and techniques we use to help ourselves understand and learn new material or skills. They help us integrate new information with what we already know in a way that makes sense. And they help us recall the information or skill later, in a different situation or place. When we are trying to learn or do a task, our strategies include what we think about, which is the cognitive aspect of the strategy, and what we physically do, which is the behavioral aspect, or the action we take.

Therefore, it is very important for teachers and parents to understand learning strategies and make specific efforts to teach students how to learn rather than to concentrate exclusively on specific curriculum content or skills (Boudah and O'Neill 1999). The following terms are associated with strategy instruction:

- A *cognitive strategy* is a strategy or group of strategies or procedures that learners use to perform academic tasks or to improve social skills. Learners often use more than one cognitive strategy at a time, depending on the individual learners and their schema for learning. In fact, research indicates that successful learners use numerous strategies. Some of these strategies include visualizing, verbalizing, making associations, chunking, questioning, scanning, underlining, accessing cues, using mnemonics, sounding out words, self-checking, and self-monitoring.

- *Cues* are visual or verbal prompts used to remind students of what they have learned or to provide an opportunity to learn something new. Strategy instruction can also use cues to prompt students to apply a strategy.

- *Independent, strategic learners* are students who use cues and strategies within their learning schema; ask clarifying questions; listen, check, and monitor their work and behavior; and set personal goals. Strategic learners know through experience the value of using particular strategies, and they are eager to learn other strategies that might also prove beneficial.

- *A learning strategy* is a set of steps to accomplish a particular task, such as taking a test, comprehending text, or writing a story.

Learners often use a first-letter mnemonic to remember the steps of the strategy.

- *Metacognition and self-regulation* refer to the understanding people have about their personal learning schema, which is how they learn—including both the strategies they use to accomplish tasks and the process they use to oversee and monitor their use of strategies.
- A *mnemonic* is a device for remembering, such as the first-letter mnemonic for writing called PLAN, which stands for *pay* attention to the prompt, *list* main ideas, *add* supporting ideas, and *number* your ideas. Other useful mnemonic devices include rhyme, rhythm, music, and key words.
- *Strategy instruction* is the process of teaching students about strategies, including how and when to use strategies, how to identify personally effective strategies, and why they should make strategic behaviors part of their learning schema.
- *Learning schema* are the sets, or mixes, of strategies that individuals use automatically to perform, produce, communicate, or learn. It can take years to develop a personal learning schema.

(Mercer and Mercer 2001)

What Has Been Learned About the Effectiveness of Strategy Instruction?

Many students' ability to learn has improved through deliberate instruction in cognitive and metacognitive strategies. This fact is especially true for students with significant learning problems. Strategy instruction is crucial for them. It has been demonstrated that when struggling students receive instruction in strategies along with ample encouragement, feedback, and opportunities to use the strategies, they improve in their ability to process information, an ability which in turn leads to improved learning. Some students find it difficult to imbed strategy use in their learning schema, so teachers need to use various approaches when teaching these strategies.

What Happens to Students When They Become Strategic?

When students become strategic in their learning, the following outcomes result:
- Students trust their minds.
- Students know there is more than one right way to do activities and accomplish tasks.
- Students acknowledge their mistakes and try to rectify them.
- Students evaluate their products and behavior.
- Students have an enhanced ability to remember.
- Students' learning increases.
- Students' self-esteem increases.
- Students feel a sense of power.
- Students become more responsible.
- Students improve in terms of work completion and accuracy.
- Students develop and use a personal study process.
- Students know how to "try."
- Students' on-task time increases; they are more engaged.

(Beckman 2002)

What Are the Most Essential Strategies to Teach?

We can determine, in large part, the most essential strategies to teach by assessing successful, efficient learners. These students use numerous strategies across subjects and tasks. They know when to use strategies and for what purposes. While we can't describe every strategy, the following often lead to improved student performance:
- Computation and problem-solving strategies include verbalizing, visualizing, chunking, making associations, and using cues.
- Memory strategies include visualizing, verbalizing, using mnemonics, making associations, chunking, and writing. These are usually more effective when learners use them in combination (Mastropieri and Scruggs 1998).

- Productivity strategies include verbalizing, self-monitoring, visualizing, and using cues.
- Reading accuracy and fluency strategies include finger pointing or tracking, sounding out unknown words, self-questioning for accuracy, chunking, and using contextual clues.
- Reading comprehension strategies include visualizing, questioning, rereading, and predicting.
- Writing strategies include planning, revising, questioning, using cues, verbalizing, visualizing, checking, and monitoring.

What Makes Up Effective Strategy Instruction?

Successful strategy instruction is an integral part of classroom teaching, regardless of the content; it is not an additional subject. In the transactional strategies instruction (TSI) model, teachers continually explain and model strategies throughout the school year. They regularly praise students for applying strategies and encourage students to help their peers do likewise. When explicitly teaching strategies, teachers should follow these steps:

- Describe the strategy. Students come to understand the strategy and its purpose—why it is important, when it can be used, and how to use it.
- Model its use. The teacher models the strategy, explaining how to perform it.
- Provide ample assisted practice time. The teacher monitors, provides cues, and gives feedback. Through practice, students do not have to "think" about using the strategy. They use it automatically.
- Promote student self-monitoring and self-evaluation of personal strategy use. Students will likely use the strategy if they see how it works for them; it will become part of their learning schema.
- Encourage continued use and generalization of the strategy. Teachers should encourage students to try the strategy in other learning situations.

(Beckman 2002)

Researchers have identified an instructional sequence in which students learn each strategy following these teacher-directed steps, which are described below: (a) pretest, (b) describe, (c) verbal practice, (d) model, (e) controlled practice, (f) feedback, (g) grade-appropriate practice, (h) posttest, and (i) generalization.

a. Usually teachers access the current level of student performance on some type of strategy pretest.
b. Students implement a procedure for learning a new strategy.
c. Teachers describe what the characteristics of the learning strategy are and when, where, why, and how students should use the strategy.
d. Teachers model how to use a strategy by "thinking aloud" as they apply the strategy to specific content material, such as a history or social studies lesson. During the verbal practice step, students memorize the strategy steps and other use requirements.
e. Controlled practice activities with ability-level materials enable students to become proficient strategy users.
f. Teachers provide specific feedback about the students' performance in using the strategy.
g. Students use the learning strategy with grade-appropriate or increasingly difficult materials.
h. Students take a posttest.
i. Teachers facilitate student generalization of the learning strategy use in other academic and even nonacademic settings.

(Boudah and O'Neill 1999)

Each strategy has multiple parts that students remember with the aid of some kind of mnemonic. For example, in the paraphrasing strategy, students learn the acronym RAP—*read* a paragraph, *ask* yourself, What are the main ideas and details? and *put* the main idea and details into your own words.

If students need to learn prerequisite skills, such as finding main ideas and details, teachers can focus on those before moving on to the learning strategy, and then reinforce student mastery of the skills during any strategy instruction. Students typically become proficient with a learning strategy by working in small groups, sometimes in a resource room, through short intensive lessons spread over several weeks.

You can find the specifics of strategies in the book *Teaching Adolescents with Learning Disabilities: Strategies and Methods* (Deshler, Ellis, and Lenz 1996). The authors identify the following components of effective and efficient learning strategies:

- They contain the steps that lead to a specific and successful outcome.
- The sequence of their steps leads to an efficient approach to the task.
- Their steps cue students to use specific cognitive strategies.
- Their steps cue students to use metacognition.
- Their steps cue students to select and use appropriate procedures, skills, or rules.
- Their steps cue students to take some type of overt action.
- All their steps take a limited amount of time to complete.
- They do not contain unnecessary steps or explanations.

The acronym DEFENDS is another strategic approach. It helps secondary students write a composition in which they take a position and defend it. Each letter stands for a strategic step:

- **D**ecide on an audience, goals, and a position.
- **E**stimate the main ideas and details.
- **F**igure the best order of main ideas and details.
- **E**xpress the position in the opening.
- **N**ote each main idea and the supporting points.
- **D**rive home the message in the last sentence.
- **S**earch for errors and correct them.

(Sturomski 1997)

The following guidelines can help a teacher design a learning strategy:

- A system for remembering an effective strategy contains seven or fewer steps. Many strategies use an easily remembered mnemonic device such as an acronym.

- Each step of the remembering system is brief and simple, and begins with an action word.
- The steps contain language that is uncomplicated and familiar to students.

We can determine the usefulness of learning strategies by considering how much they enable students to reach personal goals that are relevant to their needs. The usefulness of a given strategy generally depends on its potential applications and its ability to transfer across materials, settings, situations, and people. Most effective strategies meet the following criteria:

- They address a common but important problem that students are encountering in their settings.
- They address demands that students encounter frequently over an extended time.
- Students can apply them across a variety of situations and contexts.

(Sturomski 1997)

Resources for Learning Strategies

I have compacted a great deal of information into the previous section. It is hoped that you can see the relevance of using strategy instruction with your students. I'm sure you will recognize that you do parts of this process already, but it is important to note that LD students need such instruction in a consistent and concentrated form.

You may have heard the old saying, "Catch a man a fish, and he'll eat for a day. Teach him to fish, and he'll eat for a lifetime." Teaching students to use learning strategies is like teaching them to fish. If they have the great gift of being able to gain knowledge, they will be able to learn independently through their entire life.

Much of the research and development of learning strategies for LD students has come from researchers and educators affiliated with the

University of Kansas Center for Research on Learning. You can obtain more information from the University of Kansas in Lawrence, Kansas. Their website is http://www.ku-crl.org.

The National Information Center for Children and Youth with Disabilities (NICHCY) has also prepared an extensive bibliography of materials on learning strategies for students with learning disabilities (NICHCY 1997). There are applications to studying, thinking, test taking, reading, writing, math, science, and social skills. Another excellent resource on learning strategies is the Learning Toolbox website at http://coe.jmu.edu/ learningtoolbox. James Madison University developed this website for secondary students with LDs and ADHD as well as for teachers and parents. Its purpose is to help students become more effective learners so they can meet the increasingly rigorous academic demands of today's schools.

The website contains strategies for organization, test taking, study skills, note taking, reading, writing, math, and advanced thinking, along with examples of their application. It is designed for students to use independently, for special education teachers who wish to follow a direct and systematic teaching approach, and for parents who want to help their children learn. The Learning Toolbox is an instructional website rather than an informational one. It is unique in two respects:
1. It uses research-based special-education instructional approaches as the basis for its content.
2. Its development took into consideration the unique characteristics of students with LDs and ADHD.

Improving the Written Expression of LD Students

Many LD students struggle with expressive writing, which is defined as writing for the purpose of displaying knowledge or supporting self-expression. What is the most effective way to improve the writing of LD students? How do proficient writers plan, organize, and carry out the difficult and typically introspective task of expressive writing? Researchers have investigated this topic, and three methods stand out as reliably and consistently leading to improved outcomes:

- Adhering to a basic framework of planning, writing, and revising
- Explicitly teaching critical steps in the writing process
- Providing feedback guided by the information explicitly taught

(Gersten, Baker, and Edwards 1999)

Adhering to a Basic Framework of Planning, Writing, and Revising

Teaching students to write requires showing them how to develop and organize what they want to say and guiding them in the process of getting it down on paper. Effective interventions use a basic framework that is based on planning, writing, and revising. These steps are part of a recursive process rather than a linear one. In other words, the writer may revisit each step during the writing process, and the steps do not always proceed in the same order. In this process, teachers explicitly instruct students how to use each step, accompanying the instruction with several examples and often with a "think sheet," a prompt card, or a mnemonic.

Planning. Well-developed plans for writing result in better first drafts. To help students develop their own action plans, teachers or peers who write well can verbalize the process they use. One type of action plan, called a "planning think sheet," uses a series of sequential, structured prompts. It specifies a topic and asks the questions *Who (am I writing for)? Why am I writing? What do I know? How can I group my ideas? How will I organize my ideas?* For example, teachers can help students learn three steps for writing a paragraph. To experience success, students may need substantial modeling at each step:

1. Think about your ideas and elaborate on each part.
2. Organize the ideas you want to express. You can do this easily by using visual graphic organizers. For example, create a *mind map,* placing the main idea in a circle in the center of the page and writing the supporting facts on lines coming out of the main circle. These lines look similar to the arms of a spider or spokes on a wheel. You can use many formats for visual organizers, and different formats are appropriate for different content.

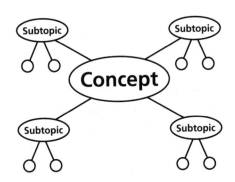

3. Analyze your graphic organizer to determine whether you included all your ideas. If you have difficulty with spelling, make a list of the more difficult or important words you may want to include in your writing. Having this reference list will help your writing flow more because you will not have to stop to think about how to spell those words.
4. Write a draft of your paragraph (or paper), focusing on the content or ideas. If you have a computer, it is best to type your draft directly on the keyboard. You will find it easier to proofread and revise.
5. You will need specific techniques and strategies to proofread, which is the process of checking your paper for appropriate punctuation, capitalization, and grammar. Then use a spell checker to help you fix your spelling.
6. Revise your paragraph, incorporating the corrections you decide to make.
7. Proofread your paragraph again, editing and revising as necessary.
8. Develop a final product, in either typed or written form.

An easy way to remember these steps is to think of the word *power:*
- **P**lan your paper (step 1).
- **O**rganize your thoughts and ideas (steps 2 and 3).
- **W**rite your draft (step 4).
- **E**dit your work (steps 5, 6, and 7).
- **R**evise your work, producing a final draft (step 8).

(Richards 1998, 1999)

Writing. Using an action plan helps students create first drafts. The plan serves as a concrete map for engaging in the writing process, and it provides students with suggestions for what to do when they feel "stuck." The action plan provides a reminder of the content and structure of the writing task.

A well-developed action plan also gives the student and teacher a common language to use when discussing the writing. The dialogue between teacher and student represents a major advance in writing instruction over traditional methods that required students to work in relative isolation.

Revising and editing. Revising and editing skills are critical to the writing process. Developing methods to help students refine and edit their work has been difficult, but a few strategies appear promising. One of these is to teach students to write opinion essays, using peer editing as an instructional strategy. Students working in pairs alternate their roles as student-writer and student-critic. The student-critic identifies ambiguities in the essay and asks the writer for clarification. With help from the teacher, the writer makes revisions. The teacher also provides the student writer with feedback on the clarity and cogency of the supportive arguments. Once the clarity and cogency of the essay meet the teacher's standard, the pair moves on to correct capitalization, spelling, and punctuation. Through this process, the student writer has to explain his or her communicative intent to the peer and then to revise the essay in a way that reflects this intent faithfully. These clarifying interactive dialogues lead the student-critic and student-writer to understand each other's perspective. In this way the trainees develop a sense of audience for their writing.

Teaching Critical Steps in the Writing Process

Explicitly teaching text structures provides a guide for the writing task, whether it is a persuasive essay, a personal narrative, or an essay comparing and contrasting two phenomena. Different types of writing have different structures. For example, a persuasive essay contains a thesis and supporting arguments, while narrative writing may contain character development and a story climax.

Instruction in text structures typically includes numerous explicit models and prompts. Different writers may proceed with the structures in a different order, and good writing involves what some researchers call "overlapping and recursive processes." These processes do not proceed in a particular order, and one process may inform another in such a way that the author returns to previous steps on a regular basis to update or revise. Again, an action plan is helpful. The plan makes text structures more visible to students and helps to demystify the writing process (Englert and Mariage 1991).

Providing Feedback Guided by the Information Explicitly Taught

A third component common to these successful interventions for teaching written expression is to provide frequent feedback to students on the overall quality of their writing, including its strengths and any missing elements. In the writing process, feedback combined with instruction strengthens the dialogue between student and teacher. Giving and receiving feedback also helps students to develop "reader sensitivity" and their own writing style.

This interactive dialogue, which leads students through multiple cycles of reflection, realization, and redress of problems, helps students "see" their thoughts and write from another's perspective. In successful writing instruction, teachers and students have an organizational framework and language to use in providing feedback on such components of writing as organization, originality, and interpretation. Successful teachers model procedures for students, providing feedback so that students will attend to the presentation of ideas as well as to the surface features like spelling and punctuation.

Specific Methods

Numerous methods for teaching written expression incorporate these three common principles. Two examples are Self-Regulated Strategy Development (SRSD) (Graham and Harris 1989) and Cognitive Strategy Instruction in Writing (Englert et al. 1995). Both contain strategies that focus on what students do before they actually write:

The SRSD technique involves self-directed prompts that require the students to do the following:
  a. Consider their audience and reasons for writing.
  b. Develop a plan for what they intend to say, using frames to generate or organize writing notes.
  c. Evaluate possible content by considering its impact on the reader.
  d. Continue the process of content generation and planning during the act of writing.

The Cognitive Strategy Instruction in Writing includes the following student strategies:
  a. Brainstorming strategies for preparing to write.
  b. Organizing strategies to relate and categorize the ideas.
  c. Comprehension strategies as students read and gather information for their writing.
  d. Monitoring strategies as students clarify both their thoughts and the relationships among their items of information.

Additional Ideas for Facilitating Written Expression

Some additional ideas have come out of research on this topic. The first set of issues concerns the mechanics versus the content of writing. Evidence suggests that writing instruction that focuses more on content will more fully capitalize on the strengths of LD students. When asked to write about complex ideas, such students often show conceptual performance beyond what would be expected on the basis of such lower-level skills as capitalization, punctuation, and spelling.

Another approach suggests that dictating to a scribe can eliminate mechanical difficulties and result in a longer, higher-quality composition. While students must eventually learn to do their own writing, these findings suggest a possible bridge to higher performance.

Daily writing instruction should include time devoted to both the mechanics and the process of writing. Teachers must address problems with the mechanics of writing in expressive writing instruction. There is a reciprocal relationship between mastery of transcription skills and growth in the quality of writing. When students have mastered the mechanics, they can devote their cognitive resources to planning, composing, and revising their work (Gersten, Baker, and Edwards 1999).

Homework Strategies for LD Students

Homework is one component of the general education curriculum that has been widely recognized as important to academic success. Teachers have long used homework to provide additional learning time, to strengthen study and organizational skills, and in some respects to keep parents informed of their children's progress. Typically, when LD students participate in the general education curriculum, they are expected to complete homework along with their peers. However, just as LD students may need instructional accommodations in the classroom, they may also need homework accommodations. Researchers have discovered five strategies to improve homework results for LD students:

1. Give clear and appropriate assignments.
2. Make accommodations in homework assignments.
3. Teach study skills.
4. Use a homework planner.
5. Ensure clear home-school communication.

Strategy 1. Give Clear and Appropriate Assignments

Teachers need to take special care when assigning homework. If the assignment is too hard, it is perceived as busywork. If it is too lengthy to complete, students might tune out and resist doing it. Never send home any task that students cannot do. Homework should be an extension of what students have learned in class. To ensure it is clear and appropriate, consider the following tips:

- Make sure students and parents have information regarding the policy on missed and late assignments, extra credit, and available adaptations. Establish a set routine at the beginning of the year.
- Assign work that the students can do.
- Assign homework in small units.
- Explain the assignment clearly.
- Write the assignment on the chalkboard and leave it there until the work is due, or provide written directions for it.
- Remind students periodically of due dates.
- Coordinate with other teachers to prevent homework overload.
- Establish a routine at the beginning of the year for how you will assign homework.
- Assign homework toward the beginning of the class period.
- Relate homework to class work, to real life, or to both.
- Explain how to do the homework, provide examples, and write directions on the chalkboard or overhead.

- Have students begin the homework in class, check that they understand how to do it, and provide assistance as necessary.
- Allow students to work together on homework.

Strategy 2. Make Accommodations in Homework Assignments

Make any necessary modifications to the homework assignment before sending it home. Identify practices that will help individual students the most and will have the potential to increase their involvement, understanding, and motivation to learn. The most common homework accommodations include the following:

- Provide additional one-on-one assistance.
- Monitor LD students' homework more closely than that of other students.
- Allow alternative response formats: for example, allow students to audiotape assignments rather than handwrite them.
- Adjust the length of the assignment.
- Provide a peer tutor or assign the student to a study group.
- Provide learning tools such as calculators.
- Adjust evaluation standards.
- Give fewer assignments.

It is important to check out all accommodations with the students, their families, and other teachers. If homework accommodations are not palatable to students, families, or teachers, they may not use them.

Strategy 3. Teach Study Skills

Both general and special education teachers consistently report that deficient basic study skills seem to exacerbate homework problems. Many students, particularly those with disabilities, need instruction in study and organizational skills. The following list of organizational strategies for students is basic to their ability to complete homework effectively:

- Identify a location that is free of distractions.
- Have all materials available and organized.
- Allocate enough time to complete activities and keep on schedule.
- Take good notes.
- Develop a sequential plan for completing multitasking assignments.
- Check assignments for accuracy and completion before turning them in.
- Know how to get help when it is needed.
- Turn in completed homework on time.

Teachers can enhance homework completion and accuracy by providing classroom instruction in organizational skills. Talk with your students' parents about how to support the application of organizational skills at home. We will devote more time to study skills in chapter 8, which addresses teaching ADHD students.

Strategy 4. Use a Homework Planner

Students with disabilities often need additional organizational support. Just as adults use calendars, schedulers, lists, and other devices to self-monitor their activities, students can benefit from these tools as well. LD students can monitor their own homework by using a planning calendar to keep track of assignments. Homework planners also can double as home-school communication tools if they include a space next to each assignment for messages from teachers and parents.

To use a homework planner to increase communication with students' families and improve homework completion rates, you might have students develop their own homework calendars. Each page in the calendar reflects one week. There is a space for students to write their homework assignments and a column for parent-teacher notes. The cover can be a heavy card stock that the student decorates. Students should take their homework planners home each day and return them to class the next day.

In conjunction with the homework planner, you can have students graph the rates for their homework return and completion. This process has proved to be an effective strategy that is linked to consistent homework completion and improved performance on classroom assessments. You might also build a reward system for returning homework and the planners. Have the students keep a self-monitoring chart in their planner. On the chart, they use the following scheme to record each time they complete and return their homework assignments:

- Color the square for the day green if they completed and returned their homework.
- Color the square for the day red if they did not complete their homework.
- Color one-half of the square for the day yellow and one-half of the square for the day red if they completed their homework late.

If students meet the success criteria, they receive a reward at the end of the week, such as fifteen extra minutes of recess. Teachers will often need different or more frequent rewards for students with emotional and behavioral disabilities.

Strategy 5. Ensure Clear Home-School Communication

Homework accounts for one-fifth of the time that successful students invest in academic tasks, yet students complete homework in environments that teachers cannot control. Given the fact that many students experience learning difficulties, this lack of control creates a major dilemma. Teachers and parents of LD students must communicate clearly and effectively with one another about homework policies, required practices, mutual expectations, student performance on homework, homework completion difficulties, and other homework-related concerns. Here are some recommended ways teachers can improve communications with parents:

- Encourage students to keep assignment books.
- Provide a list of suggestions on how parents might assist with homework: for example, by asking parents to check with their children daily about homework.
- Provide parents with frequent written communication about homework, such as progress reports, notes, letters, and forms.
- Share information with other teachers regarding student strengths and needs as well as any necessary accommodations.

Ways that administrators can support teachers in improving home-school communications include the following:

- Supply teachers with the technology needed to aid communication: for example, provide telephone answering systems, email, and homework hotlines.
- Provide incentives for teachers to participate in face-to-face meetings with parents: for example, in the form of released time and in compensation.
- Suggest that the school offer after-school sessions, peer-tutoring sessions, or both to give students extra help with homework
  (Bryan and Sullivan-Burstein 1997; Epstein et al. 1999; Warger 2001)

Certainly I could describe many more methods and materials that might help LD students. However, I can't hope to address all the possibilities in a couple of chapters. I encourage you to explore the references as well as the resources listed in this book to obtain more details or to follow up on a particular area of interest. In the next chapter we will extend the discussion to classroom practices that are intended to help the ADHD student.

References

Beckman, P. 2002. Strategy instruction. ERIC Clearinghouse on Disabilities and Gifted Education. ERIC EC Digest #E638. http://www.ericec.org/digests/e638.html.

Boudah, D. J., and K. J. O'Neill. 1999. Learning strategies. ERIC Clearinghouse on Disabilities and Gifted Education. ERIC/OSEP Digest #E577. http://www.ericec.org/digests/ e577.html.

Bryan, T., and K. Sullivan-Burstein. 1997. Homework how-to's. *Teaching Exceptional Children* 29, no. 6:32–37.

Deshler, D., E. Ellis, and B. Lenz. 1996. *Teaching adolescents with learning disabilities: Strategies and methods.* 2nd ed. Denver, CO: Love Publishing.

Englert, C. S., A. Garmon, T. V. Mariage, M. Rozendal, K. Tarrant, and J. Urba. 1995. The early literacy project: Connecting across the literacy curriculum. *Learning Disability Quarterly* 18:253–75.

Englert, C. S., and T. V. Mariage. 1991. Shared understandings:Structuring the writing experience through dialogue. *Journal of Learning Disabilities* 24, no. 6:330–42.

Epstein, M. H., D. D. Munk, W. D. Bursuck, E. A. Polloway, and M. Jayanthi. 1999. Strategies for improving home-school communication about homework for students with disabilities. *The Journal of Special Education* 33, no. 3:166–76.

Gersten, R., and S. Baker. 1999. Reading comprehension instruction for students with learning disabilities. Paper presented at the Keys to Successful Learning, Washington, DC. http://www.ncld.org/research/ncld_reading_comp.cfm.

Gersten, R., S. Baker, and L. Edwards. 1999. Teaching expressive writing to students with learning disabilities. ERIC Clearinghouse on Disabilities and Gifted Education. ERIC/OSEP Digest #E590. http://ericec.org/digests/e590.html.

Graham, S., and K. R. Harris. 1989. Improving learning disabled students' skills at composing essays: Self-instructional strategy training. *Exceptional Children* 56:201–14.

Mastropieri, M. A., and T. E. Scruggs. 1998. Enhancing school success with mnemonic strategies. *Intervention in School and Clinic* (March). http://www.ldonline.org/ld_indepth/teaching_techniques/mnemonic _strategies.html.

Mercer, C. D., and A. R. Mercer. 2001. *Teaching students with learning prob lems.* 6th ed. Upper Saddle River, NJ: Prentice Hall.

National Information Center for Children and Youth with Disabilities (NICHCY). 1997. NICHCY bibliography: Learning strategies for students with learning disabilities. NICHCY News Digest. http://www.ldonline.org/ld_indepth/teaching_techniques/nichcy _interventions_bib.html.

NICHCY. *See* National Information Center for Children and Youth with Disabilities.

Richards, R. G. 1998. *The writing dilemma: Understanding dysgraphia.* Riverside, CA: RET Center Press.

———. 1999. Strategies for dealing with dysgraphia. *LD Online* (May). http:// www.ldonline.org/ld_indepth/writing/dysgraphia_strategies.html.

Sturomski, N. 1997. Teaching students with learning disabilities to use learning strategies. *NICHCY News Digest* 25. http://www .ldonline .org/ld_indepth/teaching_techniques/nichcy_interventions.html.

Warger, C. 2001. Five homework strategies for teaching students with disabilities. ERIC Clearinghouse on Disabilities and Gifted Education. ERIC/OSEP Digest #E608. http://www.ericec.org/ digests/e608.html.

Winebrenner, S. 1996. *Teaching kids with learning difficulties in the regular classroom.* Minneapolis, MN: Free Spirit Publishing.

CHAPTER 7

Treatment Options for ADHD Students

Almost daily I hear stories containing the expression of agony of ADHD students. Parents tell me their child has expressed, in extreme frustration, thoughts such as these:

- "Mom, I just can't do it. I try to pay attention, but my brain just won't cooperate."
- "I know I'm smart enough to do this work, but it always takes me ten times longer than anybody else to get it done."
- "I hate writing. It takes me so long to write stuff out. Can't I just tell you about it instead?"

Such is the anguish of those capable students who have a brain that makes it hard for them to concentrate, inhibit responses, or complete multiple tasks effectively. As an educator, you are in a position to help reduce their pain. By making accommodations and implementing effective instructional strategies, you can enable these ADHD students to find success. You can be a crucial part of a team of professionals who help bring some enjoyment to their learning process.

Overview of Treatment for ADHD

Before getting into the specifics of classroom interventions, we need to stop and identify how educational interventions fit into the total treatment plan for ADHD students. This chapter will give a very brief overview of the parent, child, and spiritual components in helping the ADHD child. It will also include some detailed information on medication so that you as an educator can be current on the latest developments in this crucial component of treatment.

There is no cure or quick fix for attention disorders. The good news, however, is that we do know a great deal about how to help ADHD children. Numerous strategies and procedures can improve an ADHD child's behavior, self-esteem, and overall quality of life. These kinds of intervention fall into five categories:

- General education for parents about ADHD and the enhancement of parenting skills
- Teaching the child regarding self-control, attention, decision making, and social skills
- Spiritual assistance
- Medical intervention
- Educational accommodations

You can find more details about the first three categories of intervention in my earlier book *The Attention Deficit Child* (Martin 1998).

Parents

The first point of intervention for many ADHD students takes place in the home. Parents need to learn consistent management skills, including how to deal with temper outbursts and how to have family meetings and contracts. They may also need to learn how to impose immediate, frequent, and meaningful consequences on their child who has trouble with self-control. Parents can tailor to their own children such tactics as time-outs, grounding, community service, positive practice, and response cost.

Research suggests that parent-training programs work best with children under age twelve, and especially under age seven. A decline in the influence of parents on a child's misbehavior appears to become even more evident after a child turns twelve. The lesson to be learned from these findings is to start the assessment and treatment of ADHD children as early as possible (Barkley 2002).

Many parents need some basic education in ADHD, and they find support groups very helpful. Special problems, such as chronic bedwetting, may need attention. Also, since many ADHD children have significant coexisting conditions such as anxiety, depression, or bipolar disorder, additional treatment components are often necessary. Dealing with ADHD children is very hard work, and since many parents of ADHD children also have ADHD themselves, the job of maintaining consistency can be even more difficult.

Child

The second category of intervention involves teaching the child self-control, attention skills, decision-making skills, and social skills. Because each child is different, not all ADHD children need help in these areas. However, for those who do, parents, counselors, and teachers need to work together to help the child learn to stop and think, make and keep friends, and learn to recognize social cues and respond more appropriately. Problem solving, negotiation, and using words instead of fists to settle disputes are some of the areas of need for these students. They also need to learn time management, organization skills, and study skills, and we will discuss how the school can help in these areas later in the chapter.

Spiritual Dimension

As Christians, we know the spiritual dimension is a crucial part of working with the whole person. I believe ADHD children have the potential to lead creative and fulfilling lives. There is every reason for optimism regarding their ability to mature, yield fruit in season, and prosper in whatever they do (Psalm 1:3).

Parenting and teaching are difficult with any child and even more challenging with a child who has special needs. That is why the spiritual resources of a Christian parent and teacher can make all the difference. You don't have to face this task by yourself or with only your own strength and understanding. We have God's promises of direction and power. If part of God's purpose is to help a parent or a teacher develop patience and long-suffering, blessing them with a student who has ADHD could be an effective way to reach that goal.

An important injunction for parents and teachers is to present our children and our students to God in prayer. Prayer can be a simple activity. Your prayers need not be wordy or complex. A simple expression of adoration for God—followed by statements of confession, need, and thankfulness—is sufficient. The model of the Lord's Prayer is perfect (Matthew 6:9–13, Luke 11:2–4).

I suspect that you have called out to God in times of crisis and wondered whether He would answer. Why does one of your students have to struggle with problems of inattention, low self-esteem, and conflict with fellow students? We have all had feelings of being abandoned and ignored. Biblical heroes such as Jeremiah and David expressed those feelings. However, God has made some rather remarkable promises. He will answer our prayers (Mark 11:24). He never fails to keep His promises (1 Kings 8:56), and He does not lie (Titus 1:2). Remember His promises and claim them as you pray for your ADHD students.

Being a Christian educator doesn't take the hard work out of teaching ADHD children. It does, however, give you the spiritual resources to cope with the frustrations. A key ingredient in the process is your ability to learn to trust God for your students' future. The daily drain of coping with children who don't pay attention and seem to overreact to everything in their world can certainly challenge this trust.

We read in Proverbs 3:5–6, "Trust in the LORD with all your heart and lean not on your own understanding; in all your ways acknowledge him, and he will make your paths straight." These verses capture the essence of your need to trust. Your finite understanding can lead only to incomplete efforts to manage yourself and your classroom. Trusting in God demands an affirmative decision. You must move through the veil of denial that shuts out the light of God. Your path will be illuminated and made straight if you choose to let God be your guide.

Trust happens with experience, and it grows over time. At this point you may be able to give God responsibility for only part of your life, or only certain aspects of dealing with a special-needs child. That's OK. Give Him what you can. As He proves faithful in some areas, you will be willing to hand over more aspects of your life and your educational decisions. May God bless you in your efforts to meet the needs of ADHD and LD students.

Medication

The decision to proceed with medication intervention must be based on a comparison of the treatments available, especially their risks and benefits. As a teacher, you are not making the decision for the family. However, it is valuable to know the place and function of the various medications so that you will recognize what may be taking place with the ADHD students who are on medication.

A number of myths and falsehoods regarding medications have been perpetuated. By having current and scientifically sound information, you will be better able to respond to situations involving medications for ADHD. Research tells us that the single most significant treatment component for ADHD is effectively managed medication. While our focus is on classroom interventions, this section will give you a basic understanding of the medical procedures your student may undergo.

Effectiveness of Medication

Recently the National Institute of Mental Health released the Multimodal Treatment Study of Children with Attention Deficit Hyperactivity Disorder. It is the longest and most thorough study ever completed comparing treatments for ADHD. The study found that medication alone, or medication in combination with intensive behavioral therapy, was significantly superior to other types of treatment (MTA Cooperative Group 1999).

Although medication alone was found to be more effective than intensive behavioral treatment, the combination of the two led not only to a variety of improvements but also to the use of somewhat lower dosages of medication. In addition, researchers found that behavioral treatment was very beneficial and even necessary for the improvement of social skills and anger management. Medication alone does not help a child make friends or know how to resolve conflict in appropriate ways.

In general, we can say that medication intervention is a significant help to ADHD children. Stimulant medication has been shown to be effective in improving behavior, academic work, and social adjustment in 70 to 90 percent of children with ADHD. How a given student responds depends on many factors. Therefore, each situation has to be carefully evaluated to determine the best type of medication and the right dosage. There are certainly situations in which medications are improperly administered. If a child uses medication, the process must include strict controls, appropriate dosages, and careful monitoring.

Importance of Multimodality Treatment

The most important concept to emerge from the vast amounts of research about ADHD is that no treatment approach is successful alone. No single intervention—whether medical, behavioral, psychological, or educational—is adequate by itself. We must be conscious of treating the whole child or adolescent. Successful intervention makes a difference both in the short term and in the long term. We want to make changes that will help bring about the necessary confidence, competence, organization, discipline, and character in an ADHD child. We also want changes that will last a lifetime. Giving a child 10 milligrams of Adderall may help him sit in his seat and remember directions, but it will not necessarily help him make friends (Barkley 2002).

Research has shown that multidisciplinary approaches to the treatment of ADHD work better in the long term than medication alone (Cantwell 1996). Possibly one of the greatest benefits of stimulant therapy is that it maximizes the effects of concurrently applied treatments. What we often see is that the total treatment is far more effective than any of the components used alone. Medication will not make children behave well at all times, nor will it make them smarter. However, what it can do is reduce many of the students' attention difficulties so that they can tackle their problems more successfully.

How the Stimulants Work

The history of stimulant drug use dates back to 1937 when Charles Bradley discovered the therapeutic effects of Benzedrine on behaviorally disturbed children. In 1948, Dexedrine was introduced. Its advantage was that it had equal efficacy at half the dose. Ritalin was released in 1954 with the hope that it would have fewer side effects and less abuse potential. Today, Adderall, Concerta, Metadate, Ritalin, or one of the other similar medications is used in a large percentage of cases in which some type of stimulant medication is prescribed. A new nonstimulant medication, Strattera, has just been released, and it may become a favored drug if it turns out to be effective and trouble free. However, at this point stimulants are used in the vast majority of cases.

It is thought that stimulant drugs act by affecting the catecholamine neurotransmitters—especially dopamine—in the brain. Some believe that ADHD develops from a dopamine deficiency, which stimulant drug treatment can correct. At one time it was thought that stimulant drugs created a paradoxical reaction in ADHD youngsters. The paradox was the calming response to taking a stimulant drug. This possibility is no longer believed to be the case. We now have a better, although still incomplete, understanding of how the calming reaction is produced in the brain (Dougherty et al. 1999; Volkow et al. 1998).

Many parents feel guilty about having their child take medication because they mistakenly think they are tranquilizing him. This belief is simply not based on truth. The medication helps stimulate the parts of the brain needed to concentrate and attend. The decrease in external movement does not mean that the child has been tranquilized. It means he is able to focus more effectively. When children are watching television or playing a video game, they may seem oblivious of the outside world. However, that doesn't mean that the television or video game is tranquilizing them. Rather, their attention is temporarily focused, so they seem mesmerized in contrast to their more usual distractible and inattentive condition.

Attention deficit results from the malfunction of the attention system, the system that allows the brain to discriminate between situations in which focused, deliberate behavior is appropriate and situations in which quick, impulsive actions are necessary. ADHD children are not able to control their attentional skills. They may be intently concentrating when they should be aware of their surroundings. On the other hand, they may be too easily distracted and ready to run off when they should be focused. Medication works to enhance the functioning of the attentional system, enabling children to choose when to be sensitive to outside distractions and when to focus their attention. Medications stimulate the attention center, with the result that the child has better control. In other words, with medication the child is better able to put on the brakes (Goldstein and Goldstein 1990).

Short-Term Side Effects

The primary side effects noted for stimulants are insomnia, loss of appetite, weight loss, and irritability. These and other side effects are usually transitory, and they typically disappear with a reduction in drug dosage.

Other mild but less common side effects can include sadness, depression, fearfulness, social withdrawal, sleepiness, headaches, nail biting, and stomach upset. These symptoms will normally disappear spontaneously with a decrease in dosage. Some of these symptoms can be considered acceptable side effects in light of clinical improvement. The parents and physician will need to make the choice between the advantages of decreased distractibility and side effects such as nail biting.

In addition to the above side effects, perhaps fewer than 1 percent of ADHD children treated with stimulants will develop a tic disorder. Also, in 13 percent of the cases, stimulants may exacerbate preexisting tics. Therefore, it is prudent to screen children with ADHD for a personal or family history of tics or Tourette's syndrome prior to initiating stimulant therapy.

Another reported side effect is a "behavioral rebound" phenomenon. Typically, this condition is described as a deterioration in behavior that occurs in the late afternoon and evening following daytime administrations of medication. If the problem is continual or severe, adjustments in the medication dosage and scheduling should resolve the problem. The advent of the newer long-acting medications such as

Concerta, Adderall XR, Metadate CD, and Ritalin LA have greatly reduced the incidence of rebound.

The consensus is that stimulant medication is relatively safe but that side effects do occur. In the vast majority of cases, either the side effects cease after one or two weeks of continued treatment, or adjustment in the dosage alleviates the problem. It is very important that the doctor closely monitor the side effects as well as effectiveness. Most of the serious side effects show up right away. They will also disappear quickly if the drug is withdrawn. Then a trial of a different stimulant medication can be initiated (American Academy of Pediatrics 2001; Wilens 1999).

Long-Term Side Effects

There are no reported cases of addiction or serious drug dependence with these medications. Studies have examined the question of whether children on these drugs are more likely than other children to abuse other substances as teenagers. The results suggest that there is no increase in the likelihood of drug abuse. In fact, adolescents with ADHD who receive appropriate medical treatment are much less likely to abuse drugs than are untreated ADHD adolescents (Biederman et al. 1999).

Since ADHD is a long-term condition, medical treatment may be required for a prolonged period, raising the question of whether a child will become tolerant of the medication. The answer appears to be no. Over time, a child's dosages may need to be increased. However, this need probably relates more to their increasing in body weight than to their becoming tolerant of a certain dose. The doctor should continue to monitor the drug's effectiveness very closely (Wilens, Biederman, and Spencer 2002a; 2002b).

Another possible long-term side effect is the suppression of height and weight gain. Presently, it is believed that suppression in growth is a relatively transient side effect in the first year or so of treatment and that it has no significant effect on eventual adult height and weight.

Benefits of Medication

Between 70 and 95 percent of ADHD children appear to exhibit a positive response to stimulant medication. There seem to be three general categories of response to medication.

For one group of children, medication brings about a dramatic improvement. These children fall into the miraculous category. The effect is both immediate and obvious. Often within the first hour after treatment, there is a perceptible change in handwriting, talking, motility, attending, organization, and perception. Classroom teachers may notice improvement in deportment and academic productivity after a single dose. Off-task activity levels seem to decrease, and the child becomes more compliant and less aggressive. Parents report a marked reduction in troublesome sibling interactions, inappropriate activity, and noncompliance. Even peers can identify the calmer, more cooperative behavior of stimulant-treated children.

Other children who receive medication display moderate responsiveness. While parents and teachers notice improvement in their attention and self-control, the effects are not astonishing. The child is definitely easier to teach because she is not quite so fidgety and distractible, but she still requires a great deal of extra attention. Significant improvements occur, but not wholesale changes.

A final group of children are those who make minor responses. Either they don't respond at all, or they react poorly to medication. In some cases, despite all efforts to find the right medication at the right dose, there is no positive reaction. In others, there is some positive effect on attention and self-control, but because of the side effects the medication cannot be continued. It has been estimated that 1 to 3 percent of children with ADHD cannot tolerate any dose of stimulant medication (Barkley 1998).

In summary, the primary benefits of stimulant medication are the improvement of the core problems of ADHD—hyperactivity, impulsivity, and inattentiveness. Attention span seems to improve, and there is a reduction of disruptive, inappropriate, and impulsive behavior. Compliance with the commands of authority figures increases, and children's peer relations may also improve, primarily through reduction in aggression. In addition, when the dosage is carefully monitored and adjusted, medication has been found to enhance academic performance.

Medication does little to rectify any cognitive malfunctions or learning disabilities. If a child has visual- or auditory-processing deficits, medication will probably not change this learning problem. What it may do is help the child pay attention better so that remedial instruction will more likely impact the learning disability.

Although these medications are certainly helpful in the day-to-day management of ADHD, they have not been demonstrated to lead to enduring positive changes after their cessation. Research has been very clear that stimulant medications are not a panacea for ADHD and in most cases they should not be the sole treatment employed. The numerous skill deficits these children have will still need attention and remediation.

It would be a mistake to assume that all children who respond to medication have ADHD. Likewise, it is an error to say that children who do not respond to medication do not have ADHD. In other words, response to medication says nothing about whether children actually have ADHD. In addition, the problems of children who do not respond are not necessarily less real than those of the children who do respond. The key is a thorough evaluation that identifies all the child's needs, followed by a detailed treatment plan of which medication may be one component.

Current Medications Used for ADHD

Following is a description of the common medications that doctors prescribe or may prescribe in the future to treat ADHD. This overview is provided for your education only. Families must discuss the specifics of medication with their physician.

Stimulants

Psychostimulant compounds are the most widely used medications for the management of ADHD-related symptoms. Doctors began prescribing stimulant medications to children with ADHD symptoms in 1937. Researchers have studied these drugs extensively since then.

Prescribing stimulants for ADHD has changed in two fundamental ways. In the past we covered a child's symptoms only during school hours. More recently, doctors have also prescribed medication to work after school and on weekends and holidays. Second, longer-acting stimulant preparations now exist. These extended-release preparations are usually preferred because of the lack of in-school dosing requirements, improved compliance, reduced stigma and wear-off, lower risk of abuse, and lower risk of diversion of the pills to a nonprescribed consumer.

Ritalin

Ritalin, or methylphenidate, has been available since 1954 and is available in 5-, 10-, and 20-milligram tablets. Ritalin is water soluble, which means no traces of the medicine remain in the system once it has stopped providing beneficial effect. Because of this fact, Ritalin needs to be re-administered every three to four hours to maintain a therapeutic level. Ritalin is not physically addicting because of the quick absorption and depletion and because of the relatively small doses prescribed for ADHD.

Ritalin SR 20

Ritalin SR 20 is a sustained-release product having effects that last six to eight hours. The mechanism of action releases 10 milligrams initially and 10 milligrams four hours later. Some physicians report unsatisfactory reliability with the sustained-release form of Ritalin in that the child gets only about 8 milligrams of actual medication benefit. It may be necessary to administer a standard tablet of 5 to 10 milligrams in the morning, along with the SR 20.

Ritalin LA

The FDA recently approved Ritalin LA, or methylphenidate extended release, for the treatment of ADHD. This new long-acting form allows once-a-day dosing that lasts for eight to nine hours. Ritalin LA comes in 20-, 30-, and 40-milligram capsules.

Ritalin LA uses immediate- and extended-release beads within the capsule, providing a rapid onset of action followed by another release of methylphenidate approximately four hours later and thus ensuring two peak levels per day. Peaks and troughs during the day are thought to increase patient response. The older extended-release product, Ritalin SR, uses a wax matrix delivery system, which provides a slower onset and more continuous blood levels of methylphenidate over a period of six to eight hours. The new LA formulation offers patients an alternative form of dosing to improve compliance and quality of life.

Focalin

The FDA has recently approved Focalin, a refined formulation of Ritalin, for the treatment of ADHD. Whereas Ritalin contains both the D- and L-isomers of methylphenidate, Focalin contains only the more active D-isomer. (Isomers are compounds that contain the same number and type of atoms but have different structures.)

The pharmaceutical company studied the two forms of methylphenidate—dextro-methylphenidate and levo-methylphenidate—and found that the dextro form was significantly more potent than the levo form. Focalin is dextro-methylphenidate. Each tablet is described as having a faster onset of action and as requiring half the dose of Ritalin to achieve the same effect. Thus, children need half of the dose that they would need with Ritalin. Some doctors are referring to Focalin as "Focused Ritalin." It comes in 2.5-, 5-, and 10-milligram strengths. These are equivalent to the 5-, 10-, and 20-milligram Ritalin tablets. Each tablet lasts about four hours. The appropriateness of Focalin with children under age six has not been established.

Dexedrine and Dexedrine Spansules

Many people have a long benefit time from the slower-releasing medications called Dexedrine and Dexedrine Spansules. The length of time varies, but often a student can expect the therapeutic level to last around five to eight hours per dose. For a variety of reasons, teenagers often do better with one of these medications.

The amphetamines are quite similar in their pharmacologic makeup to these two medications. Dexedrine, or dextroamphetamine, has been available in the tablet form since the 1950s and comes in 5-milligram tablets; in a liquid elixir preparation with 5 milligrams per teaspoon; and in slow-release Spansule capsules of 5, 10, and 15 milligrams. The generic form, Dextrostat, comes in a 10-milligram strength.

The dosage is approximately half that of Ritalin. The slow-release, or Spansule, version of Dexedrine may work better for some children than would the Ritalin SR 20. Though dosage amounts are important, the timing of the daily medication schedule can be just as important to achieving positive results. The Spansule capsule contains small beads that release a steady dose over eight hours. The Spansule can be opened and sprinkled over food.

Since methylphenidate is not approved by the FDA for use in children under the age of six, dextroamphetamine may be preferable for children who are ages three to five (Gordon and Irwin 1997).

Generic Formulations

Methylphenidate and dextroamphetamine are also available in generic formulations. They typically cost less than the brand name drugs, and some insurance companies will provide reimbursement only for the generic formulations. Because there is greater latitude in the manufacturing process for generic versions, the pills may contain more or less of the active ingredient than the same formulation of the brand name drugs. This latitude might result in a more varied and unreliable response pattern in the child. In many cases, a child may respond the same to the generic as they do to the brand name form of the medication. Parents should talk to their physician about the choice. It might be wise to start with the brand name formulation. Then once parents have a clear idea of how their child responds, they might choose the generic for a few weeks and try to determine whether there is any difference in their child's day-to-day behavior.

Adderall

Adderall consists of mixed salts of a single-entity amphetamine product that combines amphetamine and dextroamphetamine. A company previously marketed Adderall under the name of Obetrol, which was indicated for obesity and ADHD. Then a different company, Shire Richwood, renamed the product Adderall in 1994 and completed the necessary FDA reviews. It is indicated for use in children three years of age and older. Adderall lasts longer than Ritalin or Dexedrine, perhaps by six to eight hours. This extended time may allow children to avoid the noontime dosage necessary for the other nonextended-release stimulants. No generic version is available at this time.

Adderall XR

Adderall XR is a newer extended-release formulation of Adderall. It is designed to provide symptom control in the morning and throughout the day with just one morning dose. Adderall XR capsules contain both immediate-release and delayed-release beads in a fifty-fifty ratio designed to provide a double-pulse delivery of amphetamine. Fifty percent of the beads release immediately, and 50 percent release slowly over about eight hours. Thus, for example, the Adderall XR 10 releases 5 milligrams immediately and 5 milligrams over the remaining time. Adderall XR comes in 5-, 10-, 15-, 20-, 25-, and 30-milligram capsules. Like the other capsules with beads, it can be opened and sprinkled over food.

Metadate

Metadate, a longer-acting methylphenidate, comes in two forms, Metadate ER and Metadate CD. Metadate ER is designed to last eight hours. It comes in 10-milligram and 20-milligram strengths. The Metadate ER 10 releases the equivalent of 5 milligrams initially and 5 milligrams four hours later. The Metadate ER 20 releases the equivalent of 10 milligrams immediately and 10 milligrams four hours later. Both the 10- and 20-milligram tablets are color-additive free. The surface of the tablet cannot be broken. If it is, all the medication releases immediately.

Metadate CD

The newest form of this brand, Metadate CD, lasts eight hours. It is a capsule with multiple beads inside. The capsule releases 6 milligrams initially and 14 milligrams over the remainder of the time. Unlike the Metadate ER, the capsule can be opened, and the beads can then be sprinkled over food.

Concerta

Concerta, the first once-daily treatment for ADHD, received approval in fall 1999. Because of its unique release mechanism, the therapeutic level is maintained for twelve hours. Its active ingredient is methylphenidate, and it is available as an extended-release tablet in 18-, 36-, and 54-milligram strengths of methylphenidate HCl. Each tablet is designed to be effective for twelve hours. Concerta 18 milligrams is approximately equivalent to Ritalin 5 milligrams three times a day. Concerta 36 milligrams approximately equals Ritalin 10 milligrams three times a day. Concerta 54 milligrams equals Ritalin 15 milligrams three times a day.

Concerta uses osmotic pressure to deliver methylphenidate HCl at a controlled rate. Because of its controlled release, Concerta minimizes the peaks and valleys associated with other medications when they are taken more than once per day. This once-a-day dose eliminates the need for in-school and after-school doses. Some physicians report fewer side effects with Concerta even though the active ingredient is the same as the one in Ritalin.

Concerta should be taken in the morning, with or without breakfast, and swallowed whole with a liquid. It should not be chewed, divided, or crushed. The appropriateness of its use for children under age six has not been established.

Methylphenidate Patch

Noven Pharmaceuticals is working on a once-daily MethyPatch®
(transdermal methylphenidate system). The patch incorporates
Noven's patented DOT Matrix™ patch technology in the treatment
of ADHD. DOT Matrix technology permits Noven to deliver predictable therapeutic doses of a range of prescription therapies through
discreet, comfortable, and adherent patches that are well suited to
active children. If approved by the FDA, it will be the first transdermal therapy available for ADHD (Noven Pharmaceuticals 2002).

Strattera

Recent studies have demonstrated promising results for the non-
psychostimulant Strattera, or atomoxetine. Strattera is a potent
inhibitor of the presynaptic norepinephrine transporter. Researchers
think atomoxetine works by blocking a neurotransmitter that plays an
important role in modulating the brain systems that control attention
and activity.

The need for alternative and effective nonstimulant pharmacological
treatment options is evident because some children, adolescents, and
adults with the disorder do not respond to, or cannot tolerate, a stimulant medication. Growing concern over issues related to prescribing
controlled substances over the long term, including their potential for
diversion, has also generated considerable support for the development
of alternative nonstimulant treatments. In addition, while the new all-
day stimulant formulations have succeeded in reducing the need for
multiple dosing throughout the day, their use may induce sleep disturbances, such as insomnia.

Strattera appears to offer an alternative to stimulants, showing excellent
symptom control but no abuse liability. Strattera works as it selectively

blocks the reuptake of the neurotransmitter norepinephrine, which is a chemical messenger, by certain nerve cells in the brain. This action increases the availability of norepinephrine, which is thought to be essential in regulating impulse control, organization, and attention.

Treatment with atomoxetine appears to lessen ADHD symptoms significantly and to be generally well tolerated at all doses. The relatively benign side effect profile of atomoxetine is especially promising. No serious side effects or changes in cardiac conduction have been associated with atomoxetine. Preliminary studies have shown some small amounts of weight loss (Michelson et al. 2001).

Strattera has now been approved for use and could be a valuable addition to the treatment options for ADHD. It is available in 10-, 18-, 25-, 40-, and 60-milligram capsules. It cannot be chewed or crushed. Strattera capsules should never be broken and sprinkled on food. They must be taken whole but can be taken with or without food (Brown University 2002).

Cylert

Cylert, or pemoline, is taken once a day, giving it an advantage over the shorter acting preparations. It has a gradual onset of action. Significant clinical benefits may not be evident until the third or fourth week of treatment, and they may take as long as six weeks. Because of its association with life-threatening hepatic failure, Cylert should not ordinarily be considered as first-line drug therapy for ADHD. If it is used, initial and periodic liver function tests are required.

Tricyclic Antidepressants

Tricyclic antidepressants, including Tofranil (imipramine) and Norpramine (desipramine), have also been prescribed for the treatment of ADHD. Pamelor, or nortriptyline, is another tricyclic that may be used. The bulk of the research suggests that psychostimulants tend to be superior overall to the tricyclics in managing ADHD symptoms. However, a subgroup of children, particularly those who show signs of anxiety, depression, or sleep problems or have tics or psychosis, may respond better to the tricyclics. These medications can also help those who are having trouble with anger, bed-wetting, or inability to sleep. Of these tricyclic antidepressants, desipramine may have fewer side effects and thus be preferable. Tricyclics can also be used in conjunction with stimulant medications.

The antidepressant medications are taken by mouth once or twice a day, but they do not wash out of the body as quickly as the stimulants. Therefore, it may take several weeks to build up a therapeutic level in the bloodstream. Side effects can include irregular heart rate, nervousness, sleep problems, stomach upset, dizziness, and dry mouth.

Another type of antidepressant is the selective serotonin reuptake inhibitors (SSRIs) such as Prozac (fluoxetine), Paxil (paroxetine), and Zoloft (sertraline). SSRIs increase the levels of the neurotransmitter serotonin by inhibiting the reuptake of serotonin, allowing it to remain active in the synapse for a longer period. These medications may be useful for children who have some mood disorder, including depression, anxiety, and irritability or who show a high level of aggressiveness. Improvement in attention span may result from this type of medication, but it is generally not as dramatic as the improvement seen from stimulants. Side effects can include nausea, mild weight loss, anxiety, headaches, sweating, and insomnia.

Clonidine and Tenex

Clonidine (catapres) and Tenex (guanfacine) are antihypertensive medications that can also be used to treat ADHD symptoms. Clonidine is available in transdermal skin patches that release the medicine evenly all day. Clonidine is less expensive than Tenex, but Tenex may cause less drowsiness during the day.

These medications have also been used for other disorders such as migraine headaches, schizophrenia, manic depression, obsessive-compulsive disorder, panic disorder, and anorexia nervosa. This type of medication helps control oppositional behavior, anger, aggression, cruelty, destructiveness, explosiveness, and frustration. Since these medications are also used for treatment of Tourette's syndrome, they may prove useful in ADHD children who have tics or who have developed tics on methylphenidate. The primary side effect is tiredness, along with decreased blood pressure, dizziness, and dry mouth (Hunt, Capper, and O'Connell 1990).

Some of the newer antidepressants such as Wellbutrin (bupropion), Ludiomil (maprotiline), Busbar (busiprone), Celexa (citalopram), Remeron (mirtazapine), and Effexor (venlafaxine) have also been prescribed for treating ADHD.

Teacher Participation in the Evaluation of Medical Intervention

The response of each child to medication is unique. Therefore, it is often important to collect objective data regarding changes in a child's behavior during several doses of medication. The typical approach is to determine the child's optimal dose in the context of a double-blind, placebo-controlled assessment study that includes multiple measures of the child's behavior collected from the home and school. The term *double-blind* means that the physician, teacher, and parents do not know when the child is receiving the medication and when he is taking a neutral substance, or placebo. The use of a placebo reduces the effects of positive biases that can show up on rating scales when the rater knows that the child is taking a medication.

The problem with this type of trial is that it is time-consuming, expensive, and unnecessary for most children. In most situations, observers can see improvement fairly quickly, and waiting another four to six weeks to get started with the medication regimen is unnecessary. However, four types of situations would suggest the need for the more rigorous double-blind trial.

One of these situations occurs when the parents disagree with each other about whether to consent to a medication trial. In a second type of situation, the school personnel advocate drug therapy, while the parents are strongly opposed (or vice versa). A third condition occurs when a child is so anxious about being medication free during an off-drug trial that the doctors are concerned the anxiety will interfere with an accurate assessment. In the final condition, the patients, often teenagers, are very noncompliant regarding the medication because they are convinced that they have no problems and that the medication has no effect. The trial may help show that medication does help (Gordon and Irwin 1997).

This type of trial usually takes three weeks. During one of those weeks, the patient takes a small dose of medication, such as 5 milligrams. A 10-milligram dose is often given for another week, and a placebo for still another week. Only the nurse, technician, or pharmacist who prepares or dispenses the prescriptions knows the sequence. Sometimes the physician will try a combination of medications—such as Adderall, Ritalin, and Dexedrine—during the study. Using such a combination may extend the trial to four weeks.

It is also important during this time not to make any drastic changes in school or intervention techniques. To do so would skew the observations about the medication. So if parents tell you as the teacher that a double-blind trial is underway, you should not make any significant changes in classroom instruction or management.

At the end of each week, both parents and teacher complete a rating scale of some type. This scale is meant to measure the child's behavior objectively during that particular week. The types of measures used to make the original diagnosis of ADHD now offer a comparison point for the child's performances on medication. The initial standardized score the student received allowed the clinician to compare her with other children. Now, the weekly scores provided by the parent and teacher allow her to be compared with herself. If there are any improvements in behavior that correspond to the introduction of the various medications, the doctor can assume that the changes result primarily from the medication. If one level of dosage was also accompanied by the most significant improvement in behavior, that level may become the initial therapeutic dosage. Periodic measurements are necessary to evaluate the continued efficacy of the treatment.

Whether or not the physician uses a double-blind study, some objective measures are needed. The Conner's Teacher and Parent Rating Scales Revised (CPRS-R/CTRS-R), the ADD-H Comprehensive Teacher's Rating Scale (ACTeRS), the Brown ADD Scales, and the Revised School Situations Questionnaire (SSQ) are often used to create objective measures. Their purpose is to make sure the medication is helping the child. If the data and your classroom observations don't indicate any improvement, the medication must be adjusted or stopped.

Sometimes it takes a month or two to settle on a medication program that suits the student. Therefore, the parents need to have patience and work closely with their doctor to find the right medication and dosage for their child.

Additional Suggestions for the Teacher

The school should be informed if a child is taking medication or trying new doses. As the teacher, you will need to provide regular feedback about the child's classroom behavior and academic achievement. This information is crucial in determining the medication's effectiveness. The physician or clinician provides the rating forms to use in evaluating the student's behavior. It is very important that you complete all these forms in an accurate and timely fashion.

Also, you need to inform the parents if you notice any alarming behaviors, such as twitches or social withdrawal. Remember that medication is not going to solve all the child's problems and thus the educational program must change. The effects of medication simply help determine the degree to which you will have to make changes.

Continue to look for signs such as extended in-seat activity, improvements in handwriting and organization on paper, decreased impulsiveness, and a higher frustration tolerance. Also, you need to be observant of differences in behavior at different times of day to help parents make adjustments to dosage. It is important to report any side effects, such as irritability, sadness that approaches or mimicks depression, increased restlessness, and excessive talkativeness.

Don't make statements to the child such as, "You are having a bad afternoon. Did you forget to take your pill?" Medication does not make a child "good." Also avoid such pronouncements as "You're such a good boy when you take your medicine."

School Policy for Medications

If a midday dosage is required, the parents and school will have to work out the mechanics of the process. Following are some suggested procedures for the management of medication within the school.

Policy and Procedures for Managing Medications Within the School

- Some schools prohibit students from carrying their ADHD medication to or from school. This rule necessitates having a parent, guardian, or other responsible adult deliver and remove the medication.
- ADHD medication should be provided to the school in the original pharmacy bottle, properly labeled with the student's name, the name and strength of the medication, the dosage to be administered, and the frequency and time of administration.
- One person, preferably the school nurse, should maintain primary control of the medication.
- A medication log should be maintained.

On the front of the medication log, put the following:
  - The name and grade/homeroom of the student
  - The name and strength of the medication
  - The amount of medication to be dispensed
  - The time the medication is to be dispensed
  - The duration of the order
  - A running log of the date and time of medication, and the initials of the one who dispensed it

Put the following on the back of the log:
  - The signature and initials of each person who dispenses the medication
  - An accounting of the amount of medication received by or removed from the school, signed by the deliverer and the receiver; the initials and date of the parent or guardian who is present during a physical count of the medication
  - A register of behavioral inventories or rating scales completed by the staff and to be sent to the physician

Attach these to the log:
- The signed parental permission for the school staff to administer the medication during school hours
- A written signed medication order from the doctor whose name appears on the prescription bottle

In addition to these policies and procedures, schools should not allow students to self-administer ADHD medication outside the presence of school staff so that verification can be made that the medication has, in fact, been consumed.

The drug supply should be secured in a locked room, or in a locked drawer or cabinet. Non-duplicative keys to the locked drug-storage area should be limited in number, and an inventory and accountability system for these keys should be maintained.

The school nurse should destroy unused medication that is not removed from the school by a parent or other responsible adult. It is advisable that the destruction of the medication be witnessed by at least one other person and documented.

(U.S. Department of Justice 2001)

Conclusion

The success of treatment for a child with ADHD depends on a cooperative effort between the child and a committed team of parents, caretakers, and professionals. Medication can be a significant component of treatment. However, one of its major contributions may be to provide an opportunity for a multimodal treatment program to result in maximum effectiveness. Medication may help improve the benefit of other interventions. Remember that most of the time, medication alone is not enough. The skills of self-control, not the pills, make the difference.

In the next chapter, we will look at accommodations and management practices you can use in the classroom for your ADHD students.

References

American Academy of Pediatrics. 2001. Clinical practice guideline: Treatment of the school-aged child with attention-deficit/hyperactivity disorder. *Pediatrics* 108, no. 4:1033–44.

Barkley, R. A. 1998. *Attention-deficit hyperactivity disorder: A handbook for diagnosis and treatment.* 2nd ed. New York: Guilford Press.

———. 2002. Psychosocial treatments for attention-deficit/hyperactivity disorder in children. *Journal of Clinical Psychiatry* 63, suppl. 12:36–43.

Biederman, J., T. Wilens, E. Mick, T. Spencer, and S. V. Faraone. 1999. Pharmacotherapy of attention-deficit/hyperactivity disorder reduces risk for substance use. *Pediatrics* 104:e20.

Brown University. 2002. Studies reveal atomoxetine effective treatment for ADHD. *The Brown University Child and Adolescent Psychopharmacology Update.* http://www.medscape.com/viewarticle/423374.

Cantwell, D. P. 1996. Attention deficit disorder: A review of the past 10 years. *Journal of the American Academy of Child and Adolescent Psychiatry* 35, no. 8:978–87.

Dougherty, D. D., A. A. Bonab, T. J. Spencer, S. L. Rauch, B. K. Madras, and A. J. Fischman. 1999. Dopamine transporter density in patients with attention deficit hyperactivity disorder. *The Lancet* 354:2132–3.

Goldstein, S., and M. Goldstein. 1990. *Managing attention disorders in children.* New York: John Wiley and Sons.

Gordon, M., and M. Irwin. 1997. *The diagnosis and treatment of ADD/ADHD: A no-nonsense guide for primary care physicians.* DeWitt, NY: GSI Publications.

Hunt, R., L. Capper, and P. O'Connell. 1990. Clonidine in child and adolescent psychiatry. *Journal of Child and Adolescent Psychopharmocology* 1, no. 1:87–102.

Martin, G. 1998. *The attention deficit child.* Colorado Springs, CO: Chariot Victor Books.

Michelson, D., D. Faries, J. Wernicke, et al. 2001. Atomoxetine in the treatment of children and adolescents with attention-deficit/hyperactivity disorder: A randomized, placebo-controlled, dose-response study. *Pediatrics* 108:83.

MTA Cooperative Group. 1999. A 14-month randomized clinical trial of treatment strategies for attention-deficit/hyperactivity disorder. *Archives of General Psychiatry* 56 (December): 1073–86.

Noven Pharmaceuticals. 2002. Noven submits new drug application for once-daily MethyPatch. *Press Release: June 27*. http://biz.yahoo.com/ bw/020627/272438_1.html (site now discontinued).

U.S. Department of Justice. Drug Enforcement Administration. 2001. Stimulant abuse by school age children: A guide for school officials. What precautions can schools take to ensure the safe handling of these medications? http://www.deadiversion.usdoj.gov/pubs/ brochures/stimulant/stimulant_abuse.htm#h.

Volkow, N. D., G. J. Wang, J. S. Fowler, et al. 1998. Dopamine transporter occupancies in the human brain induced by therapeutic doses of oral methylphenidate. *American Journal of Psychiatry* 155:1325–31.

Wilens, T. E. 1999. *Straight talk about psychiatric medications for kids*. New York: Guilford Press.

Wilens, T. E., J. Biederman, and T. J. Spencer. 2002a. Attention deficit/ hyperactivity disorder across the lifespan. Annual Review of Medicine 53:113–31.

———. 2002b. Attention-deficit/hyperactivity disorder: Tips to individualize drug therapy. *Current Psychiatry Online* (May): 32. http://www .currentpsychiatry.com/2002b_05/05_02_adhd.asp.

CHAPTER 8

Teaching ADHD Students

We will now look at what you the teacher can do in the classroom to assist the ADHD student. We'll start with the big picture of general principles or conditions that can be applied to the educational program. Then we will examine specific accommodations that have been found useful for this type of student. Finally, the chapter will include information about specific types of help, such as a study-skills class and a coach—useful tools for helping ADHD students become more efficient learners.

Basic Components of an Educational Program for ADHD Students

Staff Who Accept the Legitimacy of ADHD

The first step in dealing with any kind of problem is to acknowledge that it exists. While students who have struggled with the frustrations and failures associated with ADHD can certainly develop a case of

RCA, or *rotten crummy attitude,* the core reason for their struggle is their brain chemistry. All students struggle with their basic carnal nature and are in need of redemption, a fact that certainly applies to ADHD and oppositional students. However, saying that a student who has been diagnosed with ADHD really just has a spiritual problem is akin to saying that blind people can't see because they don't have enough faith in God. It simply is a falsehood, and it is a terrible injustice to those students for their educators to have that opinion.

If you encounter staff members who believe that there is really no such thing as ADHD, you need to inform them of the facts. The material in the preceding chapters should help. The many resources listed in the appendix and in the reference and resource lists in the chapters can lead you to mountains of materials that can be useful in educating both parents and fellow educators. A few additional possibilities are the book *The Attention Deficit Child* (Martin 1998) and two brochures: *Attention Deficit/Hyperactivity Disorder* (Martin 2002) and *Attention Deficit Disorder* (Martin 1994). In addition, the *International Consensus Statement on ADHD* (Barkley et al. 2002) came about in response to the mainstream media coverage about ADHD, which has historically been biased, full of misinformation, and heavily influenced by anti-psychiatry groups. In January 2002 a number of prominent medical doctors and researchers in ADHD issued this summary statement about the scientific basis for ADHD.

Knowledgeable Professionals Who Communicate

A second major component is a well-integrated and functioning team of teachers, administrators, parents, and clinicians who communicate often and work together to create a structured and supportive environment. ADHD students will fall through the cracks or revert to their old habits unless a team of helping professionals and family members work together consistently. Whether it is making sure homework assignments are clearly communicated and available for parents to access or having the bus driver consistently apply the points for the daily behavior report card, everybody must be on the same page, operating in the same fashion.

An Environment That Allows for Sufficient Monitoring, Redirection, and Accommodation

To experience success, ADHD students need frequent, immediate, and consistent feedback about their behavior. They also require more frequent redirection to tasks than do their classmates. There is certainly a practical limit to how much time a teacher can spend in prompting distractible students. However, taking extra care to make sure that ADHD students complete homework assignments, maintaining an accurate progress report process, or using a reward or point system for productive classroom behavior are techniques and procedures that have proved beneficial for ADHD students.

High Levels of Structure

ADHD students do much better when they have predictable structure and consistent application of clearly specified rules, expectations, and instructions. Teachers should implement reasonable and meaningful consequences for both compliance and noncompliance. Your classroom does not have to function as a military school or marine boot camp, but the keys are predictability and consistency.

I had a third-grade ADHD client recently whose teacher was the extreme opposite of what I am describing here. Apparently a carryover from the flower children of the '60s, this teacher would assign a homework project or spelling test for a particular day. However, more often than not, when the time came for the test, the teacher would capriciously announce an alternative activity. For example, she would say that she felt like having the class participate in a group hug: "Everybody in the class who would rather have a group hug than a spelling test, raise your hand." You can imagine the outcome of this type of vote. So the spelling test was put off for another week.

Now there's probably nothing wrong with having an occasional group hug. However, for a typical ADHD student, if you announce a test for Friday, and the parents spend hours and hours Thursday evening fighting through all the tears to practice those spelling words, there had better be a test on Friday. Otherwise, the inconsistently kept promises will produce a much greater tendency for the typical students to procrastinate and for ADHD students to think they really don't need to study. Likewise, if there are classroom rules for students regarding talking out, staying in their seat, or making animal noises with various body parts, you should enforce those rules consistently.

Accommodations to ADHD Students' Special Needs

The final component of an effective educational environment for ADHD students comprises accommodations designed to compensate for students' distractibility, limited organizational skills, and low frustration tolerance. The following section lists a number of examples of these accommodations. As was true for the lists provided earlier for LD students, not all these ideas will apply to every student, and not all these accommodations will necessarily fit in your classroom. However, teachers all over the country have used these interventions successfully at one time or another, and they are worthy of your consideration. Remember, the goal of each accommodation is to improve learning and behavior in the classroom. If you try an idea for a while and the ADHD student appears to be taking advantage in a negative way, that arrangement is not working.

I have taken ideas from many different sources and summarized them for your use. These suggestions are organized by topic according to teachers' major tasks (Bryan and Sullivan-Burstein 1997; Chapman Booth 2002; Epstein et al. 1999; ERIC Clearinghouse 1998; Fetal Alcohol Syndrome Community Resource Center n.d.; Lerner 2003; Mercer and Mercer 2001; Richards 1999; Rosenshine 1997; Warger 2001; Winebrenner 1996; Zeigler Dendy 2000).

Establishing the Proper Learning Environment

• Assign ADHD students to a traditional self-contained classroom. Four walls and one door without panoramic views of the playground or parking lots are just fine. ADHD students have great difficulty functioning in open-concept classrooms with constant transitions and many distractions.

• Try to match ADHD students with highly organized teachers who will model and encourage neatness, efficiency, and organization. A creative but informal, unpredictable, and inconsistent teacher will be difficult for ADHD children.

• Seat ADHD students near the teacher's desk, but include them as part of the regular class seating.

• Seat ADHD students away from noisy places. Avoid such distracting stimuli as air conditioners, high-traffic areas, heaters, doors, and windows.

• Seat ADHD students with well-behaved students and away from students who exhibit problem behaviors.

• Keep routines simple.

• Allow ADHD students to move. Provide opportunities for physical action: for example, allowing them to pace in the rear of the classroom, do an errand, sharpen pencils, get papers or materials, wash the blackboard, get a drink of water, or go to the bathroom. Monitor the students, however, to make sure they are not abusing the privileges. The evidence should be overall improved work production, not just more movement.

• Give the hyperactive students opportunities to work while standing or to pace while thinking as long as they learn to do so without disturbing others. You can permit activities such as running an errand or cleaning the fish tank as individual rewards for improvement and assignment completion. Just make sure the activity doesn't prove so stimulating that it causes more problems than it solves.

- Alternate classroom activities so that ADHD students have a chance to alternate standing and sitting, stillness and movement.
- Intersperse high- and low-interest activities throughout the school day. Long periods of uninterrupted seat work are hard for ADHD students. Plan for times of concentration and attention to be alternated with hands-on, multimodality, high-interest learning activities.
- Allow students to leave their seats to put a point or star on a wall chart after they finish a page.
- Have work centers in the classroom.
- Use computers and allow students to go to the computers during work time.
- Make sure ADHD students always have opportunities for physical activities. Avoid using daily recess as a time to make up missed schoolwork. Use options other than removing daily recess as punishment.
- Permit ADHD students to play with small objects they keep at their desks that they can manipulate quietly, such as a soft squeeze ball, if their playing isn't too distracting.
- Stand near ADHD students when giving them instructions.
- Provide a structured daily routine in written form and put the list where it is easy to see.
- Provide organizational aids such as charts, timelines, and compensatory strategies.
- Use materials that address students' learning styles.
- Add interest to tasks by having students work with partners, in interest centers, or in groups. Encourage peer tutoring and cooperative/collaborative learning.
- Because ADHD children do not handle change well, as much as possible avoid transitions, physical relocations, changes in schedule, and disruptions. Monitor students closely on field trips.
- For students who have trouble waiting, give verbal or motor activities to do while they wait. At the same time, encourage productive thinking, appropriate task completion, or both while waiting for

the teacher's attention. Reward them for waiting for increasing lengths of time.
- Be creative! Produce a stimuli-reduced study area. Let all students have access to the area so that ADHD students will not feel different.
- Encourage parents to provide appropriate study space at home and to set times and routines for study and to review completed homework and organization of notebooks and book bags.

Giving Instructions to Students with ADHD
- Maintain eye contact during verbal instruction.
- Keep instructions short and simple. Simplify complex directions. Avoid multiple commands.
- Make sure students comprehend instructions before beginning tasks. Ask students to repeat instructions to you and then to themselves.
- Provide a consistent, predictable schedule: tape it to the inside of the desk or student assignment book, post it in the classroom, or both.
- Write down key words on the board to aid in note-taking during instruction in lecture form.
- Provide students with a person who can take notes on classroom discussions and lectures.
- Alert students by using key phrases such as "This is important" and "Listen carefully."
- Use visual aids, charts, pictures, graphics, and transparencies and write key points on the chalkboard.
- Make directions clear and concise. Be consistent with daily instructions.
- If necessary, repeat instructions in a calm, positive manner.
- Teach ADHD students specific strategies for learning. Using strategies helps to organize the learning process and make it more meaningful. Examples include diagrams and other pictorials to help with information to be memorized; mnemonic strategies, such as HOMES for remembering the Great Lakes; mental pictures or associations to assist in storage and retrieval of information; and emphasis of critical pieces of instruction by coloring, underlining, or highlighting.

- Help students feel comfortable seeking assistance. Most children with ADHD will not ask for help. Gradually reduce the amount of assistance, but keep in mind that these children will need more help for a longer period of time than the average child does.
- Set up a specific routine and adhere to it.
- Provide ADHD students with an outline before lessons or lectures and with teacher's notes of lessons or lectures.
- Make lists to help students organize tasks.
- Use behavior contracts that specify the time allotted for activities.

Giving Assignments
- Give out only one task at a time.
- Provide students with a syllabus of the upcoming week's assignments and lessons. Keep instructions clear, and assure that instructions and assignment criteria are always available in writing by providing the syllabus at the beginning of the course and by writing the assignments on the board as you give them to the class.
- Use folders to organize materials.
- Use a different-colored folder for each subject.
- Develop a daily or weekly home-school communication system, using notes, checklists, voice mail, a homework hotline, email, or a website with homework and class timelines.
- Schedule periodic parent-teacher meetings.
- Hold regular student-teacher meetings.
- Provide families with a duplicate set of texts they can use at home for the school year.
- Develop weekly progress reports.
- Mail a schedule of class and work assignments to the students' parents.
- Encourage a team approach to homework completion. As the teacher, you will need to take the responsibility for making assignments clear and assisting parents in developing a strategy that includes the following components:
  ○ Provide a clear definition of assignments. Make sure each student correctly writes down all assignments daily. If students are not capable of this, the teacher should help them.

º Require a daily assignment notebook if necessary. There needs to be written format for communication of assignments. Provide written explanations of homework assignments for parents as well as for students.

º Implement a method for students to store and transport assignments, such as a special notebook. Sign the notebook daily to signify completion of homework assignments, and have parents sign it also.

º Make sure that students get assignments and necessary materials out the classroom door and headed for home.

º Encourage parents to check for homework on a daily basis and to communicate with teachers if questions arise about assignments.

º Encourage parents to establish and monitor the time and place for completing homework in order to ensure compliance and successful completion of assignments.

º Encourage parents to make sure assignments and school materials are in the student's possession and returned to school.

º Establish a procedure for turning in homework.

• Because many ADHD students have trouble with long-term endeavors such as term papers or social studies projects, provide regular guidance and appropriate supervision regarding planning assignments, especially extended projects that take several days or weeks to complete. Some of the most common tendencies of ADHD children are to procrastinate, to miscalculate, and to avoid unpleasant tasks until the last minute. Therefore, close guidance in planning long-term projects is important.

• Break instructions into short, sequential steps by dividing work into short mini-assignments. This method creates opportunities for reinforcement and feedback at the end of each segment. Also consider scheduling shorter work periods.

• Communicate closely with parents, emphasizing student progress when possible.

• Help children with ADHD gain a better sense of how to plan within a timed framework by modeling how to plan, coaching them through the planning process, and having them practice consistently.

- Monitor student progress frequently while maintaining a supportive attitude.
- When necessary, modify assignments. Consult with learning support personnel to determine each student's specific strengths and weaknesses.
- Adjust the curriculum to allow ADHD students to experience success. For example, modify the instruction methods to accommodate a child's difficulty in paying attention and concentrating. Use flexibility to allow for a student's low frustration tolerance.
- If necessary, shorten assignments. Consider allowing students to use computers to compensate for poor handwriting ability.
- When appropriate, divide assignments into smaller parts to help ADHD students feel successful and to provide more frequent opportunity for giving them feedback.
- Instead of assigning an amount of work to be completed, limit homework to a certain amount of time spent productively.
- Allow students to work on homework while at school.
- Select a study partner who can copy assignments or clarify them by phone.
- Allow extra-credit assignments, perhaps using alternate modalities.
- Develop a reward system for work completed both at school and at home.
- Develop an individualized education program (IEP) for individual ADHD students. If students have additional learning needs such as LDs, remember that all identified problem areas require specific individual educational programs. Make sure the IEP is relevant and comprehensive for each student's total educational needs.
- Make sure you are testing knowledge and not attention span.
- Give extra time for certain tasks. Students with ADHD may work slowly. Do not penalize them for needing extra time.
- Keep in mind that children with ADHD become frustrated easily. Stress, pressure, and fatigue can break down their self-control and lead to poor behavior.

Testing

- Allow open-book tests.
- Provide practice questions for study.
- Allow students to use one page of notes during testing.
- Vary the formats of tests.
- Read questions aloud. Allow students to respond to questions orally.
- Allow use of such technology as a calculator or word processor.
- Give multiple choice instead of short answer questions.
- Allow use of a dictionary during tests.
- Provide extra time to finish.
- Give parts of tests in more than one setting.
- Provide opportunities for students to take tests in another room or at another time of day.
- Allow students to retake tests.
- Give more frequent short quizzes and fewer long tests.

Grading

- Base grades on the amount of improvement students make.
- Base grades on modified standards, such as IEP objectives, amount of improvement, and content rather than spelling.
- Base grades on effort as well as achievement.
- Mark students' correct answers, not their mistakes, on work completed at school and at home.
- Specify the skills mastered instead of giving a letter grade.

Modifying Behavior and Enhancing Self-Esteem

Providing Supervision and Discipline

- Have preestablished consequences for misbehavior. Administer consequences immediately, and monitor behavior frequently.
- Enforce classroom rules consistently. Remain calm, state the infraction of the rule, and avoid debating or arguing with the student.
- Use discipline that is appropriate for the behavior without being harsh.

- Use immediate and frequent feedback. Redirection will often be necessary so that you minimize long periods of unproductive activity.
- Teach ADHD students hand signals or "private signs," and use them to tell students when to talk, when not to talk, and when to get back on task.
- Use mechanical and electronic devices to remind and reward.
- Be sensitive to the fact that the behavior of ADHD students can escalate. Behaviors can range from showing slight irritations to having major explosions. Find ways to distract the children from a total focus on the problem of the moment, and redirect their attention to classroom tasks. You may need to use time-outs if students become too excited.
- Know how and when to pick a battle, and be able to back off and ignore unimportant behaviors that irritate you.
- Give private, discreet cues to students to stay on task. Cue the students in advance before calling on them, and cue them before an important point is about to be made by saying, for example, "This is a major point."
- Allow adequate time after asking questions so that students can form a thoughtful answer.
- Provide the amount of support and structure individual students need—not the amount of support and structure traditional for that grade level, classroom, or subject.
- Identify the students' strengths, altering the format of a presentation to take full advantage of the strengths.
- As much as possible, use high-impact visual aids with lively oral presentations to provide a more interesting and novel presentation of lessons.
- At all times avoid using sarcasm, ridicule, and continual criticism, and avoid bringing attention to students' different needs in front of their peers.
- Recognize that students will respond significantly better when you encourage them by noticing and mentioning their positive achievements.
- Avoid reminding students publicly about taking their medication.

• Implement a home-school report card system to monitor progress. Though you may do so in many ways, an effective system has three basic components. First, identify the specific school-related behaviors that you are monitoring. The behaviors can be both uppers and downers, preferably some of both, with an emphasis on the positive. Remember, *uppers* are appropriate behaviors that children should do more often, while *downers* are inappropriate behaviors that the children should do less often. Second, implement a system of record keeping that is simple yet effective in monitoring student behavior on a daily basis. Third, create a reward system for improvement in the students' study and school-related behavior.

The following form is an example of what can be used to communicate student performance on a given day. It takes only a minute or two to complete:

Daily Behavior Report Card

Teacher: Please rate each behavior using a point system from the following scale:

> 0. Did not have a good day
> 1. Had a good day
> 2. Had a very good day

Student's name: _____ Date: _____

Behavior:
1. Completed homework   _____
2. Completed seat work   _____
3. Listened to instruction   _____
4. Cooperated with classroom rules   _____
5. Got along with classmates   _____

Total: _____

You can change the list of specific behaviors to suit the needs of your students. You or the students' parent can specify rewards for high point days. You can base rewards on weekly improvement or on the total points for a week. You can use a response cost arrangement in which you establish a weekly reward. For example, a reward can be two dollars or two hours of television time on the weekend. Every day the report card comes home with ones or twos, the reward stays the same. However, if there are any zeros, the reward decreases by twenty-five cents or fifteen minutes. You need to record or create a visual aid for each day's transaction. For instance, using a jar of marbles or making tally marks on a paper will serve the purpose. At the end of the week, the children receive the amount of their reward that remains. This type of strategy seems to work well with most ADHD children (Barkley 1996, 2000).

Providing Encouragement
- Reward children more than you punish them in order to build their self-esteem.
- Praise immediately all good behavior and performance.
- Change rewards if they are not effective in motivating behavioral change.
- Find ways to encourage children. Praise genuine accomplishments. Students can detect insincere praise.
- Praise at critical times. Praise is particularly effective when children have accomplished an especially difficult task and when they are learning new skills.
- Praise appropriately. Focus praise on ability and effort, not on task difficulty or luck. You might use the following phrases or words of encouragement:

Nobody does it better.	Marvelous work!
Now you have it!	You've mastered this.
Nothing can stop you.	You're unreal.
Great job!	Great improvement.
This made my day.	This is really great.

Tremendous!

That's awesome.

Fantastic!

That's incredible.

You make it look easy.

Keep it up.

This is better than ever.

Great effort today.

That's sensational.

Congratulations!

Outstanding.

Perfect in every way.

I am proud of you.

Wonderful!

That's great!

Good thinking.

Super!

You're doing better.

Keep up the good work.

You're learning quickly.

That's the way to do it.

That's the best ever.

You make teaching fun!

That's it.

Great going!

Too easy for you?

Good for you.

Good work.

Fine effort!

U R Great!

You're unbelievable.

That's just super!

Couldn't be better.

Beautiful to behold.

Incredible work.

Better than ever!

Your personal best.

World-class effort!

Magnificent.

Dynamite work!

It's great working with you.

You should be proud.

This is first-class work.

Now you have the hang of it.

You mastered this quickly!

You really outdid yourself.

You are very good at this.

Top-of-the-line effort.

Stupendous!

Thank you!

- Build on students' strengths. Identify their best methods of learning as well as their areas of creativity, interest, and competency. Then use those strengths for motivating students, giving them opportunities for class leadership, and building their self-esteem. Try to make sure students have at least one task each day that they can do successfully.
- Teach children to reward themselves. Encourage positive self-talk by saying, for example, "You did very well remaining in your seat today. How do you feel about that?" These types of comments encourage children to think positively about themselves.

Teaching Strategy for Secondary ADHD Students

While many of the previous accommodations can be used at all instructional levels, the following list is particularly directed to the middle school and high school classroom. These strategies can be helpful for attention deficit students. In fact, many of these suggestions would probably benefit all students and simply constitute good teaching:

- Begin lectures with a review of the previous lecture and an overview of topics for that day or an outline of the lecture.
- Use a chalkboard or overhead projector to outline and summarize lecture material, being mindful of legibility and the need to read aloud to students what is written.
- Define technical language, specific terminology, and foreign words.
- Emphasize important points, main ideas, and key concepts within the lecture, or highlight them with colored pens on an overhead projector.
- Speak distinctly at a relaxed pace, pausing occasionally to respond to questions and give students a chance to catch up in their note taking.
- Pause and respond to students' nonverbal signs of confusion or frustration.
- Try to diminish as much as possible any auditory and visual classroom distractions such as hallway noise or flickering fluorescent lights.
- Leave time for questions and answers and for periodic and end-of-lecture discussions.
- Try to determine whether students understand the material by asking volunteers to summarize, give an example, or answer a question.
- Provide periodic summaries during lectures, emphasizing key concepts.
- Offer assignments in writing as well as orally and make yourself available for clarification.
- Provide a suggested timeline when making long-range assignments and suggest appropriate checkpoints.

- Be available during office hours for clarification of lecture material, assignments, and reading.
- Select a textbook that has a study guide and offers questions and answers for review.
- Help students find study partners and organize study groups.
- For exams, provide study questions that demonstrate the format and the content.
- Ask students how you as the instructor can facilitate their learning.
- Privately discuss what was observed of students suspected of having learning difficulties and refer them as appropriate for available support services.

Helping Students Who Have Trouble with Writing or Processing Speed

Many ADHD students struggle with written work. For example, they understand the concepts and have good ideas for creative writing assignments, but they are very slow in the production of their work. Medication can often improve the quality of their handwriting, but it usually doesn't make a big difference in the quantity of work they can finish efficiently. From my discussions with colleagues and educators around the country, I have concluded that nobody has found an effective method of increasing writing speed. For this reason, accommodation seems to be the major option for this area of difficulty. Sometimes called dysgraphia, difficulty in producing written work also falls under the category of low processing speed.

Processing speed can affect more than just written work, however. Low processing speed can be the experience of students who have trouble either sustaining concentrated visual attention or working rapidly under time constraints. Such students may also have difficulty with tasks that require automatic cognitive processing and written processing.

Other factors such as medication and interest level may also impact students' ability to accomplish written work. The intent of the following compensatory strategies is to reduce distractions and to help ADHD students work more rapidly and efficiently, particularly in their written work:

- Provide clearly duplicated worksheets that contain only a few problems and plenty of white space. Double-space all printed directions. If necessary, type words in a large font with extra spaces in between. Sometimes the use of large-print textbooks may improve performance.
- Seat these students in the front row near the chalkboard for all copying activities.
- Eliminate or reduce the amount of material students must copy from the chalkboard or from a textbook. Make speed or accuracy of less importance for them than for typical students.
- Cut a window or box on a piece of cardboard so that the students can frame and separate each problem as needed. Or have the students cover part of the page that is not being worked on in order to reduce distractions.
- Point to all words and phrases while you are reading from the board.
- To develop their visual recall and perceptual speed, have students reproduce words or phrases through the use of computer games or visual discrimination tasks. The goal is to reduce the exposure time and improve perceptual speed gradually.
- Allow these students to use a finger or an index card for keeping their place in reading.
- Encourage the use of graph paper in mathematics.
- Extend the time allowed for completing written assignments.
- Provide ample time for responding in written tasks.
- Have a tutor, parent, volunteer, or fellow student act as a scribe for these students and write down what the students dictate, but without comment or editorial correction.
- Allow these students to dictate into a recording device and have an aid transcribe the words later.

- Shorten assignments so that these students may accomplish them in a reasonable time period.
- Use visual clues to organize worksheets. For example, fold paper into the shape of a box—or use a box that is already constructed—and instruct these students to place their answers in the box.
- Recommend visual tracking exercises or computer games that require rapid visual scanning.
- Allow these students to use a typewriter or word processor in order to copy letters, word sequences, or sentences. The use of a laptop computer or keyboarding device can increase writing production by up to 80 percent once a student can type thirty to thirty-five words per minute.

Two examples of such electronic note-taking devices are the AlphaSmart 3000 and the Laser PC6. The devices, which are often called "smart keyboards," cost less than $300. They are powered by AA batteries, offer a standard-size keyboard, and boot up within seconds.

The devices store text files and do not have features found on computers or personal digital assistants (PDAs). Electronic note takers are for typing notes. For people who have an easier time typing than writing, the devices can be liberating pieces of access equipment. In using electronic note takers, files save right on the devices' firmware, so there is no hassle with a disk drive. Downloading to a laptop or PC is easy, using a cable that plugs into the keyboard port of a standard PC. For AlphaSmart products, contact the company at 888-274-0680 or http://www.alphasmart.com. For Laser PC6 products, contact the company at 800-726-7086 or http://www.perfectsolutions.com.

- Teach these students verbal mediation to use when they copy material. They should say each number, letter, or word as they transfer it from one place to another.
- In some cases, obtain a developmental visual exam that assesses the functional assessment of vision and determine whether visual training or therapy would be appropriate.

• Implement speech recognition software, probably an area of greatest potential for students who struggle in writing. With this type of program, a person can dictate a report or essay into a microphone. The software translates the dictation into a text file that is compatible with most word processing programs. Students then use the word-processing program to make corrections and adjustments to the text. The programs do have to be set up, and students have to learn to make format statements for the end of sentences or paragraphs.

When considering speech recognition as a successful writing tool, note that the users have to deal with knowing basic computer skills, word processing skills, and dictation skills, with knowing when and how to use speech recognition commands, and last but not least, with feeling motivated. Yet if the students are persistent in using the program for a few days, it can become a huge time-saver.

Several programs are currently available. The IBM ViaVoice is available for both Windows and Macintosh platforms. Dragon Naturally Speaking is available only for Windows. And iListen by MacSpeech is designed for Macintosh operating systems.

Helping Students Improve Their Study Skills

Many ADHD and LD students need to improve their study skills. They don't need another study hall or an after-school study club. They need specific instruction on how to study for tests, take notes, and manage their time. Students who improve their study skills will benefit in all their subject areas. They will need less time to read long and difficult passages. They will be better able to manage their time, strengthen their memory, and study for tests.

In this section we'll look at what an effective study skills class might include. In the best scenario, this kind of class is offered as part of the regular curriculum for upper intermediate through high school students. In some schools, the class is offered as an elective, often as an English credit.

The following model works best when the class contains six to eight students. The content of the class should include such topics as these:

- Getting Ready
  - Organizational tools, such as a daily planner
  - Study environment
  - Goals
  - Motivation
- Taking in Information
  - Time management
  - Procrastination
  - Listening
  - Note taking
  - Textbook reading
  - SQ4R—survey, question, read, write, recite, review
  - Library research
  - Concentration
  - Stress management
- Processing and Recalling Information
  - Learning styles
    - Visual, auditory, and hands-on approaches to learning
  - Memory tools
    - Mind mapping, matrices, acrostics, acronyms, narrative, rhymes, imagery
- Output
  - Test preparation
  - Taking tests
  - Critical thinking and writing
  - Conducting research and writing reports
  - Methods of organization and time management
  - Using technology

As the teacher, you go through the content systematically. You provide direct instruction, starting with the most basic element of a skill and progressing to more advanced elements. The class is not a study hall. Rather, it contains detailed instruction on the most important academic skills the students will ever acquire.

Another component of the class is the coordination of class content with progress reports from the students' other teachers. The study skills teacher periodically checks with those teachers and asks about each student's performance and progress. If the progress reports indicate that certain students are not doing well on tests, the study skills teacher works with those students on additional test-taking methods. If the social studies teacher reports that a student doesn't appear to have started on an assigned South America report, the study skills teacher helps the student apply research and report-writing methods to that assignment.

The combination of systematic, direct instruction and ongoing application of the skills can make this class a tremendous help to ADHD and LD students. Of course, you can incorporate this same content into an existing subject matter class and teach it through individual modules or units. In some schools, the content has a special name, such as Advantage Plus, and extra tuition is charged to pay for staff costs. The class can be open to all students or only to students with academic deficiencies. There are many ways to implement this type of class, and I highly recommend you consider it for your school. At the end of this chapter, you will find lists of resources to help you research and implement a study skills class.

Coaching ADHD Students

Many ADHD students struggle because the school environment places demands on them to organize themselves and to work independently. However, they frequently forget to write down assignments, complete homework, or hand their work in on time. They often have difficulty using their time wisely both at home and school. In addition, they have trouble knowing how to break down long-term assignments by developing reasonable timelines and following them. They struggle with using the organizational aids that have been created.

A study skills class can do much to help ADHD students acquire the tools they need. Another ingredient that helps greatly with the ongoing application of these tools is an ADHD coach. To assist secondary students in the use of good life-management skills, a coach provides them with external structure and support. A basketball coach helps athletes become better basketball players by encouraging them and giving them new strategies and techniques for improving their game. A coach also monitors their progress. The ADHD coach goes through a similar process in order to help ADHD students become more successful in school.

The coaching model involves using someone outside the student's family. Often the coach is someone from the school setting who has good rapport with the student and a good understanding of attention deficit disorder. The coach and student work together—by phone, email, or fax, by meeting together, or by some combination of these methods—to help the student manage ADHD symptoms and behavior, build social and academic skills, and keep on task. A face-to-face contact is best for high school students, but phone, email, or fax options are better than nothing at all.

The general process is for the coach and student to develop a written plan that includes goals and objectives. Then in regular brief coaching sessions, the coach and student evaluate progress and develop new objectives. The steps of the coaching sessions could follow the acronym REAP, which stands for *review, evaluate, anticipate,* and *plan.*

In the *review* session, the coach and student review the goals established at a previous session to determine whether the student met them. *Evaluation* occurs to assess how well the goals were accomplished, how many were met, and what interfered with meeting them all. This process determines how successful the operating plan has been. In the *anticipation* step, the student previews what tasks have to be accomplished between then and the next coaching session. These tasks can include reviewing homework assignments, studying for upcoming tests or quizzes, and starting long-term assignments. The coach can check the student's assignment book to make sure all assignments are there. Finally, in the *planning* step, the student and coach develop specific plans for completing tasks to achieve the assignment goals (Dawson and Guare 1999).

Another way to outline the content of a coaching session is by using the steps described by the acronym HOPE. *H* stands for *hello,* or a short catch-up from the last contact. *O* stands for *objectives,* which are discussions of to-do lists, weekly plans, and class assignments. *P* stands for *prioritize,* which means to set up specific plans for when to do what things. The last step is *E,* or *encouragement,* meaning that the coach praises progress, and for Christians this step can include prayer and spiritual support.

An effective coach must be someone who is reliable, able to make plans and keep schedules, and able to think clearly. Good coaches need to be good problem solvers, and they need to know how to empower students to solve their own problems. Good coaches don't just lecture and instruct; they use questions and encouragement to lead students to identify for themselves solutions for the problems encountered. A coach also needs to be enthusiastic, supportive, and optimistic. When plans don't work, coaches need to be able to highlight the positive, bring students back to the long-term plan, and remind them how far they've come. Finally, good coaches need to be concerned for the students' welfare while not taking setbacks or disappointments personally (Dawson and Guare 1999).

The biggest challenge I have had working with families is finding a person who is willing to be a coach. The best option for high school students is having one of their teachers from school as their coach. Sometimes a relative such as a grandparent, aunt, or uncle will be available. A parent or sibling will not usually be an appropriate choice. Coaching is an excellent tool for high school and college students, and I encourage you to explore it with your secondary students.

Teaching Social Skills to ADHD and LD Students

Parents and teachers seem to agree that many ADHD students have difficulty with social interaction. This difficulty includes problems in making and keeping friends, handling and channeling their anger, or any combination of these skills. Observation and research clearly demonstrate that people with learning disabilities tend to be less accepted by their peers, more awkward and inappropriate in their social interactions, and less socially perceptive.

School-age children and adolescents need the acceptance and support of their peers. The social incompetence typical of LD and ADHD students often prevents them from establishing and maintaining such relationships. Consider the following comments about learning disabilities and the related social deficits:

> To become a friend means to become interested in, and somewhat knowledgeable about, the other person's interests, be sensitive to their needs and feelings, compromise on activities, laugh off differences, be supportive, allow the other person freedom to interact with others and spend time with themselves, be elated by their successes, share their sorrows sensitively, be able to communicate your pleasure, displeasure, and anger without such communication being destructive to either party, and change and grow as your friend changes and grows. I wonder whether many learning disabled adolescents possess the sensitivity, empathy, flexibility, maturity, and generate sufficient interest and excitement to maintain such friendships. (Kronick 1982)

Formal research confirms that LD and ADHD students tend to have deficient or ineffective social skills. The following descriptions are characteristic of these students; in general, they are
- More likely to choose inappropriate behaviors in social situations
- Less able to solve social problems
- Less likely to predict consequences for their social behavior
- Less likely to adjust to the characteristics of their listeners in discussions or conversations
- Less able to successfully accomplish complex social interactions, such as those involving persuading, negotiating, resisting peer pressure, and giving or accepting criticism
- More likely to be isolated or rejected by their classmates and peers
- More often the objects of criticisms, warnings, negative nonverbal reactions, and negative and nonsupportive statements
- Less adaptable to new social situations
- More likely to be judged negatively by adults after informal observation
- Less likely to receive affection from parents and siblings
- Less tolerant of frustration and failure
- Less likely to use oral language that is mature, meaningful, or concise
- Less likely to interpret or infer the language of others accurately

(Lavoie 1994)

One of the major goals of social skills training is to help students become more knowledgeable about appropriate and inappropriate social behavior. The next goal is to help students learn the specific social skills targeted and identified during the assessment process. Quite a bit of overlap occurs between training in social skills and training in self-control. Most programs will focus on the four major skill areas of social entry, conversational skills, anger management, and conflict resolution and problem solving.

As an educator, you have several options in helping your ADHD or LD students develop better social skills. You can recommend to the parents that they enroll the student in a social skills class in the community. Counseling centers, private mental health professionals, and university-affiliated clinics often offer this type of class. Sometimes you may even be able to have an ADHD- or LD-diagnosed student participate in a pro-social skills class offered by the public school in your area. For this option to be possible, an IEP would probably need to be developed for the student.

Another option is that your school could set up a class in your facility. The process might require an additional fee from the student, or it could be part of your regular offerings. This section and the end of the chapter contain information about materials for organizing such a class, which can be very effective if someone has a vision for the need of these students and will take the time to organize the content.

Another idea is to include material on social skills as part of your regular social studies or character development curriculum. You can develop short modules on specific topics such as self-control, making friends, manners, and etiquette. All students would participate, and your ADHD and LD students would benefit greatly.

The final option is to model and teach appropriate social skills continually. In this method of assisting ADHD or LD students, you need to pay particular attention to several key items. The first is how the students initiate their interactions with other people and with a group. The second is how the students start and maintain a conversation. Important social skills can include listening well, asking relevant questions, taking turns in a conversation, and showing a genuine interest in the other person. The third item is the ability to resolve conflicts, and the fourth is the students' ability to share with others.

ADHD and LD students can be one to two years behind in their social development. It is thought that this delay is related to the students' inability to pick up on the social cues and nonverbal messages present in all social contexts. Many students need help in one or more of the following areas: listening, following instructions, sharing, working and playing cooperatively, and displaying social graces. Social graces include greeting others, saying thank you, introducing others, giving or receiving compliments, offering help, apologizing, and showing sensitivity to the feelings of others. Hygiene can also be a factor related to social graces.

If students are to be helped with their social skills, it is important that the parents monitor and supervise the movies, videos, and television shows their children watch, regulating their exposure to violence and other forms of inappropriate material in books, electronic games, and computer programs.

In addition, teachers and parents can practice appropriate social behavior of the types listed earlier. Be a good model for the student. Throughout the day, label and demonstrate each of these skills, such as offering help and sharing. Point out where these behaviors are occurring in real life or on television. Reinforce and praise students when you see them demonstrate these skills. Be systematic in illustrating these social graces, but do not be overbearing and do not embarrass the students in front of their classmates.

Describing a specific way of giving feedback to students, Richard Lavoie (1994) introduced a problem-solving approach to teaching social discrimination. This method, the social autopsy, is the examination or inspection of a social error in order to determine why it happened and how to prevent it from happening in the future. When a student makes an error, the teacher uses it as an opportunity to teach the child how to correct the mistake.

To begin the process, we ask, "What do you think you did wrong? What was your mistake?" By actively involving the students in discussing and analyzing the error, we can extract from the situation a lesson that enables them to see the cause-effect relationship between their behavior and the reactions of others, or the consequences. In the next set of questions, we ask, "What happened as a result of what you did? Was that result a positive or negative outcome? What could you do that would be better?" Often, we can then walk through a rehearsal of the better way of handling the situation.

For a social autopsy to be successful, the educator must do the following:
- Make sure that all adults who have regular contact with the student know how to perform social autopsies. The list includes family members, custodial staff, cafeteria workers, bus drivers, teachers, secretaries, and administrators. This process will foster generalization by ensuring that the student participates in many relevant autopsies daily.
- Conduct social autopsies immediately after the error occurs in order to provide a direct and instantaneous opportunity to demonstrate the cause and effect of social behaviors.
- Use social autopsies to analyze socially correct behaviors as well. In doing so, you will provide reinforcement, which may assist students in repeating the appropriate behavior in another setting.
- Help students identify and classify their feelings or emotions.

This method has several advantages:
- It uses the sound learning principles of immediate feedback, positive reinforcement, and drill and practice.
- It is constructive and supportive rather than negative or punishing.
- It provides an opportunity for the active involvement of the students rather than creating an adult-controlled intervention.
- It generally involves one-on-one assistance for the students.

(Lavoie 1994)

One major theme that emerges from the evaluation of self-control and social skills training efforts for children and adolescents is the importance of active and comprehensive school and parent involvement. Attempts to improve the self-control or social skills of nonsocial ADHD or LD students will have little effect unless there is involvement from those people who are the most active change agents in the students' lives. These people usually include those closest to the students, such as parents or other close relatives, teachers, and even classmates.

Social skills development is a critical need for many ADHD and LD students. Not all of them need this extra help, of course, but it provides a vital and profound benefit for those who do. Teaching academics is important, but more students get shunned for their inappropriate interactions with peers than for being poor readers. Consider carefully what you and your school can do to help.

There are an increasing number of printed resources to help teachers and families improve social skills in their children. A list of resources is included at the end of this chapter.

Conclusion

This chapter has surveyed a wide range of treatment and accommodation ideas for ADHD students. I trust that you have found some valuable and useful ideas in this discussion. You have to be something of a super-sleuth or a researcher to make use of this material. We discussed making classroom accommodations, improving study skills, coaching ADHD junior high and high school students, and approaching social skills instruction. All these ideas have been tested, and they have produced positive results. Yet not all these ideas will be useful to you. You have to venture out and try a few of the ones that make sense to you. It is hoped that the feedback will be positive and that you will be willing to try some more experiments. The goal, of course, is to enable these special kids who happen to have ADHD to realize their full potential.

References

Barkley, R. A. 1996. Using a daily school-behavior report card. *The ADHD Report* 4, no. 6:1–2, 13–15.

———. 2000. *Taking charge of ADHD.* Rev. ed. New York: Guilford Press.

Barkley, R. A., E. H. Cook Jr., M. Dulcan, et al. 2002. International consensus statement on ADHD. Toronto, Ontario, Canada: A.D.D.O. Foundation. http://www.addofoundation.org/ consensus.htm.

Bryan, T., and K. Sullivan-Burstein. 1997. Homework how-to's. *Teaching Exceptional Children* 29, no. 6:32–37.

Chapman Booth, R. 2002. List of appropriate school-based accommodations and interventions for a 504 plan or for adaptations and modifications sections of an IEP. Oxnard, CA: Oxnard School District. http://www.oxnardsd.org/pupils/list_504_accomodations.htm.

Dawson, P., and R. Guare. 1999. *Coaching the ADHD student.* North Tonawanda, NY: Multi Health Systems. (See http://www.mhs.com.)

Epstein, M. H., D. D. Munk, W. D. Bursuck, E. A. Polloway, and M. Jayanthi. 1999. Strategies for improving home-school communication about homework for students with disabilities. *The Journal of Special Education* 33, no. 3:166–76.

ERIC Clearinghouse on Disabilities and Gifted Education. 1998. Teaching children with attention deficit/hyperactivity disorder: Update 1998. ERIC Clearinghouse on Disabilities and Gifted Education. ERIC EC Digest #E569. http://www.ericec .org/digests/e569.html.

Fetal Alcohol Syndrome Community Resource Center. 504 accommodation checklist. Fetal Alcohol Syndrome Community Resource Center. http://www.come-over.to/FAS/IDEA504.htm.

Kronick, D. 1982. *Social development of learning disabled persons.* New York: Jossey-Bass.

Lavoie, R. 1994. *Parents guide: Learning disabilities and social skills.* Alexandria, VA: PBS VIDEO.

Lerner, J. W. 2003. *Learning disabilities. Theories, diagnosis, and teaching strategies.* New York: Houghton Mifflin.

Martin, G. 1994. *Attention deficit disorder.* Colorado Springs, CO: Focus on the Family.

——. 1998. *The attention deficit child.* Colorado Springs, CO: Chariot Victor Books.

——. 2002. Attention-deficit/hyperactivity disorder. Arcadia, CA: Narramore Christian Foundation. http://www.gospelcom.net/ narramore.

Mercer, C. D., and A. R. Mercer. 2001. *Teaching students with learning problems.* 6th ed. Upper Saddle River, NJ: Prentice Hall.

Richards, R. G. 1999. Strategies for dealing with dysgraphia. *LD Online.* http://www.ldonline.org/ld_indepth/writing/dysgraphia _strategies.html.

Rosenshine, B. 1997. Advances in research on instruction. In *Issues in educating students with disabilities.* J. Lloyd, E. Kame'enui, and D. Chard, eds. Mahwah, NJ: Lawrence Erlbaum Associates, Inc.

Warger, C. 2001. Five homework strategies for teaching students with disabilities. ERIC Clearinghouse on Disabilities and Gifted Education. ERIC/OSEP Digest #E608. http://www.ericec.org/digests/ e608.html.

Winebrenner, S. 1996. *Teaching kids with learning difficulties in the regular classroom.* Minneapolis, MN: Free Spirit Publishing.

Zeigler Dendy, C. A. 2000. *Teaching teens with ADD and ADHD.* Bethesda, MD: Woodbine House.

Resources for Teaching Study Skills

Armstrong, William H. 1998. *Study is hard work: The most accessible and lucid text available on acquiring and keeping study skills through a lifetime.* 2nd ed. Boston, MA: David R. Godine.

Davis, Leslie, and Sandi Sirotowitz, with Harvey C. Parker. 1996. *Study strategies made easy: A practical plan for school success.* Plantation, FL: Specialty Press.

Dodge, Judith. 1994. *The study skills handbook (grades 4–8).* Jefferson City, MO: Scholastic Trade.

Ellis, Dave. 2002. *Becoming a master student: Tools, techniques, hints, ideals, illustrations, examples, methods, procedures, processes, skills, resources, and suggestions for success.* 10th ed. Boston, MA: Houghton Mifflin. (This is a college-level resource, but many junior high and high schools have used it.)

James, Elizabeth, and Carol Barkin. 1998. *How to be school smart: Super study skills.* Rev. ed. New York: Beech Tree Books.

Luckie, William R., and Wood Smethurst, contributor. 1997. *Study power: Study skills to improve your learning and your grades.* Newton Upper Falls, MA: Brookline Books.

Luckie, William R., Wood Smethurst, and Sara Beth Huntley. 1999. *Study power workbook: Exercises in study skills to improve your learning and your grades.* Newton Upper Falls, MA: Brookline Books.

Meagher, Linda, and Thomas Devine. 1998. *Mastering study skills.* Upper Saddle River, NJ: Prentice Hall.

Sedita, Joan. 2001. *Study skills.* 2nd ed. Prides Crossing, MA: Landmark School. See http://www.landmarkschool.org. (The strategies in this teaching guide reflect the Landmark Teaching principles, which have been developed and refined over Landmark's thirty years of teaching students with learning disabilities.)

Semones, James K. 1991. *Effective study skills: A step-by-step system for achieving student success.* Independence, KY: Thomson Learning.

Strichart, Stephen S. 1997. *Study skills and strategies for high school students in the information age.* Upper Saddle River, NJ: Prentice Hall.

Resources for Teaching Social Skills

Most of these materials can be obtained from the A.D.D. WareHouse at 800-233-9273 or http://www.addwarehouse.com or from Childswork/Childsplay at 800-962-1141 or http://www.childswork.com. Use the companies' catalogs for a complete description of these and other materials that you can use for teaching social skills, self-control, and study skills.

Berg, Berthold. *The self-control game* (Cognitive-Behavioral Resources, 265 Canterbury Dr., Dayton, OH 45429). Other titles by Berg include *The Anger Control Game, The Social Skills Game,* and *The Self-Concept Game.*

Camp, B. W., and M. A. Bash. 1985. *Think aloud: Increasing social and cognitive skills—A problem-solving program for children.* Champaign, IL: Research Press.

Duke, M., S. Nowicki, and E. Martin. 1996. *Teaching your child the language of social success.* Atlanta, GA: Peachtree Publishers.

Elardo, P., and M. Cooper. 1977. *AWARE: Activities for Social Development.* Menlo Park, CA: Addison-Wesley.

Frankel, Fred. 1996. *Good friends are hard to find.* Los Angeles, CA: Perspective Publishing.

Goldstein, A. P. 1988. *The prepare curriculum: Teaching prosocial competencies.* Champaign, IL: Research Press.

Hazel, J. S., J. Bragg Schumaker, J. A. Sherman, and J. Sheldon-Wildgen. 1981. *Asset: A social skills program for adolescents.* Video program. Champaign, IL: Research Press.

Huggins, P. 1990. *Helping kids handle anger. Teaching self-control.* Longmont, CO: Sopris West.

Huggins, P., L. Moen, and D. Wood Manion. 1995. *Teaching friendship skills: Primary version.* Longmont, CO: Sopris West.

Iannucci, Cheryl. 2001. Social development and the adolescent: A Landmark School teaching guide for enhancing the social skills of students with learning disabilities. Prides Crossing, MA: Landmark School. http://www.landmarkschool.org.

Marano, Hara Estroff. 1998. *Why doesn't anybody like me?* New York: William Morrow & Company.

McGinnis, E., and A. P. Goldstein. 1990. *Skillstreaming in early childhood.* Champaign, IL: Research Press.

———. 1997. *Skillstreaming the elementary school child.* Rev. ed. Champaign, IL: Research Press.

———. 1997. *Skillstreaming the adolescent.* Rev. ed. Champaign, IL: Research Press.

Nowicki, S., and M. Duke. 1992. *Helping the child who doesn't fit in.* Atlanta, GA: Peachtree Publishers.

Packer, Alex. 1997. *How rude! The teenagers' guide to good manners, proper behavior, and not grossing people out.* Minneapolis, MN: Free Spirit Publishing.

Walker, H.M., B. Todis, D. Holmes, and G. Horton. 1988. *The Walker social skills curriculum: The ACCESS program.* Austin, TX: Pro-Ed.

Weltmann Begun, R., ed. 2002. *Ready-to-use social skills lessons and activities for grades PreK–K.* San Francisco, CA: Jossey-Bass.

———. 2002. *Ready-to-use social skills lessons and activities for grades 1–3.* San Francisco, CA: Jossey-Bass.

———. 2002. *Ready-to-use social skills lessons and activities for grades 4–6.* San Francisco, CA: Jossey-Bass.

———. 2002. *Ready-to-use social skills lessons and activities for grades 7–12.* San Francisco, CA: Jossey-Bass.

The following websites contain excellent and detailed information on specific study skills:

http://www.marblehead.com/guidance
http://www.iss.stthomas.edu/studyguides
http://www.ucc.vt.edu/stdysk/stdyhlp.html
http://www.how-to-study.com

CHAPTER 9

Helping Students with Emotional Barriers to Learning

In chapter 1, you read about Carla, a teenager who came from a good home and seemed to have a lot going for her. But she struggled in school even though she had no learning disability or ADHD. Her parents brought her to me for counseling, and I discovered she was depressed. Part of the problem was that she hadn't connected well emotionally with her mom.

I'm happy to report that in the time I knew her, Carla made a significant turnaround. She was able to accept herself and the reality of her life. She became a "big sister" to a grade school girl who had no family, and Carla's parents made some limited changes. Several teachers spent extra time with Carla and affirmed her artistic, musical, and theatrical abilities. That helped make up for some of the limitations of her mother, although there was still some heartache there. Her grades improved, and Carla had enough confidence later that year to run for a student-body office. She no longer had to create fantasy personalities to escape reality. The depression that had made her want to destroy everything in sight was almost completely alleviated, and Carla was able to be a normal teenager.

This chapter will address situations like Carla's in which the cause for difficulty in learning is an emotional barrier. We will explore the problem areas of stress, depression, divorce in the family, and family violence. Entire books have been written about each of these complicated topics, but this chapter should give you a good idea whether any student in your classroom may be suffering from one of these problems, as well as what can help.

Emotional Barriers Due to Stress

Burnout can occur when an event or the accumulation of events demands some type of adaptation or accommodation and overwhelms the resources a person has to deal with them. When the stressors are too much, some of the signs listed in chapter 3 will appear, and the process of coping with stress begins.

Stressors occur on a continuum of severity or intensity. Because terrorist attacks have become a major concern for citizens of the United States, this section will focus on how teachers can help students deal with major stressors such as natural disasters, shootings on campus, bomb threats, and terrorist attacks.

Helping Children Deal with Stress Associated with Disasters

Like adults, children experience feelings of helplessness and lack of control when they face disasters. The intense anxiety and fear that often follow a disaster or other traumatic event can be especially troubling for children. Some may regress and demonstrate behaviors such as thumb sucking or bed-wetting. Children may be more prone to nightmares, and they may be afraid of sleeping alone. Their performance in school may suffer. Other changes in behavior patterns may include throwing tantrums more frequently, or withdrawing and becoming more solitary.

Teachers and others who care for children can help alleviate the emotional consequences of trauma. The following are some suggestions.

Wait for children to ask about the event. Watch for those teachable moments. Then evaluate how distressed the child might actually be. Adjust your response to the child's needs. Don't give more details than necessary.

Children—as well as adults—want an explanation. Why did this happen? What does it mean? A complete explanation may not be easy or possible, but we must try. We must find a balance between helping a child feel safe and acknowledging the existence of violence and danger in the world. And we must explain in a manner appropriate to the child's ability to understand.

Don't be afraid to say, "I don't know." Part of keeping a discussion of the disaster open and honest is to avoid giving in to the fear of admitting you don't know how to answer a child's questions. When facing these questions, explain to your students that disasters are extremely rare and that even adults have trouble dealing with the feelings that result from them. Temper these comments by explaining that adults will always work very hard to keep children safe and secure.

Teachers should think through their own understanding of what happened, as difficult as that might be. It is important to discuss with students the fact that we really don't know the people involved or their circumstances. A disaster also offers an opportunity to teach by exploring politics, prejudice, and the use of violence to try to solve problems or resolve disputes. A discussion of faith and morality can include how evil can coexist with good in this world and how we make our choices. You might also talk about how to reach out in a tangible way to the families involved, the survivors, and the victims, such as by doing class projects.

You can help children remember and identify how much safety is in their lives. You can help them identify what they know about their own parents' love and devotion to them. They can review good times, birthdays, Christmases, and Thanksgivings. You can remind them of getting hugs when feeling down, ill, or injured. You can also assure them that the anger of a typical parent has limits and passes quickly. This assurance provides a chance to discuss with children how to express the normal feeling of anger in an appropriate manner. With older children who can understand finer distinctions, you can discuss how a healthy relationship is one in which people can repair rifts.

Parents as well as teachers need to spend more time than usual with children, letting them be more dependent during the months following the trauma. For example, adults can let children cling to them more often than usual. Children who have experienced trauma find physical affection very comforting.

You can provide play experiences to help relieve tension. Younger children in particular may find it easier to share their ideas and feelings about the event through nonverbal activities such as drawing.

Encourage older children to speak with you and with one another about their thoughts and feelings. If they do so, their confusion and anxiety related to the trauma will decrease. Respond to questions in terms students can comprehend. Reassure them repeatedly that you care about them and that you understand their fears and concerns.

Encourage parents to limit children's media viewing because images of the disaster and the damage are extremely frightening to children. A good way for parents to do so without calling attention to their own concern is to schedule regular activities during news shows, such as reading stories, drawing, watching movies, or writing letters.

To help restore a sense of security and normalcy, families should keep regular schedules. Children benefit from knowing the times they typically participate in activities such as eating, playing, and going to bed. However, children may continue showing distress or such signs of anxiety as changes in behavior, increased aggression, nightmares, clingi-ness, headaches, tummy-aches, shyness, decreased concentration, poor sleep, or a change in appetite. If these signs persist, consider having the child evaluated by a mental health professional who specializes in car-ing for children.

Providing Spiritual Comfort

Eighty percent of the power to cope comes from people's perception of an event or a situation. If people believe they can deal with a situation, it is likely that they will handle it adequately. However, if people are mostly pessimistic about their ability to overcome an obstacle, the chances are high that they will fail. It all boils down to perception.

The psalmist captured this predicament as well as its solution when he wrote, "God is our refuge and strength, an ever-present help in trou-ble. Therefore we will not fear" (Psalm 46:1–2). The Hebrew word for *trouble* in that passage means to be in a narrow, tight place, or to be constricted, distressed, and cramped. We might put it another way by saying that trouble means being "between a rock and a hard place." This description accurately fits a stressful situation, one in which we appear trapped regardless of what we do. We think that we have nowhere to turn and that we're running out of resources.

However, Christians have hope. Solomon declared that "there is noth-ing new under the sun" (Ecclesiastes 1:9), and that statement includes stress. No matter how severe and frustrating a situation is, God is always with us. He created the laws of the universe, and those same laws affect our stress. We may not understand them all, but God does. And surely the One who makes the rules ought to be able to help us out of any bind.

We're not left to our own resources. God is for us (Romans 8:31), and that knowledge can make a big difference in our willingness to deal with stressful situations. We can walk through dark valleys without fear (Psalm 23:4). The power of God is absolute. "Nothing is too hard for you," exclaimed Jeremiah (Jeremiah 32:17). "With man this is impossible, but not with God; all things are possible with God," said Jesus to His disciples (Mark 10:27). This kind of hope can give your students the ability to cope with stress. They don't have to accomplish everything in their own power. God is there to help.

Helping in Additional Ways

Teachers can help children cope with difficult situations by providing an atmosphere of safety, security, and support. They can conduct classroom activities that may facilitate coping, and they can take care of themselves.

In times of uncertainty, children need someone, someplace, or something they can rely on for safety, security, and fulfillment. They need a place where they know that they matter and what they do matters, where their actions have consequences, where they can depend on people, and where they can count on activities that happen in predictable ways. Teachers can provide this kind of atmosphere by doing the following:

- Greet each child warmly each day. The transition from parent to teacher is important. Often mornings are extremely stressful for families. Adults may have yelled at students, hurried them, and given them breakfast in the car. A warm smile or hug as children walk in the classroom door can go a long way to help them feel accepted and wanted.
- Spend time with each child every day. Even if it's just for one or two minutes, get down on the children's level, make eye contact, listen, and watch.
- Value each child. Children learn to value themselves through the eyes and words of others. What you say or don't say to children has tremendous impact.

- Eliminate stressful situations from your classroom and routines. Ask yourself the following questions:
  - Is my room arrangement simple and easy to move through?
  - Are activity areas, such as the art area, block area, and reading/quiet area, clearly defined?
  - Do I have a balance of noisy areas, such as those for blocks and dramatic play, and quiet areas, such as those for books and manipulatives?
  - Have I planned my day so that quiet activities alternate with active ones and organized projects alternate with free play?
  - Do I stick to a routine whenever possible so that children know what to expect each day?
  - Do I listen and respond to verbal and nonverbal cues?
  - Do I notice and acknowledge things about children, keeping track of and commenting on what's going on in their lives?
  - Do I give children reassurance, support, and encouragement?
  - Do I provide structure, stability, and predictability through predictable routines, clear expectations, consistent rules, and immediate feedback?

(DeBord 1993)

Children might need extra understanding and patience, but this fact does not mean we should excessively coddle them and let them get away with inappropriate behavior. In fact, teachers should maintain their expectations for behavior and performance and should not be afraid of using discipline. At the same time, however, they should be prepared to provide extra support and encouragement.

Let children talk about experiences and express fears and concerns. Let them know that it is okay and quite natural to feel angry, sad, or frightened, and that talking about these feelings will make them feel better. You might share your own feelings. Activities that let them hear how others feel will help them realize that their feelings are not bad or unusual.

In the classroom, you can help children cope with difficulties. Suggestions include the following:

- Provide activities that encourage children to share experiences and express feelings of fear or concern.
- Conduct study projects or multidisciplinary units focused on learning about disasters. Students can learn and apply math, science, and language skills in exploring the causes and consequences of natural disasters.
- Introduce units on disaster preparedness or health and safety to give students a sense of competence, confidence, and control regarding how to handle disasters in the future.
- Encourage service projects that provide students with an opportunity to contribute to their family, school, and community.

Helping Children Cope in School

The following three shool activities can help children deal with disaster (University of Illinois Extension Disaster Resources 1998):

Storytelling
You can use oral or written storytelling to help children reenact their experiences in a constructive manner. Encouraging group discussion after the children each relate their story allows them to assist one another.

Arts Projects
You can encourage children to express their feelings by drawing what they have felt, wished, or dreamed after a disaster. As with storytelling, the children can talk about their drawings in a group discussion. Nonverbal activities promote the sharing of feelings and the beginning of grieving.

Group Projects
You can lead a group discussion in which children talk about what they could do to assist in the recovery efforts. Examples might include gathering books and toys for the relief effort or working together on a clean-up project, especially in schools that have been seriously affected.

Other Emotional Barriers to Learning

The sections that follow contain descriptions of several areas of emotional difficulty that can have a major impact on classroom performance. We'll address depression in children, the effects of divorce on children, and the effects of abuse and family violence on children.

Taking Action When You Suspect a Student Is Depressed

If you think one of your students is depressed, you should first consult with the family to see whether they are seeing the same symptoms and are also concerned for the child. You would want to inquire about any major changes or losses in the family, such as the death of a family member or a pet. If you and the parents concur about the possibility of depression, you may want to suggest the parents make a doctor's appointment for the child. The purpose would be to obtain a complete physical examination that fully explores all medical possibilities for why the child is exhibiting tiredness, lethargy, irritability, loss of appetite, or some combination of these. The parents need to tell the doctor why both of you are concerned. They might take along a copy of the previous checklist of depression symptoms and have in mind possible sources of the child's feelings.

The doctor's evaluation will consist of a history and an examination. The history is an interview. The doctor is looking for the development of the symptoms, as well as possible sources and causes. These procedures are intended to rule out any neurological or toxic causes for the depression. Medical conditions such as diabetes, thyroid problems, or calcium problems can create depression-like symptoms. A brain tumor is an example of a neurological condition that can mimic depression. The medical exam should also address the possibility of toxic conditions such as drug usage, allergies, and carbon monoxide or formaldehyde poisoning (Herskowitz 1988).

Various types of tests can rule out these physical conditions. If everything proves negative from the medical standpoint, the next step is to explore the psychological sources of the depression. If the child has a physical problem, the doctor will tell the parents how to improve their child's health. If the doctor does not find a medical basis for the depression, the next step is to consult with a mental health professional.

This counselor will probably meet with the parents to obtain background information and will then interview the child. The counselor may choose to meet with the entire family in order to understand the family dynamics and how they affect the child. The first step is to get an overview of the symptoms, of the development of the child, and of the possible stressors and their impact on the child.

This process can take place through a variety of methods. The parents and perhaps the teacher can complete several rating scales or observation forms regarding the child. The counselor may conduct a structured interview with the child, as well as give various tests. Those could include projective tests that require the child to tell stories, complete sentences, draw pictures, or describe pictures. The results of these methods can be interpreted to diagnose whether the child is depressed, and if so, why.

Other types of tests may be used when the specialist thinks they are appropriate. It is important to rule out coexisting conditions such as learning disabilities, attention deficits, or other emotional features such as mood disorders. After the diagnostic part of the process, the clinician will meet with the parents to describe the findings and propose a treatment plan.

Treatment may involve the entire family in sessions, individual therapy for the child, group counseling, or a combination of these activities. The decision depends on the needs of the child and how best to deal with them. I've encountered situations in which the diagnosis of depression was rather clear because of the child's recent behavior and mood. However, the source of the depression wasn't immediately evident. In such cases, I've told the parents I needed to spend more time with their child in building a relationship of trust. Usually, after a number of weeks of therapy, the source of the depression became clearer.

Numerous times I've had children disclose sexual abuse after several months of therapy. The child was too fearful to reveal the "secret" in the beginning. In such cases, nobody but the perpetrator and victim knew what had happened. Once the children made the disclosure, treatment could follow a definite sequence.

I've had non-abused children come out of their depression and learn to deal with life in healthier ways without my ever identifying a specific source of the problem. It was just a matter of too many little frustrations and disappointments overwhelming a child's resources and support system. Yet, in the eyes of these children, everything seemed hopeless, and their coping skills were inadequate.

In many cases, family issues were the problem. For example, by doing everything for their children, overprotective parents may limit their children's opportunity to build emotional stamina. This scenario results in children who have not had much experience in coping with problems. So when rather normal frustrations come, the children don't have the ability to persevere, and one consequence can be depression.

In other cases, one of the parents had only marginal ability to deal with life's stressors. The child sensed the tenuous balance in the home and took on some of the parent's problem. As a result, the child became vulnerable to feelings of depression in an effort to keep the parent from experiencing any more pain.

The treatment for depression can be multilevel and multidisciplinary, just like the treatment for learning disabilities and ADHD described earlier. We must acknowledge and give attention to the whole child— the intellectual, spiritual, social, emotional, and physical attributes.

Helping Children of Divorce

Divorce is a devastating process. There's no way to get through it without some pain and suffering. The experience will leave lifelong negative effects. Our goal must be to minimize the damage and do everything possible to support the children.

How Parents Can Help

You might make the following suggestions to the parents when you learn they are experiencing an impending separation or divorce:

- First and foremost, try to reconcile the marriage. I know sometimes that doesn't seem possible. Yet many broken marriages have been saved. The process is difficult, but the pain of divorce is damaging to both you and your kids. Weigh the options and consequences carefully.

- Provide your children with age-appropriate reasons for the divorce, along with a forecasting of upcoming events. Give your children some idea of the timeline, living arrangements, and other details as you learn them. Provide continuous assurance to your children that their basic needs will be meet.

- Don't make promises you can't keep. Be realistic about plans, and don't build up your kids' hopes for events that are doubtful. Avoid becoming a Disneyland parent. Both parents should share in discipline when possible.

- Help your children verbalize their feelings. They need to talk about their distress, anger, and anxiety. A chance to grieve is critical at this time. The stages of denial, anxiety, anger, depression, manipulation, unrealistic hope, and final acceptance all apply to grief over divorce. Children also need to explore with someone their understanding of why their parents are separating, as well as to verbalize their hopes.

- It's crucial to assure kids that the divorce or separation was not their fault. Explain to them that nothing they did or didn't do was responsible for your problems. Also help children understand that, by their own efforts, they can't bring you and your spouse back together. Stress these points continually because most children will constantly try to take on some of the blame.

- Give appropriate reassurances. Build hope that things will eventually work out, even if divorce does occur. Doing so means that you have to believe it in order to convey it convincingly. You should not avoid acknowledging the reality of the family struggle, yet remember that children need help in maintaining their confidence. They need to know they're not helpless in the situation. Look for ways to enhance their sense of empowerment. Give them choices to make, and affirm their strengths.
- A support system is vital. This is a crucial time to get help from extended family, church family, and other support systems. Don't be afraid to ask for assistance and to be clear about your needs. If one parent is absent, try to find a supportive big brother or sister, or increase access to someone such as a nurturing grandparent.
- Maintain consistency in routine. Keep as much predictability as possible in the daily schedule. Discuss plans with your children ahead of time, and minimize any departure from those plans.
- It may seem contradictory, but the more you as the parents can agree about issues in the parenting plan, the better your children will adjust to the realities of divorce. Research shows that the more parents fight during and after the divorce, the more their children are traumatized (Kitzmann and Emery 1994). Try to cooperate with each other. Minimize court battles. Use a mediation process if at all possible.

How Teachers Can Help

Teachers can't solve the problems of children who are experiencing parental divorce. However, you can help children learn to cope. Many children whose families are involved in the divorce process worry about abandonment. Caring teachers are in a position to reassure students. Like parents, teachers should not make promises they're powerless to keep. However, you can work to make your classroom as stable and predictable as possible. The following are some specific actions that can help children of divorce:

- Help the children feel a sense of control. During divorce, most kids experience a loss of control. Their world is turned upside down, often quite rapidly. Teachers can help by being consistent, particularly in setting limits, and by offering many choices of worthwhile activities so the children have opportunities to feel in control.
- Provide a conflict-free haven for students. Children need a buffer zone between themselves and parental conflict. Most parenting plans will specify that the parents should refrain from fighting when their children are present. But parental arguments are bound to happen. The classroom can be one place where the children are free from conflict.
- Know your students. Children of divorce often don't reveal what's happening at home. Teachers can take the initiative in identifying students who are in homes with separated or divorced parents. Check school records and confer with parents regularly to keep current on family circumstances that may affect a child's learning.
- Encourage children to talk about their feelings. Most children of divorce will have strong feelings of anger and sadness. Grief, loss, helplessness, loneliness, rejection, and anxiety are also common emotions. Children need to know that it's OK to have those feelings and that many other children have them also. Teachers may use journals, puppets and dolls, role-playing, drawing, and creative-writing strategies to encourage children to express such feelings.
- Use books to explore feelings with the children and to teach coping skills. You can read fiction books aloud or make them available for independent reading. An increasing number of juvenile books dealing with divorce are available, written from both Christian and secular perspectives.
- Help children become aware that they're not alone. Use various instructional activities to explore different family structures. Have students write stories, prepare booklets, bring pictures, and make collages that describe their respective families. As these are described and displayed, both diversity and commonality of family situations will be evident.

- Make language and assignments inclusive by taking into account the variety of family structures represented in the classroom. Grandparents, aunts, uncles, stepparents, family friends, and other caretakers may be involved in activities such as conferences, open houses, and project preparations. Explain to students that "Parents' Night" can include many different people who may want to know how the children's classroom functions. Be aware of transitions between parents, and strive to communicate with both parents so that someone monitors assignments and other classroom requirements consistently.

- Be flexible and tolerant of behavior changes. At one time or another, children are probably going to act out, show restlessness or anxiety, and struggle with concentration. Fridays and Mondays can be problematic for many children who visit with the noncustodial parent on weekends. Teachers can learn the visitation patterns for their students and try to accommodate each child's transitions. Students may need flexibility in completing assignments, time-outs to steady their emotions, or a chance to talk with the school counselor.

- Try to keep communication open with both parents. Divorce complicates communication. You may have to duplicate parent conferences or make other adjustments to keep both parents informed. Many children of divorce have to adapt to two households. They have to shuffle textbooks and assignments between homes. Teachers should do everything possible to keep parents informed of assignments and deadlines, and teachers must also be aware of transportation, guardianship, and custody issues. School policy may influence how they operate regarding these matters since kidnapping by parents is a possibility in some cases.

- Make recommendations for outside help when necessary. If you see students falling further and further behind or becoming more distraught, contact the parents and give them alternatives for counseling, tutoring, classes for children of divorce, and other community resources.

(Carlile 1991; Frieman 1993)

With understanding and strong communication, you can make a major contribution to the lives of children whose parents are experiencing conflict, separation, or even divorce. You can assist in improving the academic performance of those students, as well as in ministering to some of their emotional needs. You can't cure the problems, but you can be a critical element in helping children cope with a major stressor.

Helping Victimized Children

You might find yourself dealing with two types of situations involving an abused student. One occurs when the abuse has been disclosed and reported, and the child is currently in some type of treatment. You will find the general descriptions about the course of treatment later in this section.

In the second situation, the child reports something to you that raises the suspicion of abuse. In such cases, use the following guidelines:
- If children even hint in a vague way that sexual abuse has occurred, encourage them to talk freely. Don't make judgmental comments.
- Show that you understand and take seriously what the children are saying. Children who feel listened to and understood do much better than those who do not. The response to the disclosure of sexual abuse is critical to children's ability to resolve and heal the trauma of the abuse.
- Assure children that telling the truth was the correct action to take. Children who are close to the abuser may feel guilty about revealing the secret. The children may also feel frightened if the abuser has threatened to harm them or other family members as punishment for telling the secret.
- Tell the children they are not to blame for the sexual abuse. In attempting to make sense out of the abuse, most children will believe that somehow they caused it, or they may even view it as a form of punishment for imagined or real wrongdoings.

- Offer the children protection, and promise that you will promptly take steps to assure that the abuse stops.

(American Academy of Child and Adolescent Psychiatry 1997)

As a teacher, you are required to report any suspicion of child abuse. You can make reports by phone, in writing, or in person to a local law enforcement agency, Department of Social and Health Services, or Child Protective Services. Take the time to find out the proper procedures in your locality.

The report will consist of the name, address, and age of the child; the name and address of the adult having custody; and the nature and extent of the injury, neglect, or sexual abuse. The report should also include any other information that might help establish the cause of the abuse and the possible identity of the perpetrator.

All fifty states mandate reporting of all types of abuse, including sexual abuse. For most educational personnel, failure to report suspected child abuse is a misdemeanor. In most areas the responsibility for identifying and reporting abuse belongs to people who have direct contact with children as part of their job or profession. Although any citizen may report, most state laws name medical personnel, mental health workers, educators, and clergy. Those who report abuse are generally given immunity from liability and can remain anonymous, as long as the report was made in good faith. A report of suspected child abuse, sexual or otherwise, should be based on concern for the health and safety of the child, not on a desire to punish the caretakers. The agency receiving the report will conduct an evaluation and will take action to protect the child.

As soon as possible, a physician who specializes in evaluating and treating sexual abuse should see the child. The examining doctor will evaluate the child's condition, treat any physical problem related to the abuse, gather evidence to help protect the child, and reassure the child that he or she is all right.

While most allegations of sexual abuse made by children are true, some false accusations may arise in custody disputes and in other situations. Adults, because of their maturity and knowledge, are always to blame when they abuse children. The abused children should never be blamed.

The majority of abused children will need medical help, psychological help, or both. One in three children who come from homes where domestic violence is present will need some kind of treatment, usually for seven to eighteen months. The following describe how intervention should take place:

- The first priority is to stop the violence. This step may involve using legal procedures to remove the perpetrator, followed by a whole host of legal, social, economic, and emotional actions. The family will need support through the crisis stage—financial and medical support, assistance in job-skills training, help in learning coping skills, and many other practical forms of aid.

- The victim and the family need education and therapy. Medical attention will obviously be necessary to treat broken bones. However, while bones usually heal, the inner hurts can last a lifetime. Addressing issues of self-blame, trust, feelings of being damaged goods, identity, and empowerment is often crucial when counseling victims of abuse.

- Victimized children often need instruction in social skills. They need to learn to interact with others and increase their skills in empathizing and in dealing with feelings in such situations.

- Usually children need to have attention paid to their negative thought patterns that accompany depression and to their feelings of helplessness. Victimized children have been so overwhelmed from hearing critical conversations that they need major doses of positive and healthy input.

- The second major priority of intervention is to break the cycle of violence. There are no simple ways of doing this. For starters, we need to find ways to become a less violent society. Limiting violent television programming would help. I encourage parents to avoid letting their children use violent toys and play violent games. Above all, we need to model and teach nonviolent ways of dealing with anger and to show children alternative ways of handling their aggressiveness.

- In domestic violence situations, all the issues relating to spousal abuse need attention. Because the children often end up living in single-parent homes, the parent—usually the mother—will need help in learning how to discipline her children and deal with the aftereffects of her battering experience.

- Prevention of further abuse is the final priority. History suggests that it's a losing battle. However, as long as I have energy to give and a heart to loan out, I'm committed to the task. What can we do? We need to engage in more research on methods of prevention, develop new methods of instruction in conflict resolution, and find ways for all people to have some sense of empowerment, productivity, and fulfillment of basic needs. Above all, we must speak to the God-created vacuum that exists in everyone. Until people bring God and the person of Jesus Christ into their hearts and decision making, no permanent change will take place. As His followers, we must all do our part in bringing the good news of the gospel to a broken world.

(Martin 1987, 1992)

Counseling is important for victims of abuse and their families. However, seeking the healing touch of Jesus is most crucial of all. The treatment and prevention of child abuse and victimization makes an important distinction between good and bad touches. As Christians, we have the promise of the Christ who brought healing to those He touched (Luke 22:51). We see the cleansing touch of Jesus when He cured the leper (Matthew 8:3), the quieting touch of Jesus when He lifted the fever of Peter's mother-in-law (Matthew 8:15), the illuminating touch of Jesus when He opened the eyes of the blind men (Matthew 9:29–30), and the reassuring touch of Jesus for those who were afraid (Matthew 17:7). Finally, we see Him giving a special touch to children (Mark 10:13, 16).

My heart goes out to those who have experienced the evil effects of abuse. As Christians and thus the representatives of God, we have an opportunity to be part of the restoration process. We can claim the healing touch of the Master's hand.

Conclusion

In this chapter, we've seen how stress, depression, parental divorce, abuse, and family violence can produce emotional problems that make it hard for children to learn. We've also seen how teachers, along with parents and others, can help. But above all, we must remember that God is the Great Physician. He Himself said, "I will restore you to health and heal your wounds" (Jeremiah 30:17).

References

American Academy of Child and Adolescent Psychiatry. 1997. Responding to child sexual abuse. *Facts for Families* 28:1–2.

Carlile, C. 1991. Children of divorce: How teachers can help ease the pain. *Childhood Education* 67, no. 4:232–34.

DeBord, K. 1993. Disaster recovery: Children's needs. NC State University Cooperative Extension. http://www.ces.ncsu.edu/depts/fcs/ human-dev/disas3.html.

Frieman, B. B. 1993. Separation and divorce: Children want their teachers to know. *Young Children* (September): 58–63.

Herskowitz, J. 1988. *Is your child depressed?* New York: Pharos Books.

Kitzmann, K. M. and R. E. Emery. 1994. Child and family coping one year after mediated and litigated child custody disputes. *Journal of Family Psychology* (June): 24–38.

Martin, G. L. 1987. *Counseling in cases of family violence and abuse.* Vol. 6. Dallas, TX: Word.

——. 1992. *Critical problems in children and youth: Counseling techniques for problems resulting from attention deficit disorder, sexual abuse, custody battles, and related issues.* Dallas, TX: Word.

University of Illinois Extension Disaster Resources. 1998. Children, stress, and natural disasters: A guide for teachers. University of Illinois Cooperative Extension. http://www.ag.uiuc.edu/~disaster/teacher/csndresx.html.

CHAPTER 10

Helping Underachieving Students

Jerry was a talented junior high student. However, you wouldn't know it by looking at his grades. His parents were sure he could do better, but they weren't sure how to help him, so they brought him to me for counsel. I quickly determined he was, indeed, capable of doing well in school. So why wasn't he?

After talking with Jerry and testing him to rule out the other kinds of learning problems we've examined in this book, I decided perhaps all he needed was the right kind of motivation. I learned he was interested in flying, and his parents discovered that his school offered an after-hours aviation program run by the science teacher. Together we encouraged Jerry to give it a try.

The program included instruction and experiments in the principles of flight and aircraft design. The students were given basic flight instruction and spent time in a flight simulator at a nearby Boeing aircraft training center. Later they were paired with private pilots who became mentors to them. For the next two years, Jerry got together with his pilot mentor about once a month, and they would take the mentor's private plane on trips all over western Washington.

Jerry took to this program like a duck to water. The exposure opened his eyes to the world of flight in a way he had never experienced before. The last I heard, he was working to his full potential in school and intending to pursue a career in aviation. Who knows—he may become a member of the next generation of space station astronauts!

Jerry is a good example of the last type of learning problem we will discuss in this book. Many students who ought to be average or better students and who have no learning disabilities, no ADHD, and no serious emotional problems just aren't achieving at a level we would reasonably expect. What can we do for these students?

Also included in this discussion is the highly capable student who has the ability for outstanding academic success but is underachieving in one or more areas. Athletic, artistic, and musical abilities can also be included in a description of the capable student, though most of the discussion here will deal with academic concerns. A section at the end of the book lists more specialized resources about gifted students.

This chapter also presents the related issue of whether students should ever be retained in their current grade instead of being promoted to the next level. Often done after the kindergarten year, retention is sometimes suggested for learning-disabled, ADHD, and some underachieving students who are considered socially or academically immature. Retention can take place as late as the fourth or fifth grade. I'll note briefly the research findings concerning this practice and will make some recommendations.

Underachievement in Capable Students

It's possible for people who have special gifts to go through life with their gifts largely unrecognized. To their closest friends or family, they don't seem that different. In some cases, the family does not place any value on the special abilities and thus may not recognize them. In other cases, students may not have the opportunity to further their abilities because of economic or cultural limitations.

In our previous discussions of learning disabilities, attention deficits, and emotional problems, the goal was to remove or accommodate the problem. With capable students, the goal is to enhance, not eliminate, the characteristic. However, some students consider it a risk to demonstrate their talent. It may be the risk of stigma and social rejection for those who are intellectually, artistically, or musically superior. A high-achieving student may face criticism or ostracism by fellow students and even adults. Our cultural values emphasize self-satisfaction, group identity, immediate gratification, and superficial entertainment. Such values can make it hard for students who desire to excel in a given area.

Another kind of frustration is found in what one author calls the "conundrum kid." This is the student with high abilities in certain areas accompanied by learning disabilities in other areas. One student may have high conceptual power but low reading or writing skills. Another may have outstanding language skills but minimal math skills. Some students may excel in art or music but flounder in formal academics.

The huge discrepancies between their strengths and weaknesses cause much of the pain that these students experience academically. The greater the discrepancy, the more intense the discomfort. The unexercised talents itch because of lack of attention, and the exposed and unsupported weaknesses ache because of public exposure. Such students need help to acquire the necessary skills and assistance to nurture their talent (Vail 1987).

Causes of Underachievement

Students may fail to achieve at a level consistent with their abilities for a variety of reasons. The following are some of the most common:
- They have emotional conflicts, either in themselves or in their relationships.
- They have a dysfunctional home environment.
- They have inappropriate school programming. Schoolwork may be unchallenging and boring, content irrelevant to their personal interests, and the instructional process inappropriate to their natural learning style.
- They have a negative self-image and a negative attitude toward school.
- They experience a lack of nurturing in their classroom climate.
- They feel the effects of sexual stereotypes. Many girls achieve far less than they might because of social or cultural barriers to their selection of or progress in certain careers.
- They encounter racial or ethnic bias in identification of or programming for their abilities.
- They are capable students who have obvious disabilities and are thus overlooked or denied opportunities to achieve.

(Hallahan and Kauffman 1994)

If you have a student who is not achieving to the degree you think is appropriate, you need to take several actions. First, look at your expectations. You must differentiate between underachievement and nonproductivity. Students should not have to produce at remarkable levels all the time. They need periods of rest and recuperation, during which time their creative energies are restored, relationships are renewed, and perspective is refocused. Academic achievement, while important, should not have the highest or exclusive priority in students' total development.

Below are six principles to keep in mind as you work with your capable students. These principles reflect the importance of having goals that draw on the whole person, not just the intellect. While this section focuses on capable students, these principles apply to all students, regardless of their abilities:

- The whole person is important. While reading and math are important, character development, morality, and healthy relationships are also critical components for the well-educated person.
- Not everything people do well is necessarily enjoyable to them. Just because students have talent in a particular area doesn't mean they have to spend the rest of their life pursuing that exclusive area of interest.
- Friends are important, and they are influential. However, students should realize that it is OK to have talent and interests that their friends do not have. Students need to understand that they can even enjoy being talented in some areas that are unpopular with some of their friends, such as science or the marching band.
- Life is not a race to see who can get to the end the fastest. Capable students need a reminder to enjoy living. They need to take time to smell the roses and to value the present and the memories that they can create. Students need to know not to judge their success solely on obtaining a degree, a perfect job, or a prestigious career. Like all people, they need to be willing to take risks, even in areas in which they have not experienced success.
- Students need to feel free to ask unconventional questions. They need encouragement in becoming involved in making the world a better place. Students need instruction and modeling in how to see God-created order, or patterns, in people, places, and things.
- It is never too late to establish and pursue new goals. Regardless of earlier choices and outcomes, students need to realize they can redirect their lives and pursue their dreams.

(Delisle 1992)

In regard to underachieving students, the second action you should take is to confirm their learning abilities. What's the exact nature and range of their abilities and interests? Is there any chance that a limitation or disability may be present? Review the questions and procedures presented earlier in this book to determine whether a more comprehensive evaluation might be helpful. If there's reason to be concerned, suggest that the family have their child evaluated.

The third part of your action plan is to look for ways to encourage and motivate your underachieving students. Remember, there's no such thing as no motivation. Rather it's a matter of finding the areas in which your students are motivated. I know this assignment can be difficult. Some students seem to hide their motivational hot buttons. However, the key to unlocking your students' potential is to cultivate that dormant seed of interest.

On the basis of a review of many efforts to work with underachieving students, I've selected the following ideas for your consideration. I can't guarantee which will work with your students. You may need a counselor or learning specialist to guide you. I would remind you to never give up. Keep trying, and continue praying. Eventually, something should help your students move toward educational success.

Family Contributions to Successful Achievement in Capable Students

Academically capable and talented students probably have inherited their ability. However, the role of the family is crucial in bringing their skills to full potential. Some years ago, several well-known researchers studied a number of people who, before the age of thirty-five, had demonstrated the highest levels of accomplishment as artists, athletes, and scholars. The research included concert pianists, sculptors, Olympic swimmers, tennis players, research mathematicians, and research neurologists. The study focused partly on the role of the home in developing those competent individuals.

The most striking finding was the active role of the family—along with selected teachers and sometimes peers—in supporting, encouraging, teaching, and training these people at each stage in their development. None of them reached their high level of success on their own (Bloom 1982). The researchers found that the following characteristics were common in those who eventually achieved at the highest level:

- One or both parents, or sometimes a sibling or other relative, had a personal interest in the students' talent and provided strong support and encouragement for its development.
- There was specific parental encouragement of the students to explore and participate in home activities related to the area of developing talent. In meaningful ways, the parents rewarded even small signs of interest and capability.
- There's a great parallel between early learning of some aspects of the talent field and early learning of the mother tongue. The parents seemed to assume that their children would learn more naturally in the area of talent just as one would acquire a language. Thus they had a more relaxed set of expectations in the early childhood years.
- Most of the parents were role models, at least early in their children's development, and were highly influential in lifestyle, values, conduct, and decisions. They taught those values by modeling, by direct teaching, and by creating consequences such as rewards and punishments.
- The students' set of expected behaviors were taught on a schedule and to a standard that seemed appropriate to their families at each stage of the students' development.
- Teaching in the home took place in a great variety of informal ways. Much of the early learning was exploratory and very much like play.
- If the students demonstrated competitiveness, along with a willingness to work to achieve a high standard, these qualities became the criteria that parents used to determine whether to invest additional time and money in developing the students' talent.
- Part or all of the instruction the talented students received was one on one. A tutor, teacher, or coach diagnosed what was needed, then set learning objectives and provided instruction

with frequent feedback and correction. The teachers developed objectives and standards that addressed specific tasks, which students accomplished in their own individual ways.

- Parents worked closely with the teacher regarding what the students needed to do at home before the next lesson. Such planning included the amount of time the students needed to practice, as well as a detailed list of the tasks the students needed to accomplish.

- Parents observed the students during practice, insisted they put in the appropriate amount of practice time, and, when necessary, referred them to the procedures the teacher had suggested.

- When the students did something especially well or attained the standard of performance that the teacher set, the parents showed approval of the students and rewarded their progress.

- Even in later stages of development, the families supplied encouragement and resources, provided special outside help if needed, and helped the students consider options for the future.

- Parents encouraged participation in events such as recitals, contests, and concerts in which the students displayed their special capabilities publicly. Those activities provided significant rewards and approval for accomplishments, giving the students the motivation to apply greater effort to learning in anticipation of the public event.

- After age twelve, the talented students spent as much time on their talent field each week as their average peers spent watching television.

- The researchers noted that the families had a much harder time playing a large role in enforcing practice, homework, and maintenance of work standards if those behaviors had not become habitual for the students before the teenage years.

- The researchers observed that as the skill and age of the students increased, there might be less of a partnership between the parents and the talent teachers. This tendency is especially likely when the teacher is a renowned specialist and the talented student has already developed a practice routine, a set of standards, and a level of self-criticism that approximate the teacher's.

(Bloom 1982; Bloom and Sosniak 1981)

Your students may not be destined to become Olympic athletes or Carnegie Hall performers. However, the preceding observations still have relevance regarding how you might foster inspiration in capable youngsters who don't seem motivated.

Strategies to Reverse Patterns of Underachievement

Ideas for the Classroom

Teachers must consider several questions regarding the nature and extent of students' underachievement. On the basis of your best answer to these questions, you can begin to formulate a strategy to help the students:

- Is the underachievement chronic, situational, or temporary?
- Is the underachievement general or subject specific?
- What factors—such as poor intrinsic motivation, poor academic self-esteem, negative peer pressure, lack of family involvement, poor student-teacher relationships, and low teacher expectations—are contributing to the underachievement?

Three types of strategies have been found effective in working with underachieving students. The first is supportive strategies. This approach uses classroom techniques and designs that allow students to feel they're part of a "family" instead of a "factory." Activities include, for example, holding class meetings to discuss student concerns, designing curriculum activities that are based on the needs and interests of the students, and allowing students to bypass assignments on subjects in which they have previously shown competence.

The second type of help is intrinsic strategies. These tactics incorporate the idea that students' self-concepts as learners are tied closely to their desire to achieve academically. Thus, classrooms that invite positive attitudes are likely to encourage achievement. In classrooms of this type, teachers encourage attempts, not just successes. They value student input in creating rules and responsibilities. Teachers might also allow students to evaluate their own work before receiving a grade.

The third approach is the use of remedial strategies. Teachers who are effective in reversing underachieving behaviors recognize that students aren't perfect. These teachers understand that all students have specific strengths and weaknesses, as well as social, emotional, and intellectual needs. With remedial strategies, students get opportunities to excel in their areas of strength and interest while they receive help in specific areas of learning deficiency. Students do their work in a safe environment in which mistakes are considered a part of learning for everyone, including teachers. The key to eventual success lies in the willingness of parents and teachers to encourage students whenever their performance or attitude shifts, even slightly, in a positive direction. The use of any of the accommodation and remediation techniques described in earlier chapters would be appropriate for these students (Delisle and Berger 1990).

Ideas for Parents
The following are some broad guidelines that parents may use to prevent or reverse underachieving behavior. The same three categories of supportive, intrinsic, and remedial strategies apply to the family context. You might provide copies of this section to parents as you work together to encourage development in the capable but underachieving students.

Supportive Strategies
Many capable students thrive in a mutually respectful, nonauthoritarian, flexible, questioning atmosphere. They need reasonable rules and guidelines, strong encouragement, consistently positive feedback, and help in accepting some limitations—their own as well as those of others. These principles apply to all students. However, some parents of highly capable children believe that advanced intellectual ability results in advanced social and emotional skills. That's not necessarily true, but on the basis of this assumption, such parents may allow their children excessive decision-making power before these children have the wisdom and experience to handle the responsibility.

Capable youngsters need adults who are willing to listen to their questions without comment. Sometimes, students ask questions as a preface to giving their opinions, so quick answers prevent them from using adults as a sounding board. When problem solving is appropriate, parents should encourage students to come up with their own answers and criteria for choosing the best solution. Parents need to listen carefully and show genuine enthusiasm about children's observations, interests, activities, and goals. While being sensitive to problems, parents should avoid conveying unrealistic or conflicting expectations and solving problems their kids are capable of managing. It is wise to provide children and adolescents with a wide variety of opportunities for success, a sense of accomplishment, and a belief in themselves.

Adults can encourage students to volunteer to help others as an avenue for developing tolerance, empathy, understanding, and acceptance of human limitations. Above all, students need guidance toward activities and goals that reflect their values, interests, and needs—not just those of the parents.

Finally, families should reserve some time to have fun, to be silly, and to share daily activities. All youngsters need to feel connected to people who are consistently supportive.

Intrinsic Strategies
Whether a capable youngster uses exceptional ability in constructive ways depends, in part, on self-acceptance and self-concept. According to one expert, "An intellectually gifted student will not be happy and complete until [he or she] is using intellectual ability at a level approaching full capacity.... It is important that parents and teachers see intellectual development as a requirement for these students, and not merely as an interest, a flair, or a phase they will outgrow" (Halsted 1988).

Providing an early, appropriate educational environment can stimulate a love for learning. Young, curious students may easily be "turned off" if the educational environment is not stimulating or if class placement and teaching approaches are inappropriate. Lack of motivation can also result if students have ineffective teachers or if assignments are consistently too difficult or too easy. The ability of capable students to define and solve problems in different ways may not be compatible with traditional programs or specific classroom requirements.

We saw earlier how the learning styles of students can influence their academic achievement. Capable underachievers often have advanced visual-spatial ability but underdeveloped sequencing skills. As a result, they have difficulty learning such subjects as phonics, spelling, foreign languages, and mathematics in the way these subjects are usually taught. Knowledgeable adults can often help these students expand their learning styles. However, these students also need an environment that is compatible with their preferred ways of learning.

Older students can participate in pressure-free, noncompetitive summer activities that provide a wide variety of educational opportunities, including in-depth exploration, hands-on learning, and mentor relationships. Christian camps can offer special programs for capable and talented students, providing them with opportunities for excellence in performance and spiritual guidance in the use of their gifts.

Some students are more interested in learning than in working for grades. Such students might spend hours on a project that's unrelated to academic classes and fail to turn in required work. They should receive strong encouragement to pursue their interests, particularly since those interests may lead to career decisions and lifelong passions. At the same time, they need reminders that teachers may be unsympathetic when the required work is incomplete.

Early career guidance emphasizing creative problem solving, decision making, and setting short- and long-term goals often helps such kids to complete required assignments, pass high school courses, and plan for college. Providing real-world experiences in an area of potential career interest may also provide motivation toward academic achievement, as we saw with Jerry at the beginning of this chapter.

Remedial Strategies

Parents and teachers should avoid showing insensitivity and using silence or intimidation because these tactics may discourage students. Such comments as "If you're so bright, why did you get a D in algebra?" or "I've given you everything, so why are you so irresponsible about your schoolwork?" are never effective. Constant competition may also lead to underachievement, especially when students consistently feel like a winner or a loser. Parents need to avoid comparing their children with others. Instead, they should show their children how to function in competition and how to recover after losses.

An emphasis on achievement or outcomes rather than on effort, involvement, and desire to learn about topics of interest is a common parental pitfall. The line between pressure and encouragement is subtle but important. Pressure to perform emphasizes outcomes like winning awards and getting A's by praising students for these accomplishments. Encouragement emphasizes the effort students expend, the process they use to achieve, the steps they take toward accomplishing a goal, and the improvement they show. It leaves appraisal and evaluation to the youngster. Effective parents recognize that their underachieving children may be discouraged and in need of encouragement but that they may reject praise as artificial and inauthentic. Parents should listen carefully to their own words of praise and tell their children they are proud of their efforts.

Study-skills courses, time-management classes, and special tutoring may be ineffective if a student is a long-term underachiever. Such efforts will work only if the student is willing and eager, the teacher is chosen carefully, and the course is supplemented by additional strategies. On the other hand, special tutoring may help the concerned student who is experiencing short-term academic difficulty. In general, special tutoring is most helpful when the tutor is carefully chosen to match the interests and learning style of the student. Wide-ranging study-skills courses or tutors who don't understand the student may do more harm than good.

Some students, particularly those who are highly capable and participate in a variety of activities, appear to achieve well in a highly structured academic environment. However, they're at risk of
underachieving if they can't establish priorities, focus on a selected
number of activities, and set long-term goals. On the other hand, some
students appear to be underachievers but are not uncomfortable or discouraged. They may be quite discontented in middle or secondary
school, in part because of the organization and structure, but happy
and successful in a different environment. They may handle independence quite well. Underachievement includes a complex web of behaviors, yet parents and educators can reverse it if they consider the many
strengths and talents of the students who wear the label.

Retention of Students

Students vary in their academic performance and behavior. These variations are particularly evident in the early years of school. For students
who are lagging behind academically or who appear more immature
than their peers, retention—formerly called failing or flunking—has
often been used. The idea is to provide these students with a year to
grow or to improve their academic performance. At the early levels, the
purpose of the extra year is to give students time to acquire readiness
skills or develop prereading abilities (Shepard and Smith 1988).

Estimates place the annual retention rate in the United States at 7 to
9 percent. On the basis of this rate, we can conclude that the cumulative retention rate for a given age group entering school may be higher
than 50 percent by the time that class reaches grade twelve (Shepard
and Smith 1989).

After reviewing retention research, one author reported that one-
fourth to one-third of all kindergarten children nationwide are
retained (Nelson 1991). Some national statistics show that as much as
$10 billion each year is being spent on students who are retained need-

lessly (Mills 1992). In short, retention appears to be a widely practiced strategy for dealing with students who differ academically or behaviorally from what is considered normal (Reynolds, Temple, and McCoy 1997).

The question is whether this attempt to help students actually works. Generally speaking, the answer is no. The professional research on retention indicates that it doesn't help the delayed students and often it actually harms them. It appears to produce no significant benefits related to academic achievement. Further, most studies have found that retention has negative effects on students' self-esteem. And while one goal of retention is to give students the opportunity to experience more success and thus stay in school longer, it actually has the opposite effect. Being retained one year almost doubles a student's likelihood of dropping out of school (Dawson 1998; Foster 1994; Holmes 1989; Peterson, DeGracie, and Ayabe 1987).

Likewise, retention is generally not appropriate for LD and ADHD students. Repeating the program that failed to educate them in the first place will most likely fail the second time as well. A far better idea is to implement more appropriate instructional procedures that fit the needs of the students (Shelton 1994).

If students have struggled with kindergarten or first grade, they need some type of intervention. Promotion with remediation produces better academic results than retention. The major adjustment should be to provide experiences suited to the students' individual capacities. The curriculum and program must undergo alteration to fit their needs rather than forcing students to fit a prescribed curriculum.

Ideally, early childhood teachers would be able to provide student-centered, developmentally appropriate programs that effectively meet their students' needs. Then all students would have successful kindergarten experiences, and failures would not exist. But realistically, this scenario won't happen. Limitations of all types affect most classrooms. The fact is that some students won't do well in their first or second year of school, so we're still left with the question of what to do (Thompson and Cunningham 2000).

The preceding discussion of retention and its negative impact assumes the predominant strategy of generally sending students through the same curriculum and teaching methods a second time. That strategy is the greatest flaw of retention. As we've seen, simply retaining students will solve nothing and will likely compound their problems in the long run. Holding them back simply opens a window of opportunity in regard to their academic difficulties. If their education does not capitalize on this opportunity, the window will probably slam shut in a relatively short time.

How can we make the most of the opportunity? We need to intervene with tutoring, incentive or motivational plans, and remedial instruction—all meant to address the reasons the students are having difficulty (National Association of School Psychologists 2002). Under what conditions might retention with other accommodations and interventions be appropriate for your student? The following are some considerations:

- Students should undergo testing for academic potential. If your student is cognitively capable of completing the work, retention is not the answer. The student needs a different type of environment, perhaps with a smaller class, greater reinforcement, more definite structure, or alternative teaching methods.
- If a physically small student has a birthday near the school district's cutoff date for first grade, retention may be appropriate. Other conditions must also apply, however. Size alone is not a sufficient reason for retention.
- Retention alone is not likely to solve problems related to emotional maturity. To make changes in this area, students will need exposure to some type of social-skills training, structured socialization opportunities, or both. If students are not displaying appropriate social behavior, they need to be taught those skills and not just left to mature another year.

- A complete plan for remedial services should be developed. If an individual education plan can be developed to address the academic, social, language, speech, or behavioral needs of the students, retention will not be necessary or appropriate. In these cases, the students can advance to the next grade with their peers, but the next year's efforts must follow an overall plan.
- Teachers should decide whether the student matches well with the proposed teacher. The teaching style and expectations of next year's teacher will make a significant impact on your student. If those prospects don't look positive, another year with a good teacher may be more appropriate. Some different strategies will need to be tried, but the better teacher match should be a significant consideration.
- Teachers should think through the possible effect of retention on the family. If there's a younger sibling who would be in the same grade as the retained student, retention may not be a good idea. How will the family handle the decision? A supportive, noncritical attitude is crucial. The entire family's perspective should be that the retention represents a window of opportunity rather than a failure to achieve. The parents can set the tone by their positive attitude.
- There is a possibility that the school is motivated to retain the student for economic reasons. For example, it may be more economical for a school to retain some students in a regular kindergarten than to promote them to first grade and provide the necessary special-education services. It's crucial to do what's best for the students, not what's economical for the school.
- Some schools or teachers warn parents by the end of the second month of school when a student is in danger of being retained. In such a case, the student should not be the only focus of attention. A total appraisal of the classroom learning environment must be made, accompanied by specific intervention approaches and appropriate suggestions for the teacher (Gredler 1992; Robertson 1997).

The key consideration in retention is how to meet the developmental needs of students most effectively. When a teacher raises the question of retention, a problem exists. The student who's struggling does not benefit from our simply stating that most research does not support retention. Your goal as an educator is to find another, more appropriate way to help your student succeed. If retention seems to have merit, a detailed educational plan is still necessary. By itself, retention does not solve the problem. The major consideration must be the development and implementation of a teaching and treatment plan that will address the deficit areas of the student.

Conclusion

As we come to the end of this book, I hope that besides gaining specific knowledge about the possible needs of your students, you've also formed several general impressions. First, special-needs students aren't stupid or bad. They're just different and in need of some specialized assistance to help them learn more successfully.

Second, help is available. Whatever the nature of your students' learning problem, there's much that trained, experienced, caring professionals can do for them. Follow the procedures described in this book to get that help.

Finally, never give up. Believe in your students and in their potential. Become your students' biggest fan and advocate. God will sustain you in this vital part of your calling as a teacher.

References

Bloom, B. S. 1982. The role of gifts and markers in the development of talent. *Exceptional Children* 48:510–22.

Bloom, B. S., and L. A. Sosniak. 1981. Talent development vs. schooling. *Educational Leadership* 39:86–94.

Dawson, P. 1998. A primer on student grade retention: What the research says. *Communique* 26, no. 8:28–30.

Delisle, J. R. 1992. *Guiding the social and emotional development of gifted youth: A practical guide for educators and counselors.* New York: Longman.

Delisle, J. R., and S. L. Berger. 1990. Underachieving gifted students. Clearinghouse on Disabilities and Gifted Children. ERIC EC Digest #E478. http://www.ericec.org/digests/e478.html.

Foster, J. E. 1994. Reviews of research: Retaining children in grade. *Childhood Education* 70:38–43.

Gredler, G. R. 1992. *School readiness: Assessment and educational issues.* Brandon, VT: Clinical Psychology Publishing.

Hallahan, D. P., and J. M. Kauffman. 1994. *Exceptional children: Introduction to special education.* Boston: Allyn and Bacon.

Halsted, J. W. 1988. *Guiding gifted readers—from preschool to high school.* Columbus, OH: Ohio Psychology Publishing.

Holmes, C. T. 1989. Grade-level retention effects: A meta-analysis of research studies. In *Flunking grades: Research and policies on retention.* L. A. Shepard and M. L. Smith, eds. 16–33. Philadelphia, PA: Falmer Press.

Mills, B. 1992. Is it wise to hold back a kindergartner? *Charlotte Observer* (August 21): 1E.

National Association of School Psychologists. 2002. Position statement on student grade retention and social promotion. http://www.nasponline.org/information/pospaper_grade retent.html.

Nelson, B. 1991. Retaining children: Is it the right decision? *Childhood Education* 67:3004.

Peterson, J. S., J. S. DeGracie, and C. R. Ayabe. 1987. A longitudinal study of the effects of retention/promotion on academic achievement. *American Educational Research Journal* 24:107–18.

Reynolds, A., J. Temple, and A. McCoy. 1997. Grade retention doesn't work. *Education Week* (September 17): 17.

Robertson, A. S. 1997. When retention is recommended, what should parents do? ERIC Digest. ERIC Clearinghouse on Elementary and Early Childhood Education. http://www.ericfacility.net/databases/ERIC_Digests/ed408102.html.

Shelton, T. L. 1994. To retain or not to retain: That is the question. *The ADHD Report* 1:6–8.

Shepard, L. A., and M. L. Smith. 1988. Flunking kindergarten: Escalating curriculum leaves many behind. *American Educator* 12:34–38.

———. 1989. Introduction and overview. In *Flunking grades: Research and policies on retention.* L. A. Shepard and M. L. Smith, eds. 132–50. New York: Falmer Press.

Thompson, C. L., and E. K. Cunningham. 2000. Retention and social promotion: Research and implications for policy. ERIC Digest Number 161. ERIC Clearinghouse on Urban Education. http://www.ericfacility .net/ericdigests/ ed449241.html.

Vail, P. L. 1987. *Smart kids with school problems: Things to know and ways to help.* New York: Plume.

RESOURCES

Resources for Learning Disabilities and Educators

American Speech-Language-Hearing Association (ASHA) is an organization whose membership consists of speech/language pathologists and audiologists. It provides information and referrals to the public on speech, language, cerebral palsy, communication, and hearing disorders.
ASHA
10801 Rockville Pike
Rockville, MD 20852
800-638-8255 (Voice/TTY)
301-897-5700
http://www.asha.org

Association on Higher Education and Disability (AHEAD) is an international, multicultural organization of professionals committed to higher education for persons with disabilities. AHEAD was founded in 1977 to address the need for upgrading the services and support available to persons with disabilities in higher education.
AHEAD
PO Box 540666
Waltham, MA 02454
781-788-0003
http://www.ahead.org

Center for Accessible Technology (CforAT) began life in 1983 when a group of parents of children with disabilities came together to develop strategies for including their children in mainstream elementary school settings. With an initial focus on computer technology, these parents developed models whereby kids with disabilities could be fully included in the school curriculum.
CforAT
2547 8th St., 12-A
Berkeley, CA 94710
510-841-3224 (Voice)

510-841-5621 (TTY)
510-841-7956 (Fax)
http://www.cforat.org

Children and Adults with Attention Deficit/Hyperactivity Disorder (CHADD) is the national nonprofit organization representing children and adults with ADHD. Founded in 1987 by a group of concerned parents, CHADD works to improve the lives of people with ADHD through education, advocacy, and support. Working closely with leaders in the field of ADHD research, diagnosis, and treatment, CHADD offers its members and the public information they can trust.
CHADD
8181 Professional Pl., Ste. 150
Landover, MD 20785
800-233-4050
301-306-7070
http://www.chadd.org

Children with Disabilities is an online guide to resources for parents and children, including grants and funding, research and statistics, and a youth-to-youth page containing activities, games, and a moderated online bulletin board.
http://www.childrenwithdisabilities.ncjrs.org

The Council for American Private Education (CAPE) is a coalition of national organizations and state affiliates serving private elementary and secondary schools. CAPE member organizations represent about 80 percent of private school enrollment nationwide. Founded in 1971 to provide a coherent voice for private education, CAPE is dedicated to fostering communication and cooperation within the private school community and with the public sector to improve the quality of education for all of the nation's children. Among other goals, CAPE advocates for the equitable opportunity of private school students to participate in appropriate state and federal education programs.

CAPE
13017 Wisteria Dr., #457
Germantown, MD 20874
301-916-8460
301-916-8485 (Fax)
http://www.capenet.org

The Council for Exceptional Children (CEC) has a website geared for educators and offers a variety of links for children's disability problems. The Division of Learning Disabilities within CEC focuses on the special needs of those with learning disabilities. CEC conducts an annual conference and publishes a newsletter and magazines.
CEC
1110 N. Glebe Rd., Ste. 300
Arlington, VA 22201
703-620-3660
703-264-9446 (TTY)
http://www.cec.sped.org

The Council for Learning Disabilities (CLD) is an international organization that promotes effective teaching and research. CLD is composed of professionals who represent diverse disciplines and who are committed to the development of those with learning disabilities.
CLD
PO Box 4014
Leesburg, VA 20177
571-258-1010
http://www.cldinternational.org

ERIC Educational Resources Information Center is part of the U.S. Department of Education's Institute of Educational Sciences. ERIC responds to requests for information on special/gifted education, serves as a resource and referral center for the general public, conducts information searches, and publishes and disseminates free or low-cost information on special/gifted education research, programs, and practices. ERIC focuses on the professional literature, information, and

resources relating to the education and development of individuals of all ages who have disabilities and/or are gifted.
800-328-0272 (Voice/TTY)
http://www.eric.ed.gov

Healthfinder is a free gateway to reliable consumer health and human services information developed by the U.S. Department of Health and Human Services. It has links to over 1,700 health-related organizations.
http://www.healthfinder.gov

Higher Education and the Handicapped (HEATH) operates the national clearinghouse on postsecondary education for individuals with disabilities. The center serves as an information exchange on educational support services; policies and procedures; adaptations; and opportunities at American campuses, vocational-technical schools, adult education programs, independent living centers, and other post-secondary training entities.
The George Washington University
HEATH Resource Center
2121 K St. NW, Ste. 220
Washington, DC 20037
800-544-3284 (for general information)
202-973-0904
202-973-0908 (Fax)
http://www.heath.gwu.edu

IDEAPractices is a website maintained by two organizations, including service providers and administrators who are part of four national projects funded by the U.S. Department of Education's Office of Special Education Programs (OSEP). It delivers a common message about the landmark 1997 reauthorization of the Individuals with Disabilities Education Act (IDEA). The IDEA Partnerships inform professionals, families, and the public about IDEA 97 and strategies to improve educational results for children and youth with disabilities. This website is a good source for the latest developments regarding

IDEA legislation and application of programs.
http://www.ideapractices.org

International Dyslexia Association (IDA) is an international, non-profit scientific and educational organization dedicated to the study and treatment of dyslexia. Formerly "The Orton Dyslexia Society," IDA offers an international network that brings together professionals in the field of dyslexia and parents of dyslexic children for a common purpose. Contact IDA for referral services regarding testing and tutoring, and for free information on assistive technologies, medical and educational research, national and local conferences and seminars, legislation, public awareness, and effective teaching methods.
IDA
8600 LaSalle Rd.
Chester Bldg., Ste. 382
Baltimore, MD 21286-2044
800-ABCD123 (for general information)
410-296-0232 (for detailed information)
410-321-5069 (Fax)
http://www.interdys.org

KidsClick! was created by a group of librarians at the Ramapo Catskill Library System as a logical step in addressing concerns about the role of public libraries in guiding their young users to valuable and age-appropriate websites.
http://www.kidsclick.org

The Learning Disabilities Association of America (LDA) is a non-profit organization with an international membership of over 40,000. Its website contains information on learning disabilities and lists several other resources.
LDA
4156 Library Rd.
Pittsburgh, PA 15234-1349
888-300-6710

412-341-1515
412-344-0224 (Fax)
http://www.ldanatl.org

LD OnLine: Learning Disabilities Information and Resources has a website that provides up-to-date, in-depth information about learning disabilities. It includes introductory and detailed writings on a wide range of topics; a national calendar of events; an extensive network of national and local resources; artwork and writings by children, parents, and other individuals with learning disabilities; discussion groups with parents and national experts; a bookstore; and more.
http://www.ldonline.org

LD Resources offers a variety of resources for the learning disabilities community and a special focus on learning and technology. The site includes essays, lists of resources, software to download, and contact information for national and regional organizations, conferences, and schools.
http://www.ldresources.com

National Attention Deficit Disorder Association (ADDA) has a particular interest in the needs of adults with ADD, but their services do address children and family issues. They provide information and local resources, as well as an annual conference about adults and ADD.
ADDA
PO Box 543
Pottstown, PA 19464
484-945-2101
http://www.add.org

National Center for Learning Disabilities provides information on all aspects of learning problems in children. It offers programs nationwide to benefit children and adults with learning disabilities, their families, educators, and other helping professionals. Services comprise national information and referral, including an extensive computerized database with state-by-state resource listings of schools, diagnostic clinics, etc.; educational programs, including national and regional summits; public outreach and communications; and legislative advocacy and public policy. The organization publishes an outstanding magazine, *Their World,* and will send free information on a variety of topics.

National Center for Learning Disabilities
381 Park Ave. S., Ste. 1401
New York, NY 10016
888-575-7373 (for general information)
212-545-7510 (for detailed information)
212-545-9665 (Fax)
http://www.ncld.org

National Information Center for Children and Youth with Disabilities (NICHCY) provides free information on disabilities and related issues, focusing on children and youths (birth to age 35). Free services include personal responses, referrals, technical assistance, and general information searches. It is funded by the U.S. Department of Education.

NICHCY
PO Box 1492
Washington, DC 20013-1492
800-695-0285 (Voice/TTY)
202-884-8441 (Fax)
http://www.nichcy.org

National Institute of Child Health and Human Development (NICHD), one of the National Institutes of Health, has been conducting research on learning disabilities and related disorders.

NICHD
PO Box 3006
Rockville, MD 20847
800-370-2943

301-496-7101 (Fax)
http://www.nichd.nih.gov

National Library Service for the Blind and Physically Handicapped (NLS) administers a free program that loans recorded and Braille books and magazines, music scores in Braille and large print, and specially designed playback equipment to residents of the United States who are unable to read or use standard-print materials because of visual or physical impairment.
NLS
Library of Congress
Washington, DC 20542
800-424-8567
202-707-5100
202-707-0744 (TDD)
202-707-0712 (Fax)
http://www.loc.gov/nls

National Mental Health Information Center, formerly known as the Knowledge Exchange Network (KEN), serves as a national clearing-house for free information about mental health.
http://www.mentalhealth.org

Parents Helping Parents is a twenty-seven-year-old resource center that assists parents of special-needs children. Its website provides resources, links, and support for families.
http://www.php.com

ProQuest/bigchalk.com provides a broad spectrum of educational Internet services to teachers, students, parents, librarians, and school administrators in the K–12 educational and public library markets.
http://www.bigchalk.com

Recordings for the Blind and Dyslexic (RFB&D) was established in

1948 to provide recorded textbooks to veterans blinded in World War II. Today RFB&D provides educational materials at every academic level in recorded and computerized formats to individuals who are unable to use standard print. Books, texts, and reference materials are available to people with dyslexia or with visual, perceptual, or physical disabilities.

RFB&D
20 Roszel Rd.
Princeton, NJ 08540
800-221-4792
609-520-8031
http://www.rfbd.org

Schoolwork Ugh! This is the site for secondary school students. Students can email a librarian for assistance as well as search a comprehensive directory of resources. Schoolwork Ugh! is geared toward older students, grades 7 and up. Younger students might want to try KidsClick!
http://www.schoolwork.org

Schwab Foundation for Learning provides free information, resources, and support to parents of children with learning differences, and to kids themselves through two websites and Outreach and Community Services. The foundation was formerly known as Parents and Educators Resource Center (PERC).

Schwab Foundation for Learning
1650 S. Amphlett Blvd., Ste. 300
San Mateo, CA 94402
800-230-0988
650-655-2410
650-655-2411 (Fax)
http://www.schwablearning.org
http://www.sparktop.org

Special Education Resources on the Internet (SERI) comprises a large collection of Internet sites for those involved in special education. http://seriweb.com

U.S. Department of Education maintains a website with a variety of information, programs, and assistance. http://www.ed.gov

www.familyeducation.com is a website created by parents. It provides educational information, homework helps, craft ideas, and tips about reading skills. Also included are discussions on child development, learning disabilities, discipline, dealing with bullies, and dating. http://www.familyeducation.com

www.funschool.com is part of the online Kaboose Network. It provides original activities and educational content for children. The site contains more than 400 diverse educational games. Guidelines for parent and teacher participation are also provided. http://www.funschool.com